ANCIENT PERSIAN LEXICON
AND TEXTS

VANDERBILT UNIVERSITY STUDIES

FOUNDED BY

AUGUSTUS H. ROBINSON

AMERICAN AGENT..........LEMCKE AND BUECHNER, NEW YORK CITY

FOREIGN AGENT......OTTO HARRASSOWITZ, QUERSTRASSE, 14. LEIPZIG

A copy, in paper binding, of this number of the series will be forwarded on receipt of a Postal Order for the price (one dollar) anywhere within the limits of the Universal Postal Union upon application to the agents or to Vanderbilt University.

NASHVILLE, TENNESSEE
PUBLISHED BY VANDERBILT UNIVERSITY
1908

THE VANDERBILT ORIENTAL SERIES
EDITED BY
HERBERT CUSHING TOLMAN AND JAMES HENRY STEVENSON

ANCIENT PERSIAN LEXICON

AND THE TEXTS OF THE ACHAEMENIDAN
INSCRIPTIONS TRANSLITERATED AND
TRANSLATED WITH SPECIAL REFERENCE
TO THEIR RECENT RE-EXAMINATION

BY

HERBERT CUSHING TOLMAN
PROFESSOR OF THE GREEK LANGUAGE AND LITERATURE

NEW YORK : CINCINNATI : CHICAGO
AMERICAN BOOK COMPANY

TO
MY FORMER PUPILS
IN SANSKRIT AND AVESTAN
YALE AND VANDERBILT
1890–1908

THE VANDERBILT ORIENTAL SERIES

EDITED BY PROFESSORS

HERBERT CUSHING TOLMAN, PH.D., D.D.,

AND

JAMES HENRY STEVENSON, PH.D.

"The Vanderbilt Oriental Series deserves a word of welcome as an American undertaking."—The Nation.

VOL. I. HERODOTUS AND THE EMPIRES OF THE EAST. Based on Nikel's Herodot und die Keilschriftforschung. By the editors. Price, $1.

"A careful assembling of the valuable references in Herodotus, and a comparison of the native sources."—*Prof. Rogers, in History of Babylonia and Assyria, Vol. I., p. 264.*

VOL. II. INDEX TO THE CHĀNDOGYA UPANISHAD. By Charles Edgar Little, Ph.D. Price, $1.

"The plan as conceived is well executed."—*The Nation.*

VOL. III. ASSYRIAN AND BABYLONIAN CONTRACTS (with Aramaic Reference Notes) Transcribed from the Originals in the British Museum, with Transliteration and Translation, by J. H. Stevenson. Price, $2.50.

"Your professional colleagues ought to be very pleased with the whole book."—*E. A. Wallis Budge, British Museum.*

"Dr. Stevenson's book forms a most useful contribution to the study of Semitic epigraphy."—*Luzac's Oriental List.*

VOL. IV. HOMERIC LIFE. By Prof. Edmund Weissenborn. Translated by Gilbert Campbell Scoggin, Ph.D., and Charles Gray Burkitt, M.A. Price, $1.

"The American edition is especially valuable . . . and will prove a valuable help to every student of Homer."—*The Outlook.*

VOL. V. MYCENAEAN TROY. Based on Dörpfeld's Excavations in the Sixth of the Nine Buried Cities at Hissarlik. By H. C. Tolman and G. C. Scoggin. Price, $1.

"Laymen and even scholars will be thankful for this concise presentation. The task has been fairly and successfully performed."—*Prof. Rufus B. Richardson, in the Independent.*

"A satisfactory description of the results of Drs. Schliemann and Dörpfeld's excavations."—*Classical Review, England.*

VOL. VI. ANCIENT PERSIAN LEXICON. With texts of the Achaemenidan Inscriptions Transliterated and Translated. By H. C. Tolman. Price, $1.25.

Other volumes in the series are in preparation.

NEW YORK : CINCINNATI : CHICAGO

AMERICAN BOOK COMPANY.

PREFACE

Merivale describes the *Monumentum Ancyranum* as "a truly imperial work and probably unique in its kind," but the record of the Great Darius on the Behistan Rock is just as "unique." The text of this inscription has been made more certain by the partial rëexamination of Jackson (JAOS, 24 and 27 = Persia Past and Present) and the new collation of King and Thompson (British Museum, 1907; discussed at date of present writing by Weissbach, ZDMG, 61; Hoffmann-Kutschke, Phil. Nov. III; Tolman, Vdt. Stud. 1; Bartholomae, WZKM, 22). Their work has solved many old problems and at the same time presents new ones. I confess that I am not in sympathy with those who are bold enough to style the KT readings *Fehler*, wherever they conflict with previous emendations which were attractive and ingenious. The two English scholars have had years of experience in copying cuneiform tablets and in their long task were doubtless able to catch the most favorable effects of light and shadow upon the stone. In fact it is doubtful if another examination of the rock would now add very materially to our accurate knowledge of the text. Our chief help in the future may come from the discovery of some of the duplicate copies, written on bricks (? halat) and leather (? SU, Jensen), which Darius declares he sent into all lands, **mene (det) tuppi-me + + + + tinni (m) taiyauš marrita atima (m) u muggiya (m) taššutum-pe sapiš** (Elam. Bh. l. = Pers. Bh. iv, ll. 88–92), a fragment of which (BE, 3627 = Bh. ll. 55–58; 69–72) has already been found by Koldewey. Again in the Persepolitan Inscriptions we now have Stolze's photographs supplemented by Jackson's examination of the original (JAOS, 27). For Xerx. Van cf. Lehmann, SBAW, 1900, 625; for Dar. Suez cf. Daressy, *Révision des Textes de la Stèle de Chalouf* (*Recueil de Travaux*, Maspero, 11, 160–71); for Elvend Inscriptions cf. de Morgan, *Mission scientifique en Perse*, 2, 137; for Art. Hamadan cf. Tolman, *Rëexamination of Moldings of Columns from Ecbatana*, PAPA, 36, 32; for Kerman Inscr. cf. Jackson, JAOS, 27, 190. How accurately and painstakingly Rawlinson accomplished his great task at Behistan is newly attested by the recent rëexaminations. Jackson has noted that this patient workman inscribed his own name below the inscription he had copied, and certainly if any phrase deserves imperishable record on the Great Rock it is that of "H. C. Rawlinson, 1844." It is quite remarkable also what a number of conjectures made many years ago by Oppert is now confirmed.

My frequent references to works cited will show my obligation to modern scholars. Bartholomae's *Altiranisches Wörterbuch* (with his *Zum Altiran. Wb.* in IF, *Beiheft zum* XIX. *Band*) has been my constant *vade-mecum*, as it is of all Avestan scholars. It is hardly necessary to speak of the light thrown on the ancient language through the investigations in Middle Persian, New Persian, and the other modern dialects by Salemann (*Mittelpersisch; Grundr. d. iran. Philol.*), Hübschmann (*Persische Studien* and *Etymologie und Lautlehre der ossetischen Sprache*), Horn (*Grundriss der neupersischen Etymologie*), Justi (*Kurdische Grammatik*), Socin (*Kurdisch; Grundr. d. iran. Philol.*), Geiger (*Afgânisch, Balūcī; op. cit.*), Gray (*Indo-Iranian Phonology*) and others. The importance of the Turfan MSS. material (F. W. K. Müller; *Handschriftenreste — aus Turfan*) was not overestimated at the time of its discovery, and its bearing on the older languages is being constantly brought into greater prominence. I have used the transliteration of the Estrangelo script, which is of course hardly adapted to the character of the language, e. g. 'ûd for ud < utā; mûrdân for murdān, cf. New Pers. murda; gōkhan (Bartholomae), not gōkhun (Müller); 'ûšân (Bartholomae), not 'ôšân (Müller).

The results of their Elamite studies put forth with such assurance by Hüsing, Jensen, Bork, and others, I have used perhaps with too great caution. We are forced to admit that our knowledge of this language, notwithstanding our richly increased material (Scheil, *Textes élamites-sémitiques*, *Textes élamites-anzanites; Délég. en Perse*, 1900–1907), is still very inadequate, and I feel it is hazardous to base our interpretation of the Persian on a corresponding Elamite expression which is not absolutely certain.

Professor Weissbach wrote me a few months ago that the second *Lieferung* of his *Die altpersischen Keilinschriften* would soon be ready, and I regret that I have been unable to avail myself of it during the preparation of my manuscript. I have, however, held back the sheets that I might consult it before the volume went to press.

HERBERT CUSHING TOLMAN.

June 1, 1908.

ABBREVIATIONS

AF = Arische Forschungen

Afγ. = Afγān

AJP = American Journal of Philology

APAW = Abhandlungen der königlich-Preussischen Akademie der Wissenschaften (1904, Handschriftenreste in Estrangelo-Schrift aus Turfan, F. W. K. Müller)

Ai. Gram. = Altindische Grammatik (Wackernagel)

Altiran. Wb. = Altiranisches Wörterbuch (Bartholomae, 1904)

Art. = Artaxerxes

Assyriol. Bibl. = Assyriologische Bibliothek

Av. = Avesta or Avestan

Av. Gram. = Avesta Grammar (Jackson)

Bab. = Babylonian

BB = Beiträge zur Kunde der indogermanischen Sprachen

Bal. = Balūcī

Benfey = Die persischen Keilinschriften (1847, Benfey)

Bh. = Behistan

Dar. = Darius

de Morgan = Mission scientifique en Perse

ed. = recent edition or editions

Elam. = Elamite

Elv. = Elvend

GAv. = Gāθā Avesta

Gīl. = Gīlakī

Grundr.² = Grundriss der vergleichenden Grammatik, Zweite Bearbeitung (Brugmann)

Grundr. = Grundriss der iranischen Philologie (Awestasprache und Altpersisch, Vol. I, Bartholomae)

Grundr. = Grundriss der neupersischen Etymologie (Horn)

Ham. = Hamadan

Hdt. = Herodotus and Empires of the East (Tolman and Stevenson)

I. E. = Indo-European

IF = Indogermanische Forschungen

Ir. En. = Die iranischen Eigennamen in den Achämenideninschriften (Hüsing)

Iran. Namenbuch = Iranisches Namenbuch (Justi)

JAOS = Journal of American Oriental Society

Jn. = Jackson, who made in 1903 a partial reexamination of the Bh. rock and the inscriptions of Persepolis (JAOS, 24 and 27 = Persia Past and Present)

JRAS = Journal of Royal Asiatic Society

Jud. Pers. = Judaic Persian

Kāš = Kāšānī

Kossowicz = Inscriptiones Palaeo-Persicae (1872, Kossowicz)

Kr. = Kerman

KT = King and Thompson; The Sculptures and Inscription of Darius the Great on the Rock of Behistûn, British Museum, 1907. KT have newly copied the Persian, Elamite, and Babylonian texts

Kurd. = Kurdish

KZ = Zeitschrift für vergleichende Sprachforschung

Middle Pers. = Middle Persian

New Pers. = New Persian

NR = Naķš-i-Rustam

NS = Neupersische Schriftsprache (Grundr. d. iran. Philol., Horn)

OP. Insc. = Old Persian Inscriptions (Tolman)

Or. Litt. Ztg. = Orientalistische Litteratur-Zeitung

Oss. = Ossetic

PAPA = Proceedings of American Philological Association

Pers. = Persepolis

Pers. Stud. = Persische Studien (Hübschmann)

Phil. Nov. = Philologiae Novitates

Phl. = Pahlavī

PWb. = Sanskrit-Wörterbuch (Böhtlingk und Roth)

Rawlinson = The Persian Cuneiform Inscription at Behistun (= JRAS, Vols. x, xi; 1846, 1849)

SA = Die Sprache der Afghānen (Geiger)

SB = Die Sprache der Balūtschen (Geiger)

SBAW = Sitzungsberichte der königlich-Preussischen Akademie der Wissenschaften (1904, Handschriftenreste aus Turfan, F. W. K. Müller)

SK = Die Sprache der Kurden (Socin)

Skt. Gram. = Sanskrit Grammar (Whitney)

Spiegel = Die altpersischen Keilinschriften. 2. Auflage (Spiegel)

Stolze = Persepolis (Stolze)

Sus. = Susa

Sz. = Suez.

Turfan MSS., see APAW

Vdt. Stud. = Vanderbilt University Studies. The Behistan Inscription of King Darius, Translation and Critical Notes to the Persian Text with special reference to recent Rëexaminations of the Rock, March, 1908 (Tolman)

WB = Weissbach und Bang; Die altpersischen Keilinschriften; WB^{II} = Zweite Lieferung

WZKM = Wiener Zeitschrift für die Kunde des Morgenlandes

Xerx. = Xerxes

YAv. = Younger Avesta

ZDMG = Zeitschrift der Deutschen Morgenländischen Gesellschaft

Zum Altiran. Wb. = Zum Altiranischen Wörterbuch (= IF, Beiheft zum xix. Band, Bartholomae)

SPECIMEN OF TEXTS, Bh. Col. iv, 14.

PERSIAN.

67. θātiy dārayavauš xšāyaθiya tuvam [kā] xšāyaθiya 68. hya aparam āhy martiya [hya] draujana ahatiy hyavā [zū]rakara ₊ ₊ ahat-69. iy avaiy mā dauštā ₊ ₊ ₊ ā ufraštādiy parsā

ELAMITE.

82. aiak (m) tari-83. yamauš (m) zunkuk nanri (m) ni [(m) zunkuk (m) akka meššin] nekti (m) ruh(id)-irra titukra hupirri aini in kannenti aiak aini (m) akka appan- 84. la-ikkimme huttiš

BABYLONIAN.

105. (m) da-ri-ia]-muš [šarru] ki-a-am i-ḳab-bi man-nu at-ta šarru ša be-la-a ar-ki-ia amêlu ša u-par-ra-ṣu u amêlu UD-IŠ-A-NI 106. la ta- ₊ ₊ ₊ ₊ ₊ ₊ ₊ ₊

BASE OF COLUMN WITH XERXES INSCRIPTION
Found at Susa (trilingual)

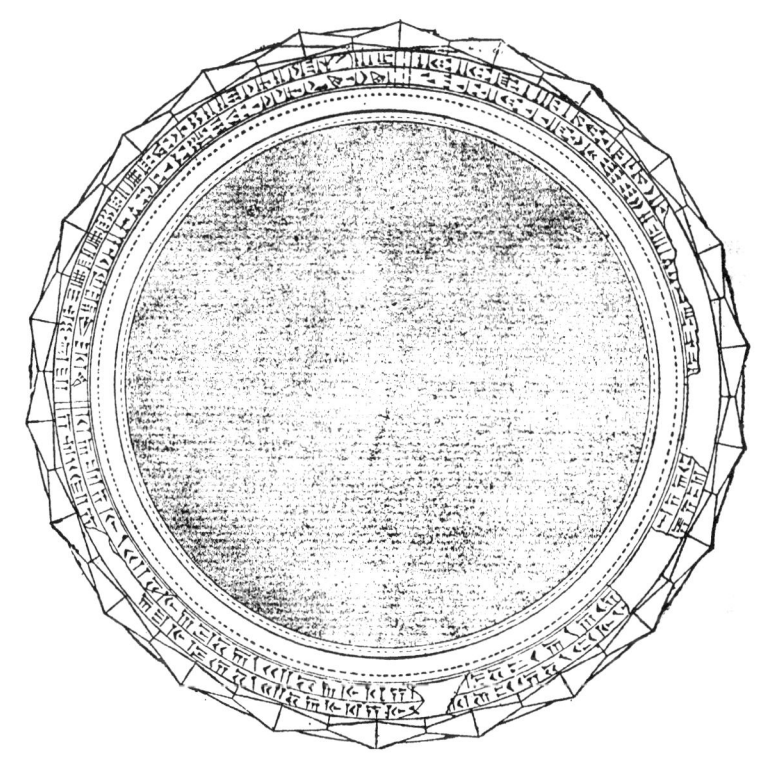

J. de Morgan, Délégation en Perse, I, 90.

Xerx. Sus.
Transliteration

1) θātiy xšayāršā xšāyaθi[ya] vašnā au[rama]zdāha 2) ima hadi[š d]ārayavauš xšāyaθiya [a]kunauš hya [manā] pit[ā]

Translation

Says Xerxes the king: By the grace of Ahura Mazda this dwelling Darius the king made who (was) my father.

(1)

PERSIAN TEXTS TRANSLITERATED

INSCRIPTIONS OF BEHISTAN (Bh.)

Col. 1.

1. 1)Adam Dārayavauš xšāyaθiya vazarka[1] xšāyaθi[ya xšāya]-θiy-2)ānām xšāyaθiya Pārsaiy xšāyaθiya dah[yūnām] V¹št-3)āspahyā puθra Aršāmahyā napā Haxāmaniš[iya

2. θ]ātiy 4)Dārayavauš xšāyaθiya manā pitā V¹štāspa V¹štāspa[hyā pit]ā Arš-5)āma Aršāmahyā pitā Ariyāramna[2] Ariyāramnahyā pit[ā Cišpiš][3] Cišp-6)āiš pitā Haxāmaniš

3. θātiy Dārayavauš xšāya[θiya ava]hyarā-7)diy vayam Haxāmanišiyā θahyāmahy hacā paruv[iyata ā]mātā[4] ama-8)hy hacā paruviyata hyā amāxam taumā xšāya[θiyā ā]ha

4. θ-9)ātiy Dārayavauš xšāyaθiya VIII manā taumāy[ā tyai]y [pa]ruvam 10)xšāyaθiyā āhaⁿ adam navama IX duvitāparanam[5] [vayam] xšāyaθi-11)yā amahy

5. θātiy Dārayavauš xšāyaθiya va[šnā] Auramazd-12)āha adam xšāyaθiya amiy Auramazdā xšaθram manā [fr]ābara

6. θ-13)ātiy Dārayavauš xšāyaθiya imā dahyāva tyā manā [pat]iyāišaⁿ vašn-14)ā Auramazdāha [a]damšām xšāyaθiya āham Pārsa Uvaja [B]ābiruš A-15)θurā Arabāya Mudrāya tyaiy drayahyā[6] Sparda Yauu[ā Māda] Armina Kat-16)patuka Parθava Zraⁿka[7] Haraiva Uvārazmiya Bāxtriš [Sug]uda Gaⁿdāra Sa-17)ka Θataguš Ha[ra]uvatiš Maka fraharavam[8] dahyāva XXIII

---

[1] vazarka, Nöldeke, Foy, Bartholomae. vazraka, ed. See voc.
[2] ariyārāmna, ed. wrongly. See voc.
[3] cⁱišpiš, see voc.
[4] ādātā, Andreas-Hüsing. See voc.
[5] duvitāparanam, Tolman, Bartholomae (with different meaning). duvitāparnam, KT, WB"; also, Hoffmann-Kutschke, who proposes an etymology contrary to philological laws. duvitātaranam, ed. wrongly. See voc.
[6] darayahyā, ed. KT, wrongly.
[7] zaraⁿka, ed.
[8] fraharavam, Bartholomae. fraharvam, KT, ed. See voc.

PERSIAN TEXTS TRANSLATED

INSCRIPTIONS OF BEHISTAN

High up on the perpendicular face of the great Behistan Rock, 65 miles west of Hamadan (Ecbatana), where are sculptured King Darius and two attendants; beneath his foot the prostrate Pseudo-Smerdis, while facing the king is the standing row of the nine captives; above is the divine symbol; below the panel the four columns of Persian text (ca. 12x6 ft.) with col. five to their right, while to their left are the three columns of Elamite version; to left of sculpture the Babylonian version on projecting block.

Col. I.

1. I (am) Darius, the great king, the king of kings,[1] the king in Persia, the king of countries, the son of Hystaspes, the grandson of Arsames, the Achaemenide.

2. Says Darius the king: My father (is) Hystaspes; the father of Hystaspes (is) Arsames; the father of Arsames (is) Ariaramnes; the father of Ariaramnes [is Teispes]; the father of Teispes (is) Achaemenes.

3. Says Darius the king: Therefore[2] we are called the Achaemenides; from long ago we have been of ancient lineage;[3] from long ago our family have been kings.[4]

4. Says Darius the king: 8 of my family (there were) who

---

[1] Cf. in Phl. the Semitic logogram malkān malkā spoken as šāhān šāh, *king of kings*, somewhat as we write Deo volente but speak the phrase as "Providence permitting."

[2] avahyarādiy. In the modern Persian dialects the survival of rādiy is noteworthy; in New Pers. rā is used in a general adverbial sense, e. g. rôz-rā, *by day*, ci-rā, *why*; cf. Horn, NS, 53, C; in Afγ. lara (metathesis for rala) is an affix for dat., e. g. γrạ (*mountain*) + lara, Geiger, SA, 17; in Balūcī rā is postposition for dat. and acc., e. g. togārā, Geiger, SB, 9; in Kurd. ra is also affix for dat., Socin, SK, 158.

[3] KT plainly record [ā]mātā. For emendation ādātā see voc. and cf. nīṣt bantī 'aṭ nī azatī, *there is neither bond nor free*, Neutest. Bruchstücke in soghdischer Sprache, Müller, SBAW, 1907. Bab. [mâr]-bânûti (pl), the same word which is used in the phrase mâr-bânûti (pl) ša it-ti-šu gab-bi= Persian martiyā tyaišaiy fratamā anušiyā.

[4] Or *our family have been royal;* cf. χšēvanêṭî, Neutest. Bruchstücke in soghdischer Sprache.

(8)

7. θātiy Dāra-18)yavauš xšāyaθiya imā dahyāva tyā manā pati[yāišaⁿ] vašnā Au-19)ramazdāha ma[n]ā baⁿdakā āhaⁿtā manā bājim abaraⁿtā [tya]šām hacāma 20)aθahya xšapavā raucapativā avā akunavayaⁿtā[1]

8. θātiy [Dāra]yava-21)uš xšāyaθiya aⁿtar imā dahyāva martiya hya āgar[tā][2] āha avam u-22)bartam abaram hya araika āha avam ufrastam aparsam vašn[ā] Auramazdā-23)ha imā dahyāva tyᵃnᵃa manā dātā[3] āpariyāyaⁿ[4] yaθāšām hacāma aθah-24)ya [a]vaθā akunavayaⁿtā[5]

9. θātiy Dārayavauš xšāyaθiya Auramazdā-25)m[aiy] imā[6] xšaθʳam frābara Auramazdāmaiy upastām abara yātā ima xšaθʳam 26)ha[ma]dārayai[y][7] vašnā Auramazdāha ima xšaθʳam dārayāmiy

10. θā-27)tiy Dārayavauš xšāyaθiya ima tya manā kartam pasāva yaθā xš-28)āyaθiya abavam Kaⁿbūjiya nāma Kūrauš puθʳa amāxam taumāy-29)ā hauvᵃmᵃ[8] idā xšāyaθiya āha avahyā Kaⁿbūjiyahyā brā-30)t[ā Bardi]ya nāma āha hamātā[9] hamapitā Kaⁿbūjiyahyā pasāva Kaⁿ-31)b[ūjiya a]vam Bardiyam avājaⁿ yaθā Kaⁿbūjiya Bardiyam avājaⁿ kārahy-32)[ā naiy] azdā abava tya Bardiya avajata[10] pasāva Kaⁿbūjiya Mudrāyam 33)[ašiya]va yaθā Kaⁿbūjiya Mudrāyam ašiyava pasāva kāra araika abava 34)[pasāva] drauga dahyauvā vasiy[11] abava utā Pārsaiy utā Mādaiy ut-35)[ā an]iyāuvā dahyušuvā

11. θātiy Dārayavauš xšāyaθiya pa-36)[sāva] I martiya maguš āha Gaumāta nāma[12] hauv udapatatā hacā Paiši-37)[yā]uvādāyā Arakadriš nāma kaufa hacā avadaša Viyaxnahya māh-38)[yā] XIV raucabiš θakatā āhaⁿ yadiy udapatatā hauv kārahyā avaθā 39)[a]durujiya adam Bardiya amiy hya Kūrauš puθʳa Kaⁿbūji-

---

[1] akunavayaⁿtā, Bartholomae. akunavyatā, ed.
[2] āgartā, Tolman, Bartholomae (with different meaning). agᵃrᵃ + + KT. The emendation daustā is impossible. See voc.
[3] tyanā manā dātā, KT. Probably dittography for tyā manā dātā. See voc. s. v. tya.
[4] āpariyāyaⁿ, Bartholomae. apariyāyaⁿ, ed. KT. See voc. s, v. hapariya.
[5] akunavayaⁿtā, Bartholomae. akunavyatā, ed.
[6] auramazdām[aiy] ima, KT.
[7] ha[ma]dārayai[y], KT. See voc.
[8] hauvᵃmᵃ, KT. Wrongly [pa]ruvam, ed.
[9] Or haplography for hamamātā, Bartholomae.
[10] avajata, KT. avājata, Gray, Bartholomae. See voc.
[11] vasiy or vasaiy. Wrongly vasiya, Müller. See voc.
[12] nāmᵃ. nāmaⁿ. Bartholomae. See voc.

were formerly kings; I am the ninth (9); long aforetime[1] we were (lit. are) kings.

5. Says Darius the king: By the grace of Ahura Mazda I am king; Ahura Mazda gave me the kingdom.

6. Says Darius the king: These are the countries which came to me; by the grace of Ahura Mazda I became king of them;— Persia, Susiana, Babylonia, Assyria, Arabia, Egypt, the (lands) which are on the sea, Sparda, Ionia, [Media], Armenia, Cappadocia, Parthia, Drangiana, Aria, Chorasmia, Bactria, Sogdiana, Ga(n)dara, Scythia, Sattagydia, Arachosia, the Macae; in all (there are) 23 countries.

7. Says Darius the king: These (are) the countries which came to me; by the grace of Ahura Mazda they became subject to me; they bore tribute to me; what was commanded to them by me night or day[2] this they did.

8. Says Darius the king: Within these countries what man was watchful[3] him well esteemed I esteemed; who was an enemy, him well punished I punished; by the grace of Ahura Mazda these countries respected my laws; as it was commanded by me to them, so they did.

9. Says Darius the king: Ahura Mazda gave me this kingdom; Ahura Mazda bore me aid until I obtained this kingdom; by the grace of Ahura Mazda I hold this kingdom.

10. Says Darius the king: This (is) what (was) done by me after that I became king; Cambyses by name, the son of Cyrus (was) of our family; he was king here; of this Cambyses there was a brother Bardiya (i. e. Smerdis) by name possessing a common mother and the same father with Cambyses; afterwards Cambyses slew that Bardiya; when Cambyses slew Bardiya, it was not known[4] to the people that Bardiya was slain; afterwards

---

[1] duvitāparanam. My interpretation (Vdt. Stud. 8) has been accepted by several critics. Bartholomae, however, writes me that he would connect duvitā with Middle Pers. dit, and render the compound *one after another*. If this view be correct, I would take the preceding numeral in connection with the word, translating *nine in succession we were kings*.

[2] Cf. Turfan MSS., šab 'ûd rôj, *night and day*, M. 88.

[3] āgar[tā]. My supplement (Vdt. Stud. 9) seems to me quite certain; cf. Turfan MSS. vîgarânêd.

[4] Cf. Turfan MSS., paṭ nîdfâr šavêd 'ô Galîlâh 'ût 'azd qarêd 'ô Šîmôn ût + + + + ['a]bârig, *at sunset* (Bartholomae; *evening*, Andreas) *go to Galilee and make known to Simon and the others*.

yahyā br-40)[ā]tā pasāva kāra haruva hamiθʳiya abava hacā Kaⁿbūjiyā abiy avam 41)[a]šiyava utā Pārsa utā Māda utā aniyā dahyāva xšaθʳam hauv 42)agarbāyatā Garmapadahya māhyā IX raucabiš θakatā āhaⁿ avaθā xša-43)θʳam agarbāyatā pasāva Kaⁿbūjiya uvāmaršiyuš amariyatā

12. θātiy 44)Dārayavauš xšāyaθiya aita xšaθʳam tya Gaumāta hya maguš adīn-45)ā Kaⁿbūjiyam aita xšaθʳam hacā paruviyata amāxam taumāyā ā-46)ha pasāva Gaumāta hya maguš adīnā Kaⁿbūjiyam utā Pārsam utā 47)Mādam utā aniyā dahyāva hauv āyasatā¹ uvāipašiyam akutā hau-48)v xšāyaθiya abava

13. θātiy Dārayavauš xšāyaθiya naiy āha martiya 49)naiy Pārsa naiy Māda naiy amāxam taumāyā kašciy hya avam Gau-50)mātam tyam magum xšaθʳam dītam caxriyā kārašim hacā daršmaⁿ² a-51)tarsa kāram vasiy avājaniyā hya paranam Bardi-yam adānā avahyar-52)ādiy kāram avājaniyā mātyamām xšnāsā-tiy tya adam naiy Bard-53)iya amiy hya Kūrauš puθʳa kašciy naiy adaršnauš cišciy θastana-54)iy pariy Gaumātam tyam magum yātā adam arasam pasāva adam Aura-55)maz[d]ām pati-yāvahyaiy³ Auramazdāmaiy upastām abara Bāgayādaiš 56)māhyā X raucabiš θakatā āhaⁿ avaθā adam hadā kamnaibiš martiyai-bi-57)š avam Gaumātam tyam magum avājanam utā tyaišaiy fratamā mar-58)tiyā anušiyā āhaⁿtā Sika[ya]uvatiš nāmā⁴ didā Nisāya nā-59)mā dahyāuš Mādaiy avadašim avājanam xšaθʳam-šim adam adīnam va-60)šnā Auramazdāha adam xšāyaθiya abavam Auramazdā xšaθʳam manā fr-61)ābara

14. θātiy Dārayavauš xšāyaθiya xšaθʳam tya hacā amāxam ta-62)umāyā parābartam āha ava adam patipadam akunavam adamšim gāθa-63)vā⁵ avāstāyam yaθā paruvamciy avaθā adam akunavam āyadan-64)ā tyā Gaumāta hya maguš viyakaⁿ adam niyaθʳārayam kārahyā abi-65)cariš⁶ gaiθāmcā māniyamcā vⁱθᵃbⁱ-šᵃcᵃa⁷ tyādiš Gaumāta h[ya] 66)maguš adīnā adam kāram gāθavā avāstāyam Pārsam[c]ā Mādam[c]-67)ā utā aniyā dahyāva yaθā paruvamciy avaθā adam tya parāba[rta]-68)m patiyābaram vašnā

---
¹āyasatā, Bartholomae. āyastā, ed., KT. ayastā, Kern.
²daršmaⁿ, Bartholomae. daršam, ed. daršama, KT. See voc.
³patiyāvahyaiy, Jn., KT. See voc.
⁴nāmᵃa. nāmāⁿ, Bartholomae. See voc.
⁵gāθvā, ed., KT, wrongly. See voc.
⁶abicariš, KT, Jn. See voc.
⁷Text as confirmed by KT and Jn. viθbiš, Justi, Tolman. viθabišaca-cā, Foy. Formerly viθaibiš, Gray, Bartholomae. viθibiš, ed. See voc.

Cambyses went to Egypt; when Cambyses went to Egypt, after that the people became hostile; after that there was Deceit to a great extent in the land, both in Persia and in Media and in the other provinces.

11. Says Darius the king: Afterwards there was one man, a Magian, Gaumâta by name; he rose up from Paishiyâuvâdâ; there (is) a mountain Arakadri by name; from there—14 days in the month Viyakhna were completing their course when he rose up; he thus deceived the people; I am Bardiya the son of Cyrus brother of Cambyses; afterwards all the people became estranged from Cambyses (and) went over to him, both Persia and Media and the other provinces; he seized the kingdom; 9 days in the month Garmapada were completing their course— then he seized the kingdom; afterwards Cambyses died by a self-imposed death.

12. Says Darius the king: This kingdom which Gaumâta the Magian took from Cambyses, this kingdom from long ago was (the possession) of our family; afterwards Gaumâta the Magian took from Cambyses both Persia and Media and the other provinces; he seized (the power) and made it his own possession; he became king.

13. Says Darius the king: There was not a man neither a Persian nor a Median nor any one of our family who could make Gaumâta the Magian deprived of the kingdom; the people feared him for his tyranny; (they feared) he would slay the many who knew Bardiya formerly; for this reason he would slay the people; "that they may not know me that I am not Bardiya the son of Cyrus;" any one did not dare to say anything against Gaumâta the Magian until I came; afterwards I asked Ahura Mazda for help; Ahura Mazda bore me aid; 10 days in the month Bâgayâdi were completing their course— then I with few men slew that Gaumâta the Magian and what foremost men were his allies; there (is) a stronghold Sikayauvati by name; there is a province in Media, Nisâya by name; here I smote him; I took the kingdom from him; by the grace of Ahura Mazda I became king; Ahura Mazda gave me the kingdom.

14. Says Darius the king: The kingdom which was taken away from our family, this I put in (its) place; I established it on (its) foundation; as (it was) formerly so I made it; the sanc-

Auramazdāha ima adam akunavam adam hamatax[šaiy] 69)yātā v¹θam tyām amāxam gāθavā avāstāyam yaθā [par]uvam[ci]y 70)avaθā adam hamataxšaiy vašnā Auramazdāha yaθā Gaumāta hya magu-71)š v¹θam tyām amāxam naiy parābara

15. θātiy Dārayavauš xšāyaθ-72)iya ima tya adam akunavam pasāva yaθā xšāyaθiya abavam

16. θātiy 73)Dārayavauš xšāyaθiya yaθā adam Gaumātam tyam magum avājanam pa-74)sāva I martiya Āθʳina nāma Upadaraⁿmahyū¹ puθ a hauv udapata[tā Uvajai]-75)y kārahyā avaθā aθaha adam Uvajaiy xšāyaθiya amiy pa[sāva] Uva-76)jiyā hamiθʳiyā abavaⁿ abiy avam [Ā]θʳinam ašiyavaⁿ hauv x[šāyaθiya] 77)abava Uvajaiy utā I martiya Bābiruviya Nadiⁿtabaira nāma Aina[ira]hy-78)ā puθʳa hauv udapatatā Bābirauv kāram avaθā adurujiya adam Nab-79)ukᵘdracara amiy hya Nabunaitahyā puθʳa pasāva kāra hya Bābiruviya 80)haruva abiy avam Nadiⁿtabairam ašiyava Bābiruš hamiθʳiya abava x-81)šaθʳam tya Bābirauv hauv agarbāyatā

17. θātiy Dārayavauš xšāya-82)θiya pasāva adam frāišayam Uvajam hauv Āθʳ[i]na basta anayatā a[biy m]ā-83)m adamšim avājanam

18. θātiy Dārayavauš xšāyaθiya pasāva adam Bā-84)birum ašiyavam abiy avam Nadiⁿtabairam hya Nabukᵘdracara aga[ubat]-ā 85)kāra hya Nadiⁿtabairahyā Tigrām adāraya avadā aištatā² utā 86)abiš nāviyā āha pasāva adam kāram maškāuvā avākanam aniyam uša-87)bārim³ akunavam aniyahyā asam⁴ frānayam⁵ Aura-[maz]dāmaiy upas[t]ām 88)abara vašnā Auramazdāha Tigrām viyatarayāmā⁶ [a]vadā avam kāram 89)tyam Nadiⁿtabairahyā adam ajanam vasiy Āθʳ[i]yādiya[hya] māhyā XXVI rau-90)cabiš θakatā āhaⁿ a[vaθ]ā hamaranam akum[ā]

19. θātiy Dārayavauš x-91)šāyaθiya pasāva a[da]m Bābirum ašiyavam aθiy⁷ Bābiru[m yaθā naiy up]-92)āyam⁸ Zāzāna nāma

---

¹ upadarmahyā, ed. upadaraⁿmahyā, Oppert, Hüsing. See voc.
² āištatā, ed.
³ ušabārim, Jn., KT. uš[tr]abārim, Bartholomae.
⁴ asam, Jn., KT. Formerly as[pā] ed., Bartholomae. See voc.
⁵ frānayam, KT. [patiy]ānayam, ed. wrongly. See voc.
⁶ viyatarayāmā, KT's cuneiform text,—ma KT's transliteration. viyatarayām[ā], Foy.
⁷ aθiy, KT.
⁸ [abiy]āyam, Foy.

tuaries which Gaumâta the Magian destroyed I restored; for the people the revenue (?) and the personal property and the estates and the royal residences[1] which Gaumâta the Magian took from them (I restored); I established the state on (its) foundation, both Persia and Media and the other provinces; as (it was) formerly, so I brought back what (had been) taken away; by the grace of Ahura Mazda this I did; I labored that our royal house I might establish in (its) place; as (it was) formerly, so (I made it); I labored by the grace of Ahura Mazda that Gaumâta the Magian might not take away our royal house.

15. Says Darius the king: This (is) what I did, after that I became king.

16. Says Darius the king: When I slew Gaumâta the Magian, afterwards there (was) one man Âθ‍ʳina by name, the son of Upadara(n)ma; he rose up in Susiana; thus he said to the people; I am king in Susiana; afterwards the people of Susiana became rebellious (and) went over to that Âθ‍ʳina; he became king in Susiana; and there (was) one man a Babylonian Nidintu-Bêl by name, the son of Aniri'; he rose up in Babylon; thus he deceived the people; I am Nebuchadrezzar the son of Nabû-na'id; afterwards the whole of the Babylonian people went over to that Nidintu-Bêl; Babylon became rebellious; the kingdom in Babylon he seized.

17. Says Darius the king: Afterwards I sent to Susiana; this Âθ‍ʳina was led to me bound; I slew him.

18. Says Darius the king: Afterwards I went to Babylon against that Nidintu-Bêl who called himself Nebuchadrezzar; the army of Nidintu-Bêl held the Tigris; there he halted and thereby was a flotilla; afterwards I placed my army on floats of skins; one part I set on camels, for the other I brought horses; Ahura Mazda bore me aid; by the grace of Ahura Mazda we crossed the Tigris; there the army of Nidintu-Bêl I smote utterly; 26 days in the month Âθ‍ʳiyâdiya were in course—then we engaged in battle.

19. Says Darius the king: Afterwards I went to Babylon; when I had not reached Babylon—there (is) a town Zâzâna by

---

[1] Cf. Turfan MSS., mânbêd visbêd zandbêd dahibêd, *lord of the house, lord of the race*, etc. visbêd = der Herr, das Haupt des Geschlechts (tōχm), das in einem vīs, *Geschlechtsdorf*, wohnt. Müller, Nachträge, SBAW, 1904, p. 110.

vardanam anuv Ufrātuvā[1] avadā [hauv Na]di^nta-93)baira hya
Nabuk^ndracara agaubatā āiš[2] hadā kārā patiš [mām hamarana]m
94)cartanaiy pasāva hama[rana]m akumā Auramazdāmaiy upastām abara [vašnā Aura]ma-95)zdāha kāram tyam Nadi^ntabairahyā
adam ajanam vasiy aniya āpi[y]ā [āhyat]ā[3] ā-96)pišim parābara
Anāmakahya māhyā II raucabiš θakatā āha^n avaθā hama[ranam
ak]umā[4]

Col. 2.

1. 1)θātiy Dārayavauš xšāyaθiya [pasā]va Nadi^ntabaira ha-2)dā
kamnaibiš asabāribiš[5] a[muθa[6] Bāb]irum ašiya-3)va pasāva adam
Bābirum ašiyavam [vašnā Auramazd]āha utā Bā-4)birum agarbāyam utā avam Nadi^ntaba[iram agarbāya]m pasāva ava-5)m
Nadi^ntabairam adam Bābirauv avāja[nam
2. θātiy D]ārayavauš x-6)šāyaθiya yātā adam Bābirauv āha[m
imā dahyāva] tyā hacāma ha-7)miθ^riyā abava^n Pārsa Uvaja Māda
Aθ[urā Mudrāya Par]θava Marguš Θa-8)taguš Saka
3. θātiy Dārayavauš x[šāyaθiya I marti]ya Martiya nā-9)ma
Ci^ncixrāiš puθ^ra Kuganakā nā[ma vardanam Pārsaiy] avadā
adāraya 10)hauv udapatatā Uvajaiy kārahyā a[vaθā aθaha adam]
Imaniš amiy U-11)vajaiy xšāyaθiya
4. θātiy Dārayavau[š xšāyaθiya] adakaiy adam ašna-12)iy āham
abiy Uvajam pasāva hacā[ma atarsa^n Uva]jiyā avam Marti-13)yam
agarbāya^n hyašām maθišta āha [utāšim av]ājana^n
5. θātiy D-14)ārayavauš xšāyaθiya I martiya Fra[vartiš nāma
Māda] hauv udapatat-15)ā Mādaiy kārahyā avaθā aθaha [adam
Xšaθrita am]iy Uvaxštrah-16)yā taumāyā pasāva kāra Māda hya
[v^iθāpatiy āha] hacāma hamiθ^riya a-17)bava abiy avam Fravartim ašiyava hauv [xšāyaθiya] abava Mādaiy
6. 18)θātiy Dārayavauš xšāyaθiya kāra Pārsa u[tā M]āda hya
upā mām ā-19)ha hauv kamnam[7] āha pasāva adam kūram frāiša-
[yam Vi]darna nāma Pārsa man-20)ā ba^ndaka avamšām maθištam
akunavam avaθāš[ām aθa]ham paraitā avam k-21)āram tyam Mā-

---

[1] ufrātauvā, ed. See voc.
[2] āiša, ed. See voc.
[3] [āhyat]ā, Kern. [aharat]ā, Oppert, KT. [a]ha^n[jat]ā, WB. See voc.
[4] akumā, Jn. [ak]umā, KT.
[5] asbāribiš, Bartholomae. See voc.
[6] a[muθa], Weissbach. ab[iy], KT.
[7] kamnam, ed. kamnama, Tolman. See voc.

name along the Euphrates—there this Nidintu-Bêl who called himself Nebuchadrezzar went with his army against me to engage in battle; afterwards we engaged in battle; Ahura Mazda bore me aid; by the grace of Ahura Mazda the army of Nidintu-Bêl I smote utterly; the enemy were driven into the water; the water bore them away; 2 days in the month Anâmaka were in course—then we engaged in battle.

Col. 2.

1. Says Darius the king: Afterwards Nidintu-Bêl with (his) few horsemen fled (and) went to Babylon; afterwards I went to Babylon; by the grace of Ahura Mazda I both seized Babylon and seized that Nidintu-Bêl; afterwards I slew that Nidintu-Bêl at Babylon.

2. Says Darius the king: While I was in Babylon, these (are) the provinces which became estranged from me, Persia, Susiana, Media, Assyria,[Egypt], Parthia, Margiana, Sattagydia, Scythia.

3. Says Darius the king: There (was) one man Martiya by name, the son of Ci(n)cikhri—there (is) a town in Persia Kuganakâ by name—here he dwelt; he rose up in Susiana; thus he said to the people; I am Imanish king in Susiana.

4. Says Darius the king: Then I was on the march to Susiana; afterwards the Susians [feared] me; they seized that Martiya who was chief of them and slew him.

5. Says Darius the king: One man Phraortes [by name, a Mede], he rose up in Media; thus he said to the people; [I am Khshathrita] of the family of Cyaxares; afterwards the Median people which [were in the palace] became estranged from me (and) went over to that Phraortes; he became [king] in Media.

6. Says Darius the king: The Persian and the Median army, which was by me, it was small; afterwards I sent forth an army; Hydarnes by name, a Persian, my subject, him I made chief of them; thus I said to them; go, smite that Median army which does not call itself mine; afterwards this Hydarnes with the army went away; when he came to Media — there (is) a town in Media Mâru by name—here he engaged in battle with the Medes; he who was the chief among the Medes did not there [withstand]; Ahura Mazda bore me aid; by the grace of Ahura Mazda my army smote that rebellious army utterly; 27 days in

dam jatā hya manā naiy gaubataiy pasāva hauv Vidarna ha-22)dā kārā ašiyava yaθā Mādam parārasa M[āru]š nāma vardanam Mā-23)daiy avadā hamaranam akunauš hadā Māda[ibi]š hya Mādaišuvā 24)maθišta āha hauv adakaiy naiy [a]vadā $_+$ $_+$[1] Auramazdāmaiy u-25)pastām abara vašnā Auramazdāha kāra [hya ma]nā[2] avam kāram t-26)yam hamiθ⁽ʳ⁾iyam aja^n vasiy Anāmakahya māh[y]ā XXVII raucabiš θakat-27)ā āha^n avaθāšām hamaranam kartam pasāva hauv [kā]ra hya manā Ka^{n}pada[3] nām-28)ā dahyāuš Mādaiy avadā mām amāniya[4] yātā adam arasam Māda-29)m

7. θātiy Dārayavauš xšāyaθiya Dādaršiš nāma Arminiya man-30)ā ba^{n}daka avam adam frāišayam Arminam avaθā[šaiy] aθaham paraidiy kā-31)ra hya hamiθ⁽ʳ⁾iya manā naiy gaubataiy avam [jad]iy pasāva Dādarši-32)š ašiyava yaθā Arminam parārasa pasāva [hamiθ⁽ʳ⁾]iyā ha^{n}gmatā parai-33)tā patiš Dādaršim hamaranam cartanaiy $_+$ $_+$ $_+$ $_+$ y nāma āvahanam A-34)rm^{i}niyaiy[5] avadā hamaranam akunava^n Au[rama]zdāmaiy upastām a-35)bara vašnā Auramazdāha kāra hya manā ava[m k]āram tyam hamiθ⁽ʳ⁾-iyam 36)aja^n vasiy Θūravāharahya māh[yā] VI[II raucabi]š θakatā āha^n avaθ-37)āšām hamaranam kartam

8. θātiy Dā[raya]vau[š xšā]ya[θ]iya patiy duv-38)itīyam hamiθ⁽ʳ⁾iyā ha^{n}gmatā parait[ā pa]tiš [Dāda]ršim hamaranam carta-39)naiy Tigra nāmā didā Arm^{i}ni[yaiy] avadā hamaranam akunava^n A-40)uramazdāmaiy upastām abara vašnā Aura[mazdā]ha kāra hya manā a-41)vam kāram tyam hamiθ⁽ʳ⁾iyam aja^n vas[iy Θūravā]harahya māhyā XVIII 42)raucabiš θakatā āha^n avaθāšām hamaranam ka[rtam]

9. θātiy Dāraya-43)vauš xšāyaθiya patiy θ⁽ʳ⁾itīyam ha[m]iθ⁽ʳ⁾[iyā] ha^{n}gmatā paraitā pat-44)iš Dādaršim hamaranam cartanaiy U[yam]ā[6] nā[m]ā didā Arm^{i}niyaiy a-45)vadā hamaranam akunava^n Auramazdāmaiy upastā[m] abara vašnā Aurama-46)zdāha kāra hya manā avam kāram tyam ham[i]θ⁽ʳ⁾i[yam] [a]ja^n vasiy Θūigarca-47)iš māhyā IX raucabiš θakatā āha^n ava[θāš]ām hamaranam kartam pasāva 48)Dādaršiš citā mām amānaya Ar[m^i]ni[ya]iy [y]ātā adam arasam Mā-49)dam

---

[1] [a]vadā $_+$ $_+$, KT. [a]vadā [āha], Tolman. See voc.
[2] [ma]nā, KT.
[3] ka^{n}pada, ed. ka^{u}pa^{n}da, Foy.
[4] amāniya, KT.
[5] armaniyaiy, ed. wrongly. See voc.
[6] wrongly u[hy]āma, ed. See voc.

the month Anâmaka were completing their course—then the battle (was) fought by them; afterwards this army of mine—there (is) a region Ka(m)pada by name in Media—there awaited me until I went to Media.

7. Says Darius the king: Dâdarshi by name, an Armenian, my subject, him I sent forth to Armenia; thus I said to him; go, the rebellious army which does not call itself mine, smite it; afterwards Dâdarshi went away; when he came to Armenia, afterwards the rebels came together (and) went against Dâdarshi to engage in battle; there is a village [Zuzza][1] by name in Armenia—here they engaged in battle; Ahura Mazda bore me aid; by the grace of Ahura Mazda my army smote that rebellious army utterly; 8 days[2] in the month Thûravâhara were completing their course—then the battle (was) fought by them.

8. Says Darius the king: A second time the rebels came together (and) went against Dâdarshi to engage in battle; there (is) a stronghold, Tigra by name, in Armenia—here they engaged in battle; Ahura Mazda bore me aid; by the grace of Ahura Mazda, my army smote that rebellious army utterly; 18 days in the month Thûravâhara were completing their course—then the battle (was) fought by them.[3]

9. Says Darius the king: A third time the rebels came together (and) went against Dâdarshi to engage in battle; there (is) a stronghold, U[yam]â by name, in Armenia—here they engaged in battle; Ahura Mazda bore me aid; by the grace of Ahura Mazda my army smote that rebellious army utterly; 9 days in the month Thâigarci were completing their course—then the battle (was) fought by them; afterwards Dâdarshi awaited me in Armenia until I came to Media.

10. Says Darius the king: Afterwards Vaumisa by name, a Persian, my subject, him I sent forth to Armenia; thus I said to him; go, the rebellious army which does not call itself mine, smite it; afterwards Vaumisa went away; when he came to Armenia, afterwards the rebels came together (and) went against Vaumisa to engage in battle; there (is) a region I[zar]â by name, in Assyria—here they engaged in battle; Ahura Mazda

---

[1] + + + + y, text; Elam. zuzza; Bab. zu-u-zu.
[2] vi[ii raucabi]š, text. Elam. version makes supplement certain.
[3] Bab. version; *they slew five hundred and forty-six and took five hundred and twenty prisoners.*

10. θātiy Dārayavauš xšāyaθiya ₊ ₊ ₊ ₊ ₊Vaumisa nāma Pārsa manā ba^n-50)daka avam adam frāišayam Arminam avaθāšaiy aθaham paraidiy kāra 51)hya hamiθ^{r}iya manā naiy gaubataiy avam jadiy pasāva Vaumisa a-52)šiyava yaθā Arminam parārasa pasāva hami[θ^{r}iy]ā ha^{n}gmatā paraitā pa-53)tiš Vaumisam hamaranam cartanaiy I ₊ ₊ ₊ ₊ ā^1 nāmā dahyāuš Aθurāy-54)ā avadā hamaranam akunava^n Auramazdā[ma]iy upastām abara vašnā Au-55)ramazdāha kāra hya manā avam kāram t[yam] hamiθ^{r}iyam aja^n vasiy 56)Anāmakahya māhyā XV raucabiš θakatā āha^n avaθāšām hamaranam 57) kartam

11. θātiy Dārayavauš xšāyaθiya patiy duvitīyam ham-58)iθ^{r}iyā ha^{n}gmatā paraitā patiš Vaumisam hamaranam cartanaiy Au-59)tiyāra nāmā dahyāuš Arminiyaiy avadā hamaranam akunava^n 60)Auramazdāmaiy upastām abara vašnā Auramazdāha kāra hya ma-61)nā avam kāram tyam hamiθ^{r}iyam aja^n vasiy Θūravāharahya māh-62)yā jiyamnam^2 patiy avaθāšām hamaranam kartam pasāva Vaumisa 63)citā mām amānaya Arminiya[iy] yātā adam arasam Mādam

12. 64)θātiy Dārayavauš xšāyaθiya pasāva adam nijāyam hacā 65)Bābirauš ašiyavam Mādam yaθā Mādam parārasam Ku^{n}d^{u}ruš nāma 66)vardanam Mādaiy avadā hauv Fravartiš hya Mādaiy xšāyaθiya a-67)gaubatā āiš^3 had[ā] kārā patiš mām hamaranam cartanaiy pasāva hamarana-68)m akumā Auramazdāmaiy upastām abara vašnā Auramazdāha kāram 69)tyam Fravartaiš adam ajanam vasiy Aduka[ni]šahya māhyā XXV ra-70)ucabiš θakatā āha^n avaθā hamaranam akumā

13. θātiy Dārayavauš x-71)šāyaθiya pasāva hauv Fravartiš hadā kamnaibiš asabāribiš amuθa Ra-72)gā nāmā dahyāuš Mādaiy avaparā^4 ašiyava pasāva adam kāram f-73)rāišayam nipadiy^5 Fravartiš āgarbī[ta]^6 anayatā abiy mām ada-74)mšai[y] utā nāham utā gaušā utā h^{a}r^{a}bānam^7 frājanam utāša-75)iy [ucaš]ma^8 avajam duvarayāmaiy basta adāriy haruvašim k-76)āra avaina pasāvašim

---

^{1}[iz]i[tuš] ed., wrongly. i[zar]ā, Tolman. i[zal]ā, Weissbach. See voc.
^{2}jiyamnam, see voc. jiyamanam, KT.
^{3}āiša, ed.
^{4}avaparā, KT.
^{5}nipadiy, KT. tyaipatiy, ed. See voc.
^{6}agarbi[ta], KT. āgarbī[ta], Bartholomae.
^{7}harbānam, KT. See voc. uzbānam, Weissbach.
^{8}ucašma, Weissbach. [ucša]m, KT. word-divider ₊cašma, Jn.

bore me aid; by the grace of Ahura Mazda my army smote that rebellious army utterly; 15 days in the month Anâmaka were completing their course—then the battle (was) fought by them.[1]

11. Says Darius the king: A second time the rebels came together (and) went against Vaumisa to engage in battle; there (is) a region Autiyâra by name in Armenia—here they engaged in battle; Ahura Mazda bore me aid; by the grace of Ahura Mazda my army smote that rebellious army utterly; at the end of the month Thûravâhara—then the battle (was) fought by them;[2] afterwards Vaumisa awaited me in Armenia until I came to Media.

12. Says Darius the king: Afterwards I went from Babylon; I went away to Media; when I went to Media—there (is) a town Ku(n)duru by name in Media—here this Phraortes who called himself king in Media went with (his) army against me to engage in battle; afterwards we engaged in battle; Ahura Mazda bore me aid; by the grace of Ahura Mazda I smote the army of Phraortes utterly; 25 days in the month Adukanisha were completing their course—then we engaged in battle.

13. Says Darius the king: Afterwards this Phraortes with a few horsemen fled; there is a region Ragâ by name in Media—along there he went; afterwards I sent forth my army in pursuit; Phraortes seized was led to me; I cut off (his) nose and ears and tongue, and I put out his eyes;[3] he was held bound[4] at my court; all the people saw him; afterwards I put him on a cross[5] at Ecbatana, and what men were his foremost allies, these I haled within the fortress at Ecbatana.

---

[1] Bab. version; *they slew two thousand and twenty-four.*

[2] Bab version; *they slew two thousand and forty-five and took one thousand five hundred and fifty-eight prisoners.*

[3] Cf. Turfan MSS., hô cašm padišt vafên[d], *they spit upon the sockets of his eyes.*

[4] Cf. Turfan MSS., bast + + + 'ô Ḥêrodôs šâh, (*he was led*) *bound to Herod, the king.*

[5] The phrase seems to mean *crucify* rather than *impale*. Almost its exact equivalent occurs in the Dârôbadagêftîg (Crucifixion), M, 18; Yîšô' sakhôn 'abyâd dârêd jê paṭ Galîlâh 'ô 'ašmâh vî'afrâšt kûm 'abispârênd 'ûṭ qarênd dârôbadag (Bartholomae; dârûbadag, Müller) ḥridig rôj 'aj mûrdân 'akhêzân, *hold in mind the saying of Jesus how in Galilee he informed you; they will give me over and put me on the cross, (but) the third day I will rise from the dead.* Qarênd < kar; dârô cf. New Pers. dâr, *wood;* bad < patiy.

Hagmatānaiy uzmayāpatiy akunavam 77)utā ma[r]tiyā tyaišaiy fratamā anušiyā āhaⁿtā avaiy Ha-78)gmatā[naiy] [aⁿta]r didām frāhaⁿjam

14. θātiy Dārayavauš xš-79)āyaθiya I mar[t]iya Ciθʳaⁿtaxma nāma Asagartiya hauvmaiy hamiθʳiya 80)abava kārahyā avaθā aθaha adam xšāyaθiya amiy Asagarta-81)iy Uvaxštra[hyā] taumāyā pasāva adam kāram Pārsam ut-82)ā Mādam fraišayam Taxmaspāda nāma Māda manā baⁿdaka avam-83)šām maθištam akunavam [a]vaθāšām aθaham paraitā k-84)āram hamiθʳiyam hya manā naiy gaubātaiy avam jatā pas-85)āva Taxmaspāda hadā kārā [a]šiyava hamaranam akunauš had-86)ā Ciθʳaⁿtaxmā Auramazdāmaiy upastām abara vašnā Auramaz-87)dāha kāra hya manā avam kāram tyam hamiθʳiyam ajaⁿ utā C-88)iθʳaⁿtaxmam agarbāya anaya abiy mām pasāvašaiy adam utā n-89)āham utā gaušā frājanam utāšaiy [u]cašma¹ avajam duvarayā-90)maiy basta adāriy haruvašim kāra a[va]i[na] pasāvašim Arbairāyā 91)uzmayāpati[y] akunavam

15. θātiy Dārayava[u]š xšāyaθiya ima tya ma-92)nā kartam Mā[da]iy

16. θātiy² Dārayavauš xšāyaθ[i]ya Parθava utā Var-93)kāna [ham]i[θʳ]iyā [aba]vaⁿ [hacā]ma Fravar[taiš aga]u[baⁿ]tā V'štāspa manā pitā ha-94)uv [Parθavaiy] āha a[va]m kāra avaha[rja³ ham]iθʳi[ya] abava pasāva V'štāspa 95)[ašiyava hadā kār]ā h[yašaiy] anuši[ya] āha Viš[pa]uz[ā]tiš nāma varda-96)[nam Parθavaiy] avadā hamaranam [a]kunau[š] hadā Parθavaibi[š] A[uramazd]āmaiy 97)[upastām abara] vašnā [A]urama[zdāha V'š]tā-[spa] avam kāra[m tyam ha]m[i]θʳiya-98)m [ajaⁿ vasiy V]iyaxnahya m[ā]hyā [XXII raucabiš] θakatā āhaⁿ avaθāšām hamaranam kartam

---

Col. 3.

1. 1)θātiy Dārayavauš xšāyaθiya pasāva adam kāra-2)m Pārsam fraišayam abiy V'štāspam hacā Ragā-3)yā yaθā hauv kāra parārasa abiy V'štāspam 4)pasāva V'štāspa āyasatā⁴ avam kāram ašiyava Patigraba-5)nā nāma vardanam Parθavaiy avadā hamaranam akunauš hadā 6)hamiθʳiyaibiš Auramazdāmaiy up-

---

¹ucašma, Weissbach. [u]cšam, KT. word-divider +cašma, Jn.
²ll. 92-98 suppl., KT.
³avaha[r +], KT. avahar[ja], Tolman. avahar[ta], Weissbach. See voc.
⁴āyasatā, Bartholomae. āyastā, ed., KT.

14. Says Darius the king: One man, Ciθʳa(n)takhma by name, a Sagartian, he became rebellious to me; thus he said to the people; I am king in Sagartia, of the family of Cyaxares; afterwards I sent forth the Persian and Median army; Takhmaspâda by name, a Mede, my subject, him I made chief of them; thus I said to them; go, the rebellious army, which does not call itself mine, smite it; afterwards Takhmaspâda went away with the army (and) engaged in battle with Ciθʳa(n)takhma; Ahura Mazda bore me aid; by the grace of Ahura Mazda my army smote that rebellious army and seized Ciθʳa(n)takhma (and) brought (him) to me; afterwards I cut off his nose and ears, and put out his eyes; he was held bound at my court; all the people saw him; afterwards I put him on a cross in Arbela.

15. Says Darius the king: This (is) what (was) done by me in Media.

16. Says Darius the king: Parthia and Hyrcania became rebellious to me and declared allegiance to Phraortes; my father Hystaspes, he was [in Parthia]; the people abandoned[1] him (and) became rebellious; afterwards Hystaspes [went with his army] which was loyal; there is a town Vish[pa]uz[â]ti' by name [in Parthia]—here he engaged in battle with the Parthians; Ahura Mazda [bore] me [aid]; by the grace of Ahura Mazda Hystaspes smote that rebellious army utterly; [22 days²] in the month Viyakna were completing their course—then the battle was fought by them.

Col. 3.

1. Says Darius the king: Afterwards I sent forth the Persian army to Hystaspes from Ragâ; when this army came to Hystaspes, afterwards Hystaspes took that army (and) went away; there (is) a town Patigrabanâ by name in Parthia—here he engaged in battle with the rebels; Ahura Mazda bore me aid; by the grace of Ahura Mazda Hystaspes smote that rebellious army

---

[1] avahar[ja]. My supplement (Vdt. Stud. 22) I regard as quite certain; cf. hêrz, *leave* in Turfan MSS. e. g. kâdôs Yîšô‘ manâstâr hêrzâ bag mârî Mânî manâ ravân bôž, *Holy Jesus, release my sins; God, lord, Mani, redeem my spirit.*

[2] So Elam. and Bab. versions.

astām abara vašnā Auramaz-7)dāha V¹štāspa avam kāram tyam hamiθ^riyam ajaⁿ vasiy Ga-8)rmapadahya māhyā I rauca θakatam[1] āha avaθāšām hamaranam ka-9)rtam.

2. θātiy Dārayavauš xšāyaθiya pasāva dahyāuš ma-10)nā abava ima tya manā kartam Parθavaiy

3. θātiy Dārayavau-11)š xšāyaθiya Marguš nāmā dahyāuš hauvmaiy hamiθ^riyā[2] abava 12)I martiya Frāda nāma Mārgava avam maθištam akunavaⁿtā pasā-13)va adam frāišayam Dādaršiš nāma Pārsa manā baⁿdaka Bāxtriy-14)ā xšaθ^rapāvā abiy avam avaθāšaiy aθaham paraidiy ava-15)m kāram jadiy hya manā naiy gaubataiy pasāva Dādaršiš hadā k-16)ārā ašiyava hamaranam akunauš hadā Mārgavaibiš[3] Auramazd-17)āmaiy upastām abara vašnā Auramazdāha kāra hya manā avam kāram 18)tyam hamiθ^riyam ajaⁿ vasiy Āθ^riyādiyahya māhyā XXIII raucabi-19)š θakatā āhaⁿ avaθāšām hamaranam kartam

4. θātiy Dārayavau-20)š xšāyaθiya pasāva dahyāuš manā abava ima tya ma-21)nā kartam Bāxtriyā

5. θātiy Dārayavauš xšāya-22)θiya I martiya Vahyazdāta nāma Tāravā nāma vardanam 23)Yautiyā nāmā dahyāuš Pārsaiy avadā adāraya ha-24)uv duvitīyama[4] udapatatā Pārsaiy kārahyā avaθā 25)aθaha adam Bardiya amiy hya Kūrauš puθ^ra pasāva 26)kāra Pārsa hya v¹θāpatiy hacā yadāyā fratarta[5] ha-27)uv hacāma hamiθ^riya abava abiy avam Vahyazdāta-28)m ašiyava hauv xšāyaθiya abava Pārsaiy

6. θā-29)tiy Dārayavauš xšāyaθiya pasāva adam kāram Pārsa-30)m utā Mādam frāišayam hya upā mām āha Artavard-31)iya nāma Pārsa manā baⁿdaka avamšām maθištam aku-32)navam hya aniya kāra Pārsa pasā manā ašiyava Mā-33)dam pasāva Artavardiya hadā kārā ašiyava Pārsam 34)yaθā Pārsam parārasa Raxā nāma vardanam Pārsaiy a-35)vadā hauv Vahyazdāta hya Bardiya agaubatā āiš[6] 36)hadā kārā patiš Artavardiyam hamaranam cartanaiy pas-37)āva hamaranam akunavaⁿ Auramazdāmaiy upastām abara va-38)šnā Auramazdāha kāra hya manā avam kāram tyam Vahya-39)zdātahya ajaⁿ vasiy Θūravāharahya māhyā XII raucabiš θaka-40)tā āhaⁿ avaθāšām hamaranam kartam

---

[1] θakatam, KT. See voc.
[2] hamiθ^riyā, KT. Wrongly hašitiyā, ed.
[3] mārgavaibiš, KT. Wrongly mārgayaibiš, ed.
[4] duvitīyama, Bartholomae. duvitiyam, ed.
[5] yadāyā fratarta, KT. ya[u]dāyā fratarta, Foy. See voc.
[6] āiša, ed.

utterly; 1 day in the month Garmapada was completing its course—then the battle (was) fought by them.[1]

2. Says Darius the king: Afterwards it became my province; this (is) what (was) done by me in Parthia.

3. Says Darius the king: There (is) a region Margiana by name; it became rebellious to me; one man Frâda, a Margian, him they made chief; afterwards I sent forth Dâdarshi by name, a Persian, my subject, satrap in Bactria against him; thus I said to him; go, smite that army which does not call itself mine; afterwards Dâdarshi with the army went away (and) engaged in battle with the Margians; Ahura Mazda bore me aid; by the grace of Ahura Mazda my army smote that rebellious army utterly; 23 days in the month Âθ^riyâdiya were completing their course—then the battle (was) fought by them.[2]

4. Says Darius the king: Afterwards it became my province; this (is) what (was) done by me in Bactria.

5. Says Darius the king: One man Vahyazdâta by name; there (is) a town Târavâ by name; there (is) a region Yautiyâ by name in Persia—here he dwelt; he was the second to rise against me in Persia; thus he said to the people; I am Bardiya the son of Cyrus; afterwards the Persian army which (was) in the palace cast aside their loyalty; they became estranged from me (and) went over to that Vahyazdâta; he became king in Persia.

6. Says Darius the king: Afterwards I sent forth the Persian and the Median army which was by me; Artavardiya by name, a Persian, my subject, him I made chief of them; the rest of the Persian army went with me to Media; afterwards Artavardiya with the army went to Persia; when he came to Persia—there (is) a town Rakhâ by name in Persia—here this Vahyazdâta who called himself Bardiya went with (his) army against Artavardiya to engage in battle; afterwards they engaged in battle; Ahura Mazda bore me aid; by the grace of Ahura Mazda my army smote that army of Vahyazdâta utterly; 12 days in the

---

[1] Bab. version; *he slew six* (?) *thousand five hundred and seventy and took four thousand one hundred and ninety-two prisoners.*

[2] Bab version; *he slew fifty-five thousand* (sic!) *two hundred and + + three and took six thousand five hundred and seventy-two prisoners.* The Koldewey fragment reads; *six thousand nine hundred and seventy, + + + prisoners.*

7. θātiy Dārayavauš xšāyaθi-41)ya pasāva hauv Vahyazdāta hadā kamnaibiš asabāribiš a-42)muθa ašiyava Paišiyāuvādām hacā avadaša kāram āyasa-43)tā[1] hyāparam āiš[2] patiš Artavardiyam hamaranam cartana-44)iy Parga[3] nāma kaufa avadā hamaranam akunava[n] Auramazdāma-45)iy upastām abara vašnā Auramazdāha kāra hya manā ava-46)m kāram tyam Vahyazdātahya aja[n] vasiy Garmapadahya māh-47)yā V raucabiš θakatā āha[n] avaθūšām hamaranam kartam utā ava-48)m Vahyazdātam agarbāya[n] utā martiyā tyaišaiy fratam-49)ā anušiyā āha[n]ta[4] agarbāya[n]

8. θātiy Dārayavauš xš-50)āyaθiya pasāva adam avam Vahyazdātam utā martiyā 51)tyaišaiy fratamā anušiyā āha[n]ta[4] Uvādaicaya nāma var-52)danam Pārsaiy avadašiš uzmayāpatiy akunavam

9. θū-53)tiy Dārayavauš xšāyaθiya ima tya manā kartam Pārsaiy

10. 54)θātiy Dārayavauš xšāyaθiya hauv Vahyazdāta hya Bardiya 55)agaubatā[5] hauv kāram frāišaya Harauvatim Vivāna 56)nāma Pārsa manā ba[n]daka Harauvatiyā xšaθrapāvā abiy ava-57)m utāšām I martiyam maθištam akunauš avaθūšām a-58)θaha paraitā Vivānam jatā utā avam kāram hya Dāraya-59)vahauš xšāyaθiyahyā gaubataiy pasāva hauv kāra ašiya-60)va tyam Vahyazdāta frāišaya abiy Vivānam hamaranam cartanaiy K-61)āpišakūniš nāmā didā avadā hamaranam akunava[n] Auramazdāmai-62)y upastām abara vašnā Auramazdāha kāra hya manā avam kāram tya-63)m hamiθ[r]iyam aja[n] vasiy Anāmakahya māhyā XIII raucabiš θakatā āha[n] a-64)vaθāšām hamaranam kartam

11. θātiy Dārayavauš xšāyaθiya patiy h-65)yāparam hamiθ[r]iyā ha[n]gmatā paraitā patiš Vivānam hamaranam cartana-66)iy Ga[n]dum(?)ava[6] nāmā dahyāuš avadā hamaranam akunava[n] Auramazdāma-67)iy upastām abara[7] vašnā Auramazdāha kāra hya manā avam kāram t-68)yam hamiθ[r]iyam aja[n] vasiy Viya[x]nahya māhyā VII raucabiš θakatā 69)āha[n] avaθāšām hamaranam kartam

12. θātiy Dārayavauš xšāyaθiya 70)pasāva hauv mart[iya] hya avahyā kārahyā maθ[išta ā]ha tyam Va-71)hyazdāta frāišaya abiy

---

[1] āyasatā, Bartholomae. āyastā, ed., KT.
[2] āiša, ed.
[3] paraga, KT, ed.
[4] āha[n]ta, KT as Rawlinson; certainly not a "schreibfehler Rawlinsons."
[5] agauratā, text, stone-cutter's blunder.
[6] ga[n]dutava, KT. ga[n]dumava, Justi.
[7] ar[a]r[a], text, stone-cutter's blunder for abara.

month Thûravâhara were completing their course—then the battle (was) fought by them.

7. Says Darius the king: Afterwards this Vahyazdâta with few horsemen fled (and) went to Paishiyâuvâdâ; from thence he took an army (and) again went against Artavardiya to engage in battle; there (is) a mountain Parga by name—here they engaged in battle; Ahura Mazda gave me aid; by the grace of Ahura Mazda my army smote that army of Vahyazdâta utterly; 5 days in the month Garmapada were completing their course—then the battle (was) fought by them and they seized that Vahyazdâta and what men were his foremost allies they seized.

8. Says Darius the king: Afterwards—there (is) a town in Persia Uvâdaicaya by name—here, that Vahyazdâta and what men were his foremost allies, them I put on the cross.

9. Says Darius the king: This (is) what (was) done by me in Persia.

10. Says Darius the king: This Vahyazdâta, who called himself Bardiya, he sent forth an army to Arachosia—there (was) Vivâna by name, a Persian, my subject, satrap in Arachosia—against him (he sent an army) and one man he made chief of them; thus he said to them; go, smite Vivâna and that army which calls itself of Darius the king; afterwards this army, which Vahyazdâta sent forth, went against Vivâna to engage in battle; there (is) a stronghold Kâpishakâni by name—here they engaged in battle; Ahura Mazda bore me aid; by the grace of Ahura Mazda my army smote that rebellious army utterly; 13 days in the month Anâmaka were completing their course—then the battle (was) fought by them.

11. Says Darius the king: Again the rebels came together (and) went against Vivâna to engage in battle; there (is) a region Ga(n)dum(?)ava by name—here they engaged in battle; Ahura Mazda bore me aid; by the grace of Ahura Mazda my army smote that rebellious army utterly; 7 days in the month Viyakhna were completing their course—then the battle (was) fought by them.

12. Says Darius the king: Afterwards this man, who was chief of that army which Vahyazdâta sent against Vivâna, he fled with a few horsemen (and) went away—there (is) a stronghold Arshâdâ by name in Arachosia—he went thereby; afterwards Vivâna with an army went in pursuit of them; here he seized him and what men were his foremost allies he slew.

Vivānam hauv am[uθa¹ ha]dā kamnaib-72)iš asabāribiš ašiyava Aršādā nāmā didā [Ha]rauvatiyā a-73)vaparā² atiyāiš³ pasāva Vivāna hadā kārā nipadi[y] t[ya]iy⁴ ašiya-74)va avadāšim agarbāya u[t]ā martiyā tyaišaiy fratamā anušiyā 75)āhaⁿtā avājaⁿ

13. θātiy Dārayavauš xšāyaθiya pasāva dahyāuš ma-76)nā abava ima tya manā kartam Harauvatiyā

14. θātiy Dārayavauš xšā-77)yaθiya yātā adam Pārsai[y] u[t]ā Mādaiy āham patiy duvitīyam 78)Bābiruviyā hamiθʳiyā abavaⁿ hacāma I martiya Arxa nāma [Arm]ini-79)ya Halditahya puθʳa hauv udapatatā Bābirauv Dubāla nāmā [da]hyā-80)uš hacā avadaša hauv [k]ārahyā avaθā adurujiya adam Nabukud-81)racara amiy Nabunaitahya puθʳa pasāva kāra Bābiruviya hacāma ha-82)miθʳiya abava abiy avam Arxam ašiyava Bābirum hauv agarbāyat-83)ā hauv xšāyaθiya abava Bābirauv

15. θātiy Dā[rayavau]u[š xš]āyaθi-84)ya pasāva adam kāram frāišayam Bābirum Viⁿdafar[nā] nāma Pā[rsa] manā 85)baⁿdaka avamšām maθištam akunavam avaθāšām aθaham para[itā ava]m kāram 86)Bābiruvi[ya]m⁵ jatā hya manā naiy [ga]ubātaiy⁶ pasāva [V]iⁿda[farn]ā hadā kār-87)ā ašiyava Bābirum Auramazdāmaiy upast[ām] a[bara] vašnā Auramaz-88)dāha Viⁿda[far]nā Bābiruvi[y]ā ajaⁿ⁷ utā [bastā anaya]⁸ + + + + + + + māhyā XXII ra-89)ucabiš [θaka]tā āhaⁿ avaθā avam A[rxam hya Nabuku]dracara a-90)gauba[tā⁹ ut]ā martiyā tyā i + + + + nuši + + + + + 91)+ + + + + + [hauv Arxa u]tā [mart]iyā t[yaišaiy f]rata[m]ā a[n]-92)[u]ši[y]ā āhaⁿtā Bābira[u]v [uzmay]āpatiy akariyaⁿtā¹⁰

Col. 4.

1. 1)θātiy Dūraya[vauš] xšāyaθiya ima t-2)ya manā kartam [Bābirau]v

¹ am[uθa], KT. Wrongly maθ[išta], ed.
² avaparā, KT.
³ atiyā[i]ša, ed. See voc.
⁴ t[ya]iy, KT. See voc.
⁵ bābiruvi[ya]m, KT. Wrongly bābirauv, ed.
⁶ [ga]ubātaiy, KT. [ga]ubataiy, ed.
⁷ bābiruvi[y]ā ajaⁿ, KT. Wrongly bābirum agarbāya, ed.
⁸ [bastā anaya], Tolman.
⁹ ll. 90-91, a-90)gauba[tā ut]ā martiyā tyai[šaiy fratamā a]nušiyā [āhaⁿtā agarbāya pa]-91)sāva [niya]štāyam, Weissbach. See voc. s. v. kar.
¹⁰ akariyaⁿtā, Bartholomae, WBⁱⁱ. asariyatā, KT. ākariyaⁿtām, WBⁱ. See voc.

13. Says Darius the king: Afterwards the province became mine; this (is) what (was) done by me in Arachosia.

14. Says Darius the king: When I was in Persia and in Media, a second time the Babylonians became estranged from me; one man, Arkha by name, an Armenian son of Haldita, he rose up in Babylon; there (is) a region, Dubâla by name—from here he thus lied to the people; I am Nebuchadrezzar, the son of Nabû-na'id; afterwards the Babylonian people became estranged from me (and) went over to that Arkha; he seized Babylon; he became king in Babylon.

15. Says Darius the king: Afterwards I sent forth my army to Babylon; Intaphernes by name, a Persian, my subject, him I made chief of them; thus I said to them; go, smite that Babylonian army which does not call itself mine; afterwards Intaphernes with an army went to Babylon; Ahura Mazda bore me aid; by the grace of Ahura Mazda Intaphernes smote the Babylonians; and [he led them bound to me]; 22 days in the month + + + +[1] were completing their course—then that Arkha, who called himself Nebuchadrezzar, and the men who [were his foremost allies they seized and bound];[2] [this Arkha] and what men were his foremost allies were put on the cross at Babylon.

Col. 4.

1. Says Darius the king: This (is) what was done by me in Babylon.

2. Says Darius the king: This (is) what I did; by the grace of Ahura Mazda in the same year[3] after that I became king I

---

[1] The Elam. version gives the month Markazanash.

[2] Supplied from Elam. version; see voc. akariyaⁿtā, s. v. kar.

[3] Weissbach's interpretation (see voc. s. v. θard) is very probable, yet I would note the following objections: 1)The lacuna before Bab. MUANNA fits gab-bi, *all*, very well; cf. Oppert's old interpretation, *dans toute l'anne, toujours, dans toute ma vie*, to which I would add Turfan MSS. hâv-sâr, *eius modi*. So KT, *always*. 2)The omission of the det. AN (which invariably occurs in expressions of time) from the corresponding Elam. phrase. 3)The congestion of all these recorded events in one year. Weissbach in a personal letter to me (quoted in voc.) would avoid this difficulty by supposing that Darius' words are not literally true here; that the rebellions broke out in one and the same year but putting them down required a longer time, a difficult explanation when we read the express words of the king who is recording what *he*, not others, accomplished.

2. θātiy D-3)ārayavauš xš[āyaθi]ya ima tya adam akuna-4)vam vašnā Aura[mazd]āha[1] hamahyāyā θar-5)da pasāva yaθā x[šāya-θiya] abavam XIX hamaran-6)ā akunavam vašn[ā Aura]mazdāha adamšim[2] a-7)janam utā IX xš[āyaθiy]ā agarbāyam I Gaumāta 8)nāma maguš āha [hauv ad]urujiya avaθā aθaha adam 9)Bardiya amiy [hya Kū]rauš puθ'a hauv Pārsam ha-10)miθ'iyam akunau[š I Āθ'i]na nāma Uvajiya hauv adu-11)rujiya avaθā a[θaha adam] xšāyaθiya amiy Uvajaiy 12)hauv Uvajam ha[miθ'iya]m akunauš [ma]nā [I Na]di'tabaira n-13)āma Bābiruviya hauv adurujiya avaθā aθaha 14)adam Nabukudra[cara amiy] hya Nabunaitahya puθ'a 15)hauv Bābirum [hami]θ'iyam akunauš I Martiya nā-16)ma Pārsa hauv [ad]u[ruj]iya avaθā aθaha adam Imani-17)š amiy Uvajai[y xšāya]θiya hauv Uvajam hamiθ'iya-18)m akunauš I Fravar[ti]š nāma Māda hauv adurujiya 19)avaθā aθaha a[da]m [X]ša[θr]ita amiy Uvaxštrahya taumāy-20)ā hauv Mādam [hami-θ'iyam] akunauš I Ciθ'a'taxma nāma Asa-21)gartiya hauv [adu]-rujiya avaθā aθaha adam xšāyaθ-22)iya amiy Asaga[rtaiy] Uvaxš-trahya taumāyā hauv 23)Asagartam hamiθ'i[yam] akunauš I Frāda nāma 24)Mārgava hauv a[d]u[r]ujiya avaθā aθaha adam 25)xšāyaθiya a[miy Mar]gauv hauv Margum hamiθ'i-26)yam akunauš [I Vahya]zdāta nāma Pārsa hauv a-27)durujiya ava[θā aθaha] adam Bardiya amiy hya Kū-28)rauš puθ'a ha[uv Pār]sam hamiθ'iyam akunauš I Ar-29)xa nāma Armin[iya hauv] adurujiya avaθā aθaha adam Nab-30)ukudracara amiy [hya Nabu]naitahya puθ'a hauv Bābirum ham-31)iθ'iyam akunauš

3. θā[t]iy Dārayavauš xšāyaθiya imaiy 32)IX xšāyaθiyā [ada]m agarbāyam a'tar imā hamaranā

4. 33)θātiy Dāraya[vauš xšā]yaθiya dahyāva imā tyā hamiθ'iy-34)ā abava" drauga di[š hamiθ'iy]ā akunauš tya imaiy kāram adur-35)ujiyaša" pasāva di[š Auramaz]dā manā dastayā akunauš yaθā mām k-36)āma avaθā di[š akunavam]

5. θātiy Dārayavauš xšāyaθi-37)ya tuvam kā x[šāyaθiya h]ya aparam[3] āhy[4] hacā draugā daršam 38)patipayauvā mart[iya hya drau]jana abatiy avam ufraštam[5] parsā ya-39)diy avaθā man[iyā-hay][6] dahyāušmaiy duruvā ahati-40)y

* [1] aura[mazd]āha, WB." a[uramazdāha] āha, ed.
[2] adamšim, KT. Wrongly adamšām, ed.
[3] apara-ma, Bartholomae. See voc.
[4] ahy, ed., KT., wrongly in all places. See voc
[5] ufraštam, KT. See voc.
[6] ma[niyāhy], ed.

engaged in 19 battles; by the grace of Ahura Mazda I waged them and I seized 9 kings; there was one, Gaumâta by name, a Magian; he lied; thus he said; I am Bardiya the son of Cyrus; he made Persia rebellious; there (was) one, Âθʳina by name, a Susian; he lied; thus he said; I am king in Susiana; he made Susiana rebellious to me; there (was) one, Nidintu-Bêl by name, a Babylonian; he lied; thus he said; I am Nebuchadrezzar the son of Nabû-na'id; he made Babylon rebellious; there (was) one, Martiya by name, a Persian; he lied; thus he said; I am Imanish, king in Susiana; he made Susiana rebellious; there (was) one, Phraortes by name, a Mede; he lied; thus he said; I am Khshathrita, of the family of Cyaxares; he made Media rebellious; there (was) one, Ciθʳa(n)takhma by name, in Sagartia; he lied; thus he said; I am king in Sagartia, of the family of Cyaxares; he made Sagartia rebellious; there (was) one, Frâda by name, a Margian; he lied; thus he said; I am king in Margiana; he made Margiana rebellious; there (was) one, Vahyazdâta by name, a Persian; he lied; thus he said; I am Bardiya the son of Cyrus; he made Persia rebellious; there (was) one, Arkha by name, an Armenian; he lied; thus he said; I am Nebuchadrezzar the son of Nabû-na'id; he made Babylon rebellious.

3. Says Darius the king: These 9 kings I seized within these battles.

4. Says Darius the king: These (are) the provinces which became rebellious; the Lie made them rebellious so that these deceived the people; afterwards Ahura Mazda gave them into my hand; as was my will so [I did] unto them.

5. Says Darius the king: O thou who shalt be king in the future, protect thyself strongly from Deceit; whatever man shall be a deceiver,[1] him well punished, punish, if thus thou shalt think "may my country be secure."

6. Says Darius the king: This (is) what I did; by the grace of Ahura Mazda I did (it) in the same year; O thou who shalt examine this inscription in the future, let it convince thee[2] (as to) what (was) done by me; regard it not as lies.

7. Says Darius the king: Ahura Mazda is my surety that this (is) true (and) not false (which) I did in the same year.

---

[1] Cf. Turfan MSS., drôzaniy.
[2] Cf. Turfan MSS., nê varovâd, *is not believed;* par varnū, *by belief*, Neutest. Bruchstücke in soghdischer Sprache.

6. θātiy Dā[raya]va[uš] xšāyaθiya ima tya adam akunavam 41)vašnā Auramazdāha [ha]ma[h]yāyā θarda akunavam tuvam kā hya 42)aparam imām dipi[m] patiparsāhy tya manā kartam varnavatām 43)θuvām mātya [drauj]īyāhy[1]

7. θātiy Dārayavauš xšā-44)yaθiya Auramazd[ām upāva]rtaiy[a]iy[a2] yaθā ima hašiyam naiy duru-45)xtam adam akuna[vam hama]hyāyā θarda

8. θātiy Dārayavauš xšāya-46)θiya vašnā Aura[mazdāha ap]imaiy aniyašciy vasiy astiy karta-47)m ava ahyāyā d[i]p[iy]ā naiy nipištam avabyarādiy naiy n-48)ipištam māt[ya hya apa]ram imām dipim patiparsātiy avah-49)yā paruv θa[dayā[3] tya] manā kartam naiš[im] ima[4] varnavātaiy d-50)uruxtam maniyā[taiy][5]

9. θātiy Dārayavauš xšāyaθiya tyaiy 51)paruvā xšāyaθ[iyā y]ātā āha[n] avaišām avā naiy astiy kar-52)tam yaθā manā va[šnā] Auramazdāha hamahyāyā θarda kartam

10. θā-53)tiy Dārayavauš x[šā]yaθiya nūram[6] θuvām varnavātām tya man-54)ā kartam avaθā kā[rahyā θ]ā[hy avahya]rādiy[7] mā apagaudaya yadiy imām 55)ha[n]dugām naiy [a]pa[gau]da[yāh]y kārahyā θāhy Auramazdā θuvām 56)dauštā bīyā utā[ta]iy taumā vasiy bīyā utā dargam jīvā

11. 57)θātiy Dārayavauš [xšāya]θiya yadiy imām ha[n]dugām apagaudayā-58)hy naiy θāhy [k]āra[hyā] Auramazdātay jatā bīyā utātaiy taum-59)ā mā bīyā

12. θātiy Dārayavauš xšāyaθiya ima tya adam akunavam 60)hamahyāyā θarda [vašn]ā Auramazdāha akunavam Auramazdāmaiy upas-61)tām abara utā an[iyāha ba]gāha tyaiy ha[n]tiy

13. θātiy Dārayavau-62)š xšāyaθiya avah[ya]rā[diy] Auramazdā upastām abara utā ani-63)yāha bagāha tyai[y ha[n]tiy yaθ]ā naiy arai[ka] āham naiy draujana āham na-64)iy zūrakara āham

---

[1] [drauj]īyāhy, Bartholomae. [duruj]iyāhy, KT, WB[n]. [duruxtam man]iyāhy, ed.

[2] Dittography for auramazd[ām upāva]rtaiy, Tolman. See voc. auramazd[a] + + + + + rtaiyiya, KT. auramaz[diya] taiyiya, WB. auramazd[ā va]rtiyaiy, Bartholomae.

[3] θadayā, Bartholomae. θad[a] + +, Jn. θā[dutiy], KT. See voc.

[4] naiš[im] ima, Tolman. naiš[aiy] ima, Weissbach. naiš + + im, KT.

[5] maniy[ātiy], ed.

[6] nuram, KT, Jn. + + + nuram, ed. wrongly.

[7] sā + + + + d + + + + + + ādiy, KT. kā[rahyā θ]ā[hy avahya]rādiy, Tolman.

8. Says Darius the king: By the grace of Ahura Mazda much else (was) done by me that (is) not written[1] on this inscription; for this reason it (is) not written lest whoever shall examine this inscription in the future, to him what has been done by me should seem too much; and it should not convince him, but he should think (it) false.

9. Says Darius the king: Who were the former kings, while they lived, by these nothing (was) thus done as (was) done by me through the grace of Ahura Mazda in the same year.

10. Says Darius the king: Now let it convince thee (as to) what (was) done by me; thus [tell it to the people];[2] do not conceal (it); if thou shalt not conceal this record (but) tell (it) to the people, may Ahura Mazda be a friend to thee and may there be unto thee a family abundantly and mayest thou live long.

11. Says Darius the king: If thou shalt conceal this record (and) not tell (it) to the people, may Ahura Mazda be a smiter unto thee and may there not be unto thee a family.

12. Says Darius the king: This (is) what I did in the same year; by the grace of Ahura Mazda I did (it); Ahura Mazda bore me aid and the other gods which are.

13. Says Darius the king: For this reason Ahura Mazda bore me aid and the other gods which are, because I was not an enemy, I was not a deceiver, I was not a wrong-doer, neither I nor my family; according to rectitude [I ruled] nor against the slave(?) nor the lowly(?) did I exercise oppression;[3] the man who helped my house, him well esteemed, I esteemed; (the man) who would destroy it, him well punished, I punished.

14. Says Darius the king: O thou who shalt be king in the future, whatever man shall be a deceiver or whoever shall be a

---

[1] Cf. nipis, *write*, Neutest. Bruckstücke in soghdischer Sprache, Müller, SBAW, 1907; New Pers. nivēsa∂.

[2] I would read avaθā kā[rahyā θ]ā[hy avahya]rādiy, *tell it thus to the people*; *for this reason*, which can fit the few traces of characters on the rock. Since KT do not give the extent of the lacuna, I feel some doubt whether the space justifies the supplement of the last word. KT however read the Elam. as hu[pentukkime], *wherefore*. I would add that my reading is in full accord with Weissbach's emendation of the Bab. version, u amat kit- tum a-na u-ḵu ki-[bi?], *and declare(?) the true record to the people*, ZDMG, 61, 729.

[3] See voc. s. v, + + + tᵘnᵘuvᵃtᵃmᵃ

[naiy a]da[m na]imaiy taumā upariy arštām¹ upariy-65)[axša-yaiy]² naiy šakauri[m³ naiy] ₊ ₊ tᵘnᵘuvᵃtᵃmᵃ⁴ zūra akunavam martiya hya hamata-66)xšatā manā v¹θi[yā a]vam ubartam a[ba]ram hya viyanā[sa]ya⁵ avam ufrasta-67)m aparsam

14. θātiy Dārayavauš xšāyaθiya tuvam [kā] xšāyaθiya 68)hya aparam⁶ āhy martiya [hya] draujana ahatiy hyavā [zū]rakara₊₊⁷ ahat-69)iy avaiy mā dauštā [bīy]ā⁸ ufraštādiy parsā

15. θātiy Dāra-70)yavauš xšāyaθiya [tu]vam kā hya aparam imām dipim vaināhy ty-71)ām adam niyapi[ša]m [i]maivā patikarā mātya vikanāhy⁹ yāvā dᵃ(?)-72)tᵃsᵃ(?)¹⁰ āhy avaθāštā¹¹ pari[ba]rā¹²

16. θātiy Dārayavauš xšāyaθiya ya-73)[diy] imām di[pim] vainā[hy] imaivā patikarā naiydiš vikanāhy⁹ utā-74)taiy yāvā taumā [ahatiy] paribarāh(i)diš¹³ Auramazdā θuvām dauštā bīy-75)ā utātaiy tau[mā] vasiy bī[y]ā utā dargam jīvā utā tya kunavāhy 76)avataiy Auramazdā [ukarta]m¹⁴ kunautuv

17. θātiy Dārayavauš xšā-77)yaθiya yadiy im[ā]m dipim imaivā patikarā vaināhy vikanāh(i)diš¹⁵ ut-78)ātaiy yāvā tau[m]ā ahati[y nai]ydiš paribarāhy¹⁶ Auramazdātaiy jatā b-79)īyā utātaiy taum[ā mā bīyā] utā tya kunavāhy avataiy Auramazd-80)ā nikᵃⁿtuv

18. θātiy Dā[ra]yavauš xšāyaθiya imaiy martiyā tyaiy 81)adakaiy avadā [ā]haⁿtā yātā adam Gaumātam tyam magum avājanam 82)hya Bardiya aga[uba]tā adakai[y] imaiy martiyā hamataxšaⁿtā anušiyā man-83)ā Viⁿdafarnā nā[ma] Vā[ya]sp[āra]hyā puθʳa Pār[sa U]tā[na n]āma Θuxrah[y]ā 84)[puθʳa] Pārsa [Gaubr]u-

---
¹ arštām, Foy, Jn., KT. See voc.
² upariy[āyam], ed., upariy[axšayaiy], Tolman. See voc.
³ šᵃkᵃurᵃi[mᵃ], KT. š-kᵃurᵃi(?)mⁿ, Jn. See voc.
⁴ tᵘnᵘuvᵃtᵃmᵃ, KT. mᵃnᵘuvᵃtᵃmᵃ, Jn. See voc.
⁵ viyanā[sa]ya, KT. viyanā[θa]ya, Foy.
⁶ apara-ma, Bartholomae.
⁷ [zu]rakara, KT, Müller, Foy. See voc.
⁸ [bīy]ā (Opt. 2 sg.), Tolman, Weissbach. ₊ ₊ ₊ ā, KT.
⁹ vikanāhy, Jn. visanāhy, KT. See voc.
¹⁰ da(?)tas(?) ahy, KT. āmātaāhy, Tolman. tava ahy, Hoffmann-Kutschke.
¹¹ avaθā štā, Hoffmann-Kutschke.
¹² pari[ba]rā, KT. Wrongly parikarā, ed. See voc.
¹³ wrongly parikarāh[i]diš, ed.
¹⁴ [ukarta]m, Tolman. [vazarka]m, Oppert, Foy. See voc.
¹⁵ vikanāh[i]diš, Jn. visanāhadiš, KT.
¹⁶ wrongly parikarāhy, ed.

wrong-doer (be) not a friend to these; punish (them) with severe punishment.

15. Says Darius the king: O thou who shalt see this inscription in the future which I have written or these sculptures, thou shalt not destroy (them) as long as thou shalt be powerful(?); thus thou shalt guard them.

16. Says Darius the king: If thou shalt see this inscription or these sculptures (and) shalt not destroy them and shalt guard them as long as thy family[1] shall be, may Ahura Mazda be a friend to thee and may there be unto thee a family abundantly and mayest thou live long and whatever thou shalt do, this for thee (let) Ahura Mazda make [successful].

17. Says Darius the king: If thou shalt see this inscription or these sculptures (and) shalt destroy them and shalt not guard them as long as thy family shall be, may Ahura Mazda be a smiter unto thee and may there not be unto thee a family and whatever thou shalt do, this let Ahura Mazda destroy for thee.

18. Says Darius the king: These (are) the men who were there then when I slew Gaumâta the Magian, who called himself Bardiya; then these men coöperated as my allies; Intaphernes by name, the son of Vâyaspârâ, a Persian; Otanes by name, the son of Thukhra, a Persian; Gobryas by name, the son of Mardonius, a Persian; Hydarnes by name, the son of Bagâbigna, a Persian; Megabyzus by name, the son of Dâtuhya, a Persian; Ardumanish by name, the son of Vahauka, a Persian.

19. Says Darius the king: O thou who shalt be king in the future, preserve [the family of] these men.

20. Says Darius the king: By the grace of Ahura Mazda this inscription + + + + which I made + + + + + + + + I have written; this inscription + + + me afterwards the inscription + + + + + throughout the provinces + the people.[2]

---

[1] Here and in the following section Bartholomae renders taumā, by *power* (i. e. *as long as will be possible*), connecting the word with the root *tu, to be strong,* Av. tu. Cf. Foy. KZ. 35, 47; WZKM. 24, 288; Bang. ZDMG. 43, 533; Reichelt, KZ. 39, 74. The Elam. translates the word by patta, which Foy. interprets *possibility.* See voc. s. v. tauman.

[2] For Hoffmann-Kutschke's interpretation of Elam. version (Bh. L.) cf. Or. Lit. Ztg., Sept., 1906; also Jensen, ZDMG, 55.

va nāma Marduniyahya [puᶿʳa] [P]ārsa [Vi]darna nāma Ba-
85)g[ā]bignah[yā p]uᶿʳa Pārsa Ba[gab]uxša nāma [Dātu]hyahyā
puᶿʳa Pārsa 86)Ar[duma]n[iš nāma] Vahau[kahya p]uᶿʳa Pārsa

19. θātiy Dārayavauš xšāyaθ-87)iya tuvam [kā] xšāya[θ]iya hya aparam[1] āhy tyām imaišām martiyā u-88)₊ ₊ ₊ ₊ ₊ ₊ imām ₊ ₊ ₊ ā ₊ ₊ ₊ ₊ par[ibar]ā[2]

20. θātiy Dārayavauš xšāyaθiya vašnā [A]u-89)[ramaz]dā[ha] i[yam] dipi ₊ ₊ ₊ ₊ ₊ [ty]ām[3] akunavam ₊ ₊ tišam a ₊ ₊ ā ₊ ₊ t ₊ avast-90)[ā]ya[m] ₊ ₊ ₊ ₊ āxar ₊ ₊ ₊ ₊ [niyap]išam iya [d]ipi ₊ ₊ ₊ nam aθahavaja ₊ ₊ ₊ ₊ iš ₊ ₊ ₊ ₊ ādā 91)₊ ₊ ₊ ₊ ₊ m utā ₊ ₊ ₊ ₊ i ₊ ₊ i ₊ ₊ ᵐi ā ₊ ₊ ₊ taiy ₊ ₊ ₊ ₊ ya ₊ i ₊ iyā mā[m] pasāva ima d-92)ipi ₊ ₊ ₊ ima ₊ ₊ ₊ āvatā ₊ ₊ ₊ ₊ ₊ ₊ ₊ ₊ aⁿtar dahyā[va k]āra hama amaxamatā[4]

Col. 5.

1. 1)θāt[iy D]ārayava[uš x]šāyaθiya 2)ima t[ya ada]m aku[na-vam]₊ ₊ ₊ ₊ tiya a ₊ ₊-3)mca θʳ[itīyām][5] θardam ₊ ₊ [pasāva ya]θā xšāya-4)θiya [abavam U]vaja [nāmā da]hyauš hau-5)v ha-[cāma hamiθʳiya] abava [I martiya] ₊ mamaita nāma U-6)vaji[ya avam maθ]išta[m akunavaⁿ]tā pasāva ada-7)m kā[ram frāiša]yam U[vajam I martiya] Gaubruva 8)nāma [Pārsa man]ā baⁿdaka [avamšām] maθištam aku-9)navam pa[sāva hauv Gau]bruva [hadā kār]ā ašiyava 10)Uvajam [hamaranam a]kuna[uš hadā] Uvajiyai-biš[6] pas-11)āva Ga[ubr]uva ₊ ₊ ₊ ₊ ₊ ₊ [av]āja ⁿ utā daiy[7] marda 12)utā [tyamšām][8] maθ[ištam] agarbāya anaya abi-13)y mā[m utāši]m ada[m avā]janam pasāva dahyā-14)uš [manā abava]

2. θāt[iy Dā]rayavauš xšāyaθi-15)ya a[dakaiy Uvaj]iyā [atar-

---

[1] apara-ma, Bartholomae. See voc.

[2] tyām imaišām martiyānā-88)m taumām [ubart]ā[m] par[ibar]ā, Weissbach.

[3] [ariy]ām, WBⁿ.

[4] [k]āra hama amaxahyatā, Weissbach. See voc. ll. 88-90 are supposed to correspond to Elam. Bh.L. referring to duplicate copies sent to all lands. Cf. fragment BE. 8627 found by Dr. Koldewey at Babylon = Bh. 55-58; 69-72.

[5] θʳ[itiyam], WBⁿ., better read θʳ[itīyām]. KT record traces of first character as θʳ or p; the latter might be initial of Persian word for *fifth*.

[6] uvajiyaibiš, KT. hamiθʳiyaibiš, ed. wrongly

[7] utā daiy, KT. utā šiš, Tolman. utāšim, Foy.

[8] [tvamšām]. WBⁿ.

Col. 5.

1. Says Darius the king: This (is) what I did [in the third?] year [when I became] king; (there is) a province Susiana [by name]; this became estranged from me; [one man] ₊ ₊ ₊ mamaita by name, a Susian, him they made chief; afterwards I sent forth (my) army to Susiana; [one man] Gobryas by name, [a Persian] my subject, [him] I made chief [of them]; afterwards this Gobryas with an army went to Susiana; he engaged in [battle] with the Susians; afterwards Gobryas smote ₊ ₊ ₊ and annihilated them (?) and seized their chief and brought him to me and I slew him; afterwards the province [became mine].

2. Says Darius the king: Then the Susians [feared] and Ahura Mazda gave them [into my hand]; I offered thanks; by the grace of Ahura Mazda, as was my will, thus I did unto them.

3. Says Darius the king: Whoever shall worship Ahura Mazda, as long as [his family] shall be, and life ₊ ₊ ₊ ₊ ₊ ₊

4. Says Darius the king: With (my) army I went to Scythia; unto Scythia ₊ ₊ ₊ ₊ the Tigris[1] ₊ ₊ ₊ ₊ ₊ ₊ ₊ ₊ ₊ ₊ unto the sea ₊ ₊ ₊ I crossed in rafts (?); the Scythians I smote; one part I seized [and they were brought] bound to me and [I slew] them; ₊ ₊ ₊ Sku(n)kha by name, him I seized ₊ ₊ ₊ ₊ there another I made chief as was my will; afterwards the province became mine.

5. Says Darius the king: ₊ ₊ ₊ ₊ ₊ not Ahura Mazda ₊ ₊ ₊ ₊ I gave thanks to Ahura Mazda; by the grace of Ahura Mazda, as was my [will, thus] I did unto them.

6. Says Darius the king: [Whoever] unto Ahura Mazda shall give worship [as long as his family shall be] ₊ ₊ ₊

Bh. a.

Persian and Elamite over the figure of king Darius; Babylonian wanting.

1. I (am) Darius, the great king, king of kings, king in Persia, king of the countries, the son of Hystaspes, the grandson of Arsames, the Achaemenide.

---

[1] KT's record, sakām, makes hardly possible Foy's attractive supplement; see voc. s. v. tigrā.

saⁿ]¹ utā[š]ām Aurama-16)zdā [manā dastayā] a[kunauš] ayadaiy vašnā A-17)urama[zdāha yaθā] mā[m kāma āha ava]θādiš akunavam

3. 18)θ[ātiy Dāraya]vauš [xšāyaθ]iya hya Auramazdā-19)m ya[dātaiy]² yā[vā taumā a]hatiy utā jīvah-20)yā + + + + + + + + + yā + +

4. [θāti]y Dārayavauš xš-21)āya[θiya hadā kār]ā Sa[kām³ adam aš]iyavam abiy Sak-22)ām + + + + + + + + i + + + + + + m Tigrām bᵃrᵃtᵃ-23)yᵃ⁴ + + + + + + + + + + + + + + iya abiy draya⁵ a-24)vā + + + + + + + + ā h + + + + + + ā pisā viyatara-25)yam + + + + + + + Sak[ā av]ājanam⁶ aniyam aga-26)rb[āyam + + + + + ba]sta [anayatā a]biy mām ut-27)āš[im avājanam] + + šn + + + + S[kuⁿ]xa nāma avam aga-28)rb[āyam] + + + + y + + + + + + avadā aniyam maθ-29)iš[tam ak]unavam ya[θā mām k]āma⁷ āha pasāva da-30)h[yāuš ma]nā [aba]va

5. [θāti]y Dārayavauš xšāya-31)θi[ya] + + + + + ˢ + + ā + + + + + ₘtā naiy Auramazd-32)ā + + i + + [A]ura[mazdām a]yadaiy⁸ vašnā Aurama-33)z[dāha yaθā m]ām [kāma āha avaθādi]š akunavam

6. θāt-34)i[y Dārayavauš xš]ā[yaθiya hya] Auramazdām⁹ yadāta-35)i[y yāvā] t[aumā ahatiy¹⁰ u]tā jīvahyā utā 36)+ + + + + + + + +

Bh. a.

1. 1)Adam Dārayavauš xšāyaθiya vazarka xšāya-2)θiya xšāyaθiyānām xšāyaθiya Pārsaiy xš-3)āyaθiya dahyūnām V¹štāspahyā puθʳa 4)Aršāmahyā napā Haxāmanišiya

2. θātiy Dāra-5)yavauš xšāyaθiya manā pitā V¹štāspa V¹-6)štāspahyā pitā Aršāma Aršāmahyā pi-7)tā Ariyāramna Ariyāramnahyā pitā 8)Cišpiš Cišpaiš pitā Haxāmaniš

3. 9)θātiy Dārayavauš xšāyaθiya avahya-10)rādiy vayam Haxā-

---

¹ [atarsaⁿ], KT.
² ya[dātaiy], Tolman.
³ [hadā kār]ā sa[kām], KT.
⁴ sakū t[yaiy haumavargā utā tyaiy xaudā]m tigrām baraⁿt[i]y, Foy, but text confirmed by KT.
⁵ daraya, KT. darayam, ed. wrongly. See voc.
⁶ sak[iyā av]ājanam, KT.
⁷ ya + + + [n]āma, KT.
⁸ [a]ura[mazdām a]yadaiy, Tolman. + + ura + + [ā]yadaiy, WBⁿ.
⁹ [hya] auramazdām, WBⁿ.
¹⁰ [utā yāvā] t[aumā ahatiy], WBⁿ.

2. Says Darius the king: My father (is) Hystaspes; the father of Hystaspes (is) Arsames; the father of Arsames (is) Ariaramnes; the father of Ariaramnes (is) Teispes; the father of Teispes (is) Achaemenes.

3. Says Darius the king: Therefore we are called Achaemenides; from long ago we have been of ancient lineage; from long ago our family have been kings.

4. Says Darius the king: 8 of my family (there were) who were formerly kings; I am the ninth (9); long aforetime we are kings.

Bh. b.

Persian, Elamite, Babylonian under prostrate form.

This Gaumâta the Magian lied; thus he said: I am Bardiya, the son of Cyrus; I am king.

Bh. c.

Persian, Elamite over first standing figure; Babylonian below.

This Âθʳina lied; thus he said: I am king in Susiana.

Bh. d.

Persian, Elamite over second standing figure; Babylonian below.

This Nidintu-Bêl lied; thus he said: I am Nebuchadrezzar, the son of Nabû-na'id; I am king in Babylon.

Bh. e.

Elamite above third standing figure; Persian on the garment; Babylonian below.

This Phraortes lied; thus he said: I am Khshathrita of the family of Cyaxares; I am king in Media.

Bh. f.

Persian, Elamite above fourth standing figure; Babylonian below.

This Martiya lied; thus he said: I am Imanish, king in Susiana.

Bh. g.

Persian, Elamite above fifth standing figure; Babylonian below.

This Ciθʳa(n)takhma lied; thus he said: I am king in Sagartia, of the family of Cyaxares.

manišiyā θahyā-11)mahy hacā paruviyata ā[m]ātā 12)amahy hacā paruviyata hyā amā-13)xam taumā xšāyaθiyā āha

4. θā-14)tiy Dārayavauš xšāyaθiya VIII ma-15)nā taumāyā tyaiy paruva-16)m xšāyaθiyā āha^n adam na-17)vama IX duvitāparanam[1] vayam x-18)šāyaθiyā amahy

Bh. b.

1)Iyam Gaumā-2)ta hya maguš a-3)durujiya 4)avaθā aθaha adam Ba-5)rdiya amiy hya K-6)ūrauš pu$θ^r$a adam xš-7)āyaθiya amiy

Bh. c.

1)Iyam Āθ^r-2)ina adu-3)rujiya 4)avaθā 5)aθaha a-6)dam x-7)šāyaθ-8)iya am-9)iy U-10)vajaiy

Bh. d.

1)Iyam Nadi^{n}tabaira 2)adurujiya ava-3)θā aθaha adam Nab-4)ukudracara ami-5)y hya Nabunaita-6)hya pu$θ^r$a adam x-7)šāyaθiya amiy B-8)ābirauv

Bh. e.

1)Iyam Fra-2)vartiš 3)aduru-4)jiya ava-5)θā aθaha adam 6)Xšaθrita amiy 7)Uvaxštrahya 8)taumāyā adam 9)xšāyaθiya amiy 10)Mū-11)daiy

Bh. f.

1)Iyam Martiya a-2)durujiya a-3)vaθā aθaha a-4)dam Imaniš am-5)iy Uvajaiy x-6)šāyaθi-7)ya

Bh. g.

1)Iyam Ciθ^{r}a^n-2)taxma ad-3)urujiya 4)avaθā a-5)θaha adam 6)xšāyaθi-7)ya Asaga-8)rtaiy Uva-9)xštrahya 10)taumāy-11)ā[2]

Bh. h.

1)Iyam Vahya-2)zdāta adu-3)rujiya ava-4)θā aθaha ada-5)m Bardiya a-6)miy hya K-7)ūrauš pu$θ^r$a 8)adam xšā-9)yaθiya amiy

Bh. i.

1)Iyam Arxa 2)aduruj-3)iya avaθā 4)aθaha adam 5)Nabuku[d]ra-6)cara amiy 7)hya Nabuna-8)itahya pu-9)θ^{r}a adam xšā-10)yaθiya amiy 11)Bāb[i]rauv

---

[1] duvitāparanam. See critical note to Bh. 1, l. 10.

[2] Reading of KT's cuneiform text. Their transliteration, however, has ami-8)y asaga-9)rtaiy uva-10)xštrahya 11)taumāy-12)ā.

Bh. h.
Persian, Elamite above sixth standing figure; Babylonian below.
This Vahyazdâta lied; thus he said: I am Bardiya, the son of Cyrus; I am king.

Bh. i.
Persian, Elamite above seventh standing figure; Babylonian below.
This Arkha lied; thus he said: I am Nebuchadrezzar, the son of Nabû-na'id; I am king in Babylon.

Bh. j.
Persian, Elamite above eighth standing figure; Babylonian below.
This Frâda lied; thus he said: I am king in Margiana.

Bh. k.
Persian, Elamite above ninth standing figure.
This (is) Sku(n)kha, the Scythian.

INSCRIPTIONS OF PERSEPOLIS

Dar. Pers. a.
On the door-posts of the tacara, above sculpture of the king; Persian, Elamite, Babylonian.
Darius the great king, king of kings, king of the countries, the son of Hystaspes, the Achaemenide, who built this tacara.

Dar. Pers. b.
On the garment of the king.
Darius the great king, the son of Hystaspes, the Achaemenide.

Dar. Pers. c.
Repeated on the window cornice.
Stone window cornice made in the royal house of King Darius.

Bh. j.

1)Iyam Frāda 2)aduru-3)jiya avaθā aθaha 4)adam xšāyaθ-5)iya amiy Marga-6)uv

Bh. k.

1)Iyam Skuⁿ-2)xa hya Saka

INSCRIPTIONS OF PERSEPOLIS

Dar. Pers. a.

1)Dārayavauš xšāyaθiya 2)vazarka xšāyaθiya xšā-3)yaθiyanām xšāyaθiya 4)dahyūnām Vištāspahy-5)ā puθ^ra Haxāmanišiya h-6)ya imam tacaram akunauš

Dar. Pers. b.

Dārayavauš XŠ vazarka Vištāspahyā puθ^ra Haxāmanišiya

Dar. Pers. c.

Ardastāna aθaⁿgaina Dārayavahauš XŠhyā viθiyā karta

Dar. Pers. d.

1. 1)Auramazdā vazarka hya maθišta bag-2)ānām hauv Dārayavaum xšāyaθi-3)yam adadā haušaiy xšaθ^ram frāba-4)ra vašnā Auramazdāhā Dārayavau-5)š xšāyaθiya

2. θātiy Dārayavauš 6)xšāyaθiya iyam dahyāuš Pār-7)sa tyām manā Auramazdā frāba-8)ra hyā naibā uvaspā umarti-9)yā vašnā Auramazdāhā manac-10)ā Dārayavahauš xšāyaθiyahy-11)ā hacā aniyanā naiy tarsat-12)iy

3. θātiy Dārayavauš xšāya-13)θiya manā Auramazdā upastām 14)baratuv hadā viθⁿibiš bagai-15)biš utā imām dahyāum Aura-16)mazdā pātuv hacā haināy-17)ā hacā dušiyārā[1] hacā dra-18)ugā abiy[2] imām dahyāum mā 19)ājamiyā mā ha[i]nā mā duš-20)iyāram[3] [m]ā drauga aita adam 21)yānam[4] jadiyāmiy[5] Auramazd-

---

[1] dušiyārā, Jn.
[2] abiy, Stolze.
[3] dušiyāram, Jn.
[4] yānam, Jn. Wrongly yān + + m, ed. Stolze's Phot. shows defect in stone, not lacuna.
[5] jadiyā[m]iy, Stolze's Phot. jadiyāmiy, Jn. See voc.

Dar. Pers. d.
On the south retaining wall of terrace.

1. The great Ahura Mazda, who (is) the greatest of the gods,[1] he made Darius king; he gave him the kingdom; by the grace of Ahura Mazda Darius (is) king.
2. Says Darius the king: This (is) the country Persia which Ahura Mazda gave me, which, beautiful, possessing good horses, possessing good men, by the grace of Ahura Mazda and (by the achievements) of me Darius the king, does not fear an enemy.
3. Says Darius the king: Let Ahura Mazda bear me aid with the royal[2] gods and let Ahura Mazda protect this country from an evil host, from famine,[3] from Deceit; may not an evil host nor famine nor Deceit come upon this country; this favor I pray of Ahura Mazda with the royal[2] gods; this let Ahura Mazda give me with the royal[2] gods.

Dar. Pers. e.
On the south retaining wall of terrace.

1. I (am) Darius the great king, king of kings, king of many countries, the son of Hystaspes, the Achaemenide.
2. Says Darius the king: By the grace of Ahura Mazda these (are) the countries which I have brought into my possession with the help of this Persian army, (and) which feared me (and) brought to me tribute; Susiana, Media, Babylonia, Arabia, Assyria, Egypt, Armenia, Cappadocia, Sparda, the Ionians who (are) of the main land (and) those who (are) on the sea, and the countries which (are) on the east, Sagartia, Parthia, Drangiana, Aria, Bactria, Sogdiana, Chorasmia, Sattagydia, Arachosia, India, Ga(n)dara, Scythia, the Macae.
3. Says Darius the king: If thus thou shalt think, "May I not fear an enemy," protect this Persian people; if the Persian people shall be protected, Welfare for a long time undisturbed will through Ahura descend upon this royal house.

---

[1] Cf. Turfan MSS., bagân bagîystôm; also šmâχ baγânîq 'azûnt 'îštâ, *ye are sons of God*, Neutest. Bruchstücke in soghdischer Sprache, Müller, SBAW, 1907.

[2] See voc. s. v. vⁱⁱᶿᵃⁱbᵃⁱšᵃ.

[3] Cf. Turfan MSS., dûšyârîy, *need*.

22)ām hadā viθᵃibiš¹ bagaibiš a-23)i[tamai]y² [Au]ramazdā dadāt-24)u[v hadā vi]θᵃ[i]biš bagaibiš

Dar. Pers. e.

1. 1)Adam Dārayavauš xšāyaθiya vaz-2)arka xšāyaθiya xšāya-θiyānā-3)m xšāyaθiya dahyūnām tyai-4)šām parūnām Vištāspa-hyā 5)puθʳa Haxāmanišiya

2. θātiy Dāra-6)yavauš xšāyaθiya vašnā Aurama-7)zdāhā imā dahyāva tyā adam 8)adaršiy³ hadā anā Pārsā kā-9)rā tyā hacāma atarsaⁿ manā bāj-10)im abaraⁿ Uvaja Māda Bābiru-11)š Arabāya Aθurā Mudrāy-12)ā Armina Katpatuka Sparda Ya-13)unā tyaiy uškahyā utā tya-14)iy drayahyā⁴ utā dahyāva t-15)yā pᵃrᵃu-[vᵃ]iyᵃ⁵ Asagarta Parθava Zraⁿ-16)ka⁶ Haraiva Bāxtriš Sug[u]da Uv-17)ārazmiya Θataguš Harauvatiš H-18)iⁿduš Gaⁿdāra Sakā Maka

3. θātiy 19)Dārayavauš xšāyaθiya yadiy 20)avaθā maniyāhay⁷ hacā aniya-21)nū mā [ta]rsam imam Pārsam kāram pādi-22)y yadiy kāra Pārsa pāta⁸ ahatiy hyā 23)duvaiš[ta]m šiyātiš axšatā hauvci-24)y Aurā nirasātiy abiy imām viθam

Xerx. Pers. a [aa, ab, ac, ad].

1. 1)Baga vazarka Auramazdā hya imām būmim a-2)dā hya avam asmānam adā hya martiyam 3)adā hya šiyātim adā marti-yahyā hya 4)Xšayāršām xšāyaθiyam akunauš aivam 5)parūnām xšāyaθiyam aivam parūnām fram-6)ātāram

2. adam Xšayāršā xšāyaθiya vazarka 7)xšāyaθiya xšāyaθiyā-nām xšāyaθiya dahy-8)ūnām⁹ paruv zanānām xšāyaθiya ahyāy-9)ā¹⁰ būmiyā vazarkāyā dūraiy apiy Dā-10)rayavahauš¹¹ xšāyaθi-yahyā puθʳa Hāxāmaniš-11)iya¹²

---

¹ viθᵃibiš read viθaibiš or viθibiš. See voc.
² ai[tamai]y, Jn.
³ adaršiy, Bartholomae. See voc.
⁴ darayahyā, ed. wrongly.
⁵ Stone-cutter's blunder for paruvaiy. Jn. records a blank space as occupying the lacuna; so Westergaard.
⁶ zaraⁿka, ed.
⁷ maniyāhay, Bartholomae. maniyāhy, ed.
⁸ Jn. records traces of the word-divider after pāta, where Westergaard believed was a blank space; cf. Stolze's Phot.
⁹ da-8)hyūnām, ac, ad.
¹⁰ ahyā-9)yā, ac, ad.
¹¹ d-10)ārayavahauš, ac, ad.
¹² written wrongly for haxāmanišiya. -11)šiya, ac, ad.

Xerx. Pers. a [aa, ab, ac, ad].

Four times repeated on propylaea of Xerxes, above the sculptured winged bulls; Persian, Elamite, Babylonian.

1. A great god (is) Ahura Mazda who created this earth, who created yonder heaven, who created man, who created welfare for man, who made Xerxes king, one king of many, one lord of many.

2. I (am) Xerxes the great king, king of kings, king of the countries possessing many kinds of people, king of this great earth far and wide, the son of Darius the king, the Achaemenide.

3. Says Xerxes the great king: By the grace of Ahura Mazda, this colonnade (for the representatives) of all countries I made; much else (that is) beautiful (was) done throughout Persia which I did and which my father did; whatever work seems beautiful, all that we did by the grace of Ahura Mazda.

4. Says Xerxes the king: Let Ahura Mazda protect me and my kingdom and what (was) done by me and what (was) done by my father, (all) this let Ahura Mazda protect.

Xerx. Pers. b.

On wall beside the magnificent sculptured staircase of the Column Hall of Xerxes.

1. A great god (is) Ahura Mazda who created this earth, who created yonder heaven, who created man, who created welfare for man, who made Xerxes king, one king of many, one lord of many.

2. I (am) Xerxes the great king, king of kings, king of the countries possessing many kinds of people, king of this great earth far and wide, the son of Darius the king, the Achaemenide.

3. Says Xerxes the great king: What (was) done by me here and what (was) done by me afar, all this I did by the grace of Ahura Mazda; let Ahura Mazda protect me with the gods, and my kingdom and what (was) done by me.

3. θātiy Xšayāršā xšāyaθiya vašnā 12)Auramazdāhā imam duvarθim visadahyum[1] 13)adam akunavam vasiy aniyašciy naibam[2] 14)kartam anā Pārsā tya adam akunavam 15)utamaiy tya pitā akunauš tyapatiy ka-16)rtam[3] vainataiy naibam ava visam vašnā A-17)uramazdāhā[4] akumā

4. θātiy Xšayāršā 18)xšāyaθiya[5] mām Auramazdā pātuv utamai-19)y xšaθ^ram[6] utā tya manā kartam utā tyamai-20)y piθ^ra[7] kartam avašciy Auramazdā pātuv.

Xerx. Pers. b.

1. 1)Baga vazarka Auramazdā 2)hya imām būmim 3)adā hya avam asmā-4)nam adā hya martiya-5)m adā hya šiyāti-6)m adā martiyahyā 7)hya Xšayāršām xšā-8)yaθiyam akunauš ai-9)vam parūnām xšāyaθ-10)iyam aivam parūnām 11)framātāram

2. adam X-12)šayāršā xšāyaθiya 13)vazarka xšāyaθiya xš-14)āyaθiyānām xšāyaθ-15)iya dahyūnām paruvza-16)nānām xšāyaθiya 17)ahiyāyā būmiyā va-18)zarkāyā dūraiy a-19)piy Dārayavahauš xš-20)āyaθiyahyā puθ^ra Hax-21)āmanišiya

3. θātiy X-22)šayāršā xšāyaθiya va-23)zarka tya manā kartam 24)idā utā tyamaiy 25)apataram kartam ava v-26)isam vašnā Auramazdā-27)ha akunavam mām Aura-28)mazdā pātuv hadā ba-29)gaibiš utāmaiy xšaθ^ra-30)m utā tyamaiy kartam

Xerx. Pers. ca, cb.[8]

1. 1)[1]Baga vazarka Auramazdā hya [2]imām būmim 2)adā hya [3]avam asmānam adā hya [4]marti-3)yam adā hya šiy[5]ātim adā martiyahyā 4)[6]hya Xšayāršām XŠm aku[7]nauš aivam pa-5)rūnām XŠ[8]m aivam parūnām fram[9]ātāram

2. 6)adam Xšayāršā [10]XŠ vazarka XŠ XŠānām XŠ 7)[11]dahyūnām paruv zanā[12]nām XŠ ahyāyā b-8)ūmi[13]yā vazarkāyā dūraiy a[14]piy Dārayava-9)hauš XŠhy[15]ā puθ^ra Haxāmanišiya

3. θ[16]ātiy X-10)šayāršā XŠ vazar[17]ka vašnā Aurahya mazdāha [18]i-11)ma hadiš Dārayavauš XŠ [19]akunauš hya manā

---

[1] visadahyu-13)m, ac, ad.
[2] naiba-14)m, ac, ad.
[3] kar-16)tam, ac, ad.
[4] au-17)ramazdāhā, ac, ad.
[5] xš-18)āyaθiya, ac.
[6] utamaiy 19)xšaθ^ram, ac. utama-19)iy, ad.
[7] tyamaiy 20)piθ^ra, ac. tyama-20)iy, ad.
[8] Square brackets [ ] inclose the line-numbers of Xerx. Pers. cb, db, eb, and Art. Pers. b.

Xerx. Pers. ca, cb.

Repeated^{ca} on huge door-jamb and^{cb} beside the south stairs of tacara of Darius; Persian, Elamite, Babylonian.

1. A great god (is) Ahura Mazda who created this earth, who created yonder heaven, who created man, who created welfare for man, who made Xerxes king, one king of many, one lord of many.

2. I (am) Xerxes the great king, king of kings, king of the countries possessing many kinds of people, king of this great earth far and wide, son of Darius the king, the Achaemenide.

3. Says Xerxes the great king: By the grace of Ahura Mazda this dwelling Darius the king made who (was) my father; let Ahura Mazda protect me with the gods, and what (was) done by me and what (was) done by my father Darius the king, (all) this let Ahura Mazda protect with the gods.

Xerx. Pers. da, db.

Repeated^{da} on two slabs and^{db} on wall beside the steps in the palace of Xerxes; Persian, Elamite, Babylonian.

1. A great god (is) Ahura Mazda who created this earth, who created yonder heaven, who created man, who created welfare for man, who made Xerxes king, one king of many, one lord of many.

2. I (am) Xerxes the great king, king of kings, king of the countries possessing many kinds of people, king of this great earth far and wide, son of Darius the king, the Achaemenide.

3. Says Xerxes the great king: By the grace of Ahura Mazda this dwelling I made; let Ahura Mazda protect me with the gods, and my kingdom and what (was) done by me.

Xerx. Pers. ea, eb.

Above the sculpture of the king, repeated on door-posts^{ea} on north and^{eb} on east; Persian, Elamite, Babylonian.

Xerxes the great king, king of kings, the son of Darius the king, the Achaemenide.

12)pit[20]ā mām Auramazdā pātu[21]v hadā baga-13)ibiš utā t[22]yamaiy kartam utā tyamai[23]y 14)piθʳa Dārayavahauš XŠhy[24]ā kartam avašciy 15)Auramaz[25]dā pātuv hadā bagaibiš

Xerx. Pers. da, db.[1]

1. 1)[1]Baga vazarka Auramazdā [2]hya i-2)mām būmim [3]adā hya avam 3)asmā[4]nam adā hya martiya-4)[5]m adā hya šiyāti[6]m adā mar-5)tiyahyā [7]hya Xšayāršām x-6)šā[8]yaθiyam akunauš ai[9]vam par-7)ūnām xšāyaθ[10]iyam aivam parū-8)nām [11]framātāram

2. adam X[12]šayārš-9)ā xšāyaθiya [13]vazarka xšāyaθiya 10)xš[14]āyaθiyānām xšāyaθ[15]iya dahy-11)ūnām paruvza[16]nānām xšāyaθiya 12)[17]ahiyāyā būmiyā va[18]zarkāyā 13)dūraiy a[19]piy Dārayavahauš xš-14)[20]āyaθiyahyā puθʳa Hax[21]āmani[š]iya

3. 15)θātiy X[22]šayāršā xšāyaθiya [23]va-16)zarka vašnā Auramaz[24]dāha ima had-17)iš adam [25]akunavam mām Auramaz-18)[26]dā pātuv hadā bagai[27]biš utama-19)iy xšaθʳam [28]utā tyamaiy kartam

Xerx. Pers. ea, eb.[1]

1)[1]Xšayāršā xšāyaθiya vazar-2)[2]ka xšāyaθiya xšāyaθiyā-3)[3]nām Dārayavahauš xšāyaθ-4)iya[4]hyā puθʳa Haxāmanišiya

Art. Pers. a [aa, ac, ad], b.[1]

1. 1)[1] Baga vazarka Auramazd[2]ā hya 2)imām būmām [3]adā hya a-3)vam[2] asmān[4]ūm adā hya marti-4)yam [5]adā hya šāyatūm[3] a[6]dā mart-5)ihyā[4] hya mā[7]m Artaxšaθʳā xšāya-6)θi-[8]ya[5] akunauš aivam pᵃrᵘuvᵃ[9]nᵃamᵃ[6] 7)xšāyaθiyam aiva[10]m pᵃrᵘuvᵃnᵃamᵃ[6] 8)framatāram[7]

2. [11]θātiy Artaxšaθʳā 9)xš[12]āyaθiya[8] vazarka xšāya[13]θiya 10)xšāyaθiyanām [14]xšāyaθiya 11)DAHyūnām [15]xšāyaθiya

---

[1] Square brackets [ ] inclose the line-numbers of Xerx. Pers. cb, db, eb, and Art. Pers. b.
[2] hya 3)avam, ac.
[3] šāytām (for šyātām), Marquart, Foy.
[4] thus written for martiyahyā. -5)yā, ac.
[5] xšāyaθi-6)ya, ac.
[6] thus written for parūnām. See voc.
[7] written thus for framātāram.
[8] x-9)šāyaθiya, ac.

Art. Pers. a [aa, ac, ad], b.

Repeated on three slabs at north of palace of Artaxerxes and beside the western steps of tacara of Darius.

1. A great god (is) Ahura Mazda who created this earth, who created yonder heaven, who created man, who created welfare for man, who made me, Artaxerxes, king, one king of many, one lord of many.

2. Says Artaxerxes the great king, king of kings, king of countries, king of this earth: I (am) the son of Artaxerxes, the king; Artaxerxes (was) the son of Darius the king; Darius (was) the son of Artaxerxes the king; Artaxerxes (was) the son of Xerxes the king; Xerxes (was) the son of Darius the king; Darius was the son of Hystaspes by name; Hystaspes was the son of Arsames by name, the Achaemenide.

3. Says Artaxerxes the king: This stone staircase (was) made by me.

4. Says Artaxerxes the king; Let Ahura Mazda and the god Mithra protect me and this country and what (was) done by me.

INSCRIPTIONS OF NAKŠ-I-RUSTAM

On one of four similar Achaemenidan tombs at Nakš-i-Rustam near Persepolis, cruciform with the entrance in the tetrastyle transverse section; above is a double row of figures supporting platform where Darius stands before a burning altar; higher up is the divine symbol; Persian, Elamite, Babylonian.

Dar. NRa.

1. A great god is Ahura Mazda who created this earth, who created yonder heaven, who created man, who created welfare for man, who made Darius king, one king of many, one lord of many.

2. I (am) Darius the great king, king of kings, king of the countries possessing all kinds of people, king of this great earth far and wide, son of Hystaspes, the Achaemenide, a Persian, the son of a Persian, an Aryan, of Aryan lineage.

ahyāyā [16]BŪMIyā ada-12)m Artaxšaθ^rā x[17]šāya-13)θiya[1] puθ^ra Artaxšaθ^rā [18]Dārayavau-14)š xšāyaθiya [19]puθ^ra Dārayavauš A-15)rtaxša[20]θ^rā[2] xšāyaθiya puθ^ra Arta[21]xša-16)θ^rā[3] Xšayāršā xšāya[22]θiya puθ^ra X-17)šayāršā Dāra[23]yavauš xšāyaθ-18)iya puθ^ra [24]Dārayavauš V^{i}štāspa-19)hy[25]ā nāma puθ^ra V^{i}štāspahy[26]ā 20)Aršāma nāma puθ^ra Ha[27]xāmaniši-21)ya

3. θātiy A[28]rtaxšaθ^rā xšāyaθi-22)ya [29]imam[4] ustašanām aθa^{n}ga[30]nām[5] mā-23)m upā[6] mām [31]kartā

4. θātiy Arta-24)xšaθ^r[32]ā[7] xšāyaθiya mām Aura[33]mazdā[8] 25)utā M$^i\theta$ra baga pā[34]tuv utā imā-26)m[9] DAIIyum [35]utā tya mām kartā

INSCRIPTIONS OF NAKŠ-I-RUSTAM

Dar. NRa.

1. 1)Baga vazarka Auramazdā hya im-2)ām būmim adā hya avam asm-3)ānam adā hya martiyam adā h-4)ya šiyātim adā martiyahyā 5)hya Dārayavaum xšāyaθiyam ak-6)unauš aivam p^{a}r^{n}uv^{a}n^{a}am^a[10] xšāyaθ-7)iyam aivam p^{a}r^{n}uv^{a}n^{a}am^a[10] framāta-8)ram[11]

2. adam Dārayavauš xšāyaθiya va-9)zarka xšāyaθiya xšāyaθiyānām 10)xšāyaθiya dahyūnām vispazanā-11)nām xšāyaθiya ahyāyā būmi-12)yā vazarkāyā dūraiapiy[12] Višt[ā]s-13)pahyā puθ^ra Haxāmanišiya Pārsa [P]-14)ārsahyā puθ^ra Ariya Ariya c[i]-15)θ^ra

3. θātiy Dārayavauš xšā[ya]-16)θiya vašnā Auramazdāhā im[ā] 17)dahyāva tyā ada[m] agarbāya[m] 18)apataram hacā Pārsa adamšām 19)patiyaxšayaiy[13] manā bājim aba[ra^n] 20)tyašām[14] hacāma aθah[ya ava a]-21)kunava^n dātam tya manā ava[d]iš 22)adā-

---

[1] xšā-13)yaθiya, ac.
[2] arta-15)xšaθ^rā, ac.
[3] artaxšaθ^rā 16)xšayāršā, ac.
[4] 22)imam, ad.
[5] thus written for aθa^{n}gainām.
[6] mām 23)upā, ad.
[7] artax-24)šaθ^rā, ad.
[8] auramazd-25)ā, ad.
[9] i-26)mām, ad.
[10] thus written for parūnām. See voc.
[11] thus written for framātāram.
[12] dūraiapiy, Stolze's Phot.
[13] patiyaxšayaiy, Stolze's Phot. See voc.
[14] h(?) tyašām, Stolze's Phot., showing a careless stroke of stone-cutter.

3. Says Darius the king: By the grace of Ahura Mazda these (are) the provinces which I seized afar from Persia; I ruled them; they brought tribute to me; what was commanded to them by me, [this] they did; the law which (is) mine, that was established for them; Media, Susiana, Parthia, Aria, Bactria, Sogdiana, Chorasmia, Drangiana, Arachosia, Sattagydia, Ga(n)dara, India, the Amyrgian Scythians, the pointed-capped Scythians, Babylon, Assyria, Arabia, Egypt, [Armenia], Cappadocia, Sparda, Ionia, the Scythians beyond the sea, Skudra, the sea-faring (?)[1] Ionians, the Pu(n)tians, Kushians, Maxyes, Karkians.

4. Says Darius the king: Ahura Mazda, when he saw this earth in commotion, afterwards gave it to me; he made me king; I am king; by the grace of Ahura Mazda I established it on (its) foundation; what I commanded to them, this they did as was my will. If thou shalt think: "something limited in number are these countries which Darius the king held," look at the picture (of those) who are bearing my throne, thus thou wilt know them; then it will be known to thee (that) the spear of a Persian man hath gone forth afar; then it will be known to thee (that) a Persian man fought his foe far from Persia.

5. Says Darius the king: This (is) what (was) done; all this by the grace of Ahura Mazda I did; Ahura Mazda bore me aid while I was doing my deeds; let Ahura Mazda protect me from evil and my royal house and this country; this I pray of Ahura Mazda; this let Ahura Mazda give me.

6. O man, what (is) the precept[2] of Ahura Mazda, may it not seem to thee repugnant; do not leave the true[3] path; do not sin.

Dar. NRb.

1. A great god is Ahura Mazda who + + + + + + + created welfare for man + + + made + + + + + + + + + Darius the king + + + + + + + + + +

---

[1] See voc. s. v. takabara.

[2] Cf. Turfan MSS., Qatriyônân vâ 'istratiyôtân 'aj Pîlatiš framân 'ôh padgrift, *as for the centurions and soldiers a command was received for them from Pilate.*

[3] Cf. Turfan MSS., râst, *true;* râstêît bagpûhar 'ast, *the son of God is truth,* M. 18.

riy[1] Māda Uvaja Parθava [Harai]-23)va Bāxtriš Suguda Uvāra-[zm]-24)iš Zra^nka[2] Harauvatiš Θatagu[š Ga^n]-25)dāra Hi^nduš Sakā Haumavar[kā[3] Sa]-26)kā Tigraxaudā Bābir[uš A]-27)θurā Arabāya Mudrāyā [Armina] 28)Katpatuka Sparda Yauna Sakā tyai[y ta]-29)radraya Skudra Yaunā Takabarā Pu^n[tiy]-30)ā[4] Kušiyā Maciyā Karkā

4. θātiy D-31)ārayavauš xšāyaθiya Auramaz[dā yaθ]-32)ā avaina imām būmim yau + + + +[b] 33)pasāvadim manā frābara mā[m xšā]-34)yaθiyam akunauš adam xšā[yaθ]iya 35)amiy vašnā Auramazdāh[ā] a-36)daṃšim gāθavā niyašādayam [tya]šā-37)m adam aθaham ava akunava^n [6] [yaθā] mām 38)kāma āha yadipatiy[7] maniyā[ha]-39)y[8] ciyakaram[9] a[vā[10] dahy]ā[va] 40)tyā Dāraya[va]uš [x]šāya[θ]iya 41)adāraya patikaram dīdiy [tya]i[y manā] g-42)āθ- um bara^ntiy [avad]ā[11] xšnās[āh(i)diš] 43)adataiy azdā bavā[t]iy Pār[sa]h[yā] 44)martiyahyā dūraiy[12] ar[šti]š pa-45)rāgmatā adataiy azdā ba[v]āti-46)y Pārsa martiya dūrayapiy[13] [hac]ā Pā-47)rsā hamaram patiyajatā

5. θā[t]iy Dā-48)rayavauš xšāyaθiya aita t[ya] karta-49)m ava visam vašnā Auramazdāhā ak-50)unavam Auramazdāmaiy upa[s]tām aba-51)ra yātā kartam akuna[vam mā]m A-52)uramazdā pātuv hacā s^ar^a+[14] utāma-53)iy viθam utā imām dahyāum aita ada-54)m Auramazdām jadiyāmiy aitama-55)iy Auramazdā, dadātuv

6. 56)martiyā hyā Auramazdāh-57)ā framānā hauvtai,y gaз-58)tā mā θadaya paθim 59)tyām rāstām mā 60)avarada mā starava[15]

---

[1] adāraya, Foy.
[2] zara^nka, ed.
[3] haumavar[kā], see voc.
[4] pu[tiy]ā, ed.
[5] yau[da^ntim], Bartholomae. yu[diyā], WB[I]. yau$_{ta}^{di}$ + +, WB[II]. See voc.
[6] akunava^n, Bartholomae. akunava^ntā, ed.
[7] yadipatiy, Stolze's Phot. yadipad[i]y, ed. wrongly.
[8] maniyā[ha]y, Stolze's Phot. mani[yāhy t]ya, ed.
[9] ciya^nkaram, ed. See voc.
[10] a[va], ed.
[11] [avad]ā, Stolze's Phot.
[12] dūraiy, Stolze's Phot.
[13] dūrayapiy, Stolze's Phot.
[14] sarā, Jn. saranā, Justi. gastā, Foy. See voc.
[15] starava, Bartholomae, WB[II]. stakava, WB[I]. See voc.

2. Says Darius the king: By the grace of Ahura Mazda + + + + done by me +

Dar. NRc.

Gobryas, a Patischorian, spear-bearer of Darius the king.

Dar. NRd.

Aspathines, bow-bearer (?),[1] a server of the arrows (?)[2] of Darius the king.

Dar. NRe.

These (are) the Maxyes.

INSCRIPTIONS OF SUSA

Dar. Sus. a.

On tablet now in Louvre.

[I am Darius the great king, king of kings, king of countries,] son of Hystaspes, the Achaemenide. Says Darius the king + + + + + + this I did + + + + I give due reverence (?).

Dar. Sus. b.

On tablet now in Louvre.

[I am Darius the great king, king of] kings, king of countries, king of this earth, son of Hystaspes, the Achaemenide.

Art. Sus. a.

On four pedestals of Column Hall; Persian, Elamite, Babylonian.

Says Artaxerxes the great king, king of kings, king of countries, king of this earth, the son of Darius the king: Darius (was) the son of Artaxerxes the king; Artaxerxes (was) the

---

[1] vaθrabara, see voc.
[2] See voc. s. v. dārayantā.

Dar. NRb.

1. 1)Baga vazarka Auramazdā hya adā + + + + + + 2)+ + + + + tya + + + + + adā ši-3)yātim martiyahyā + + [ak]u[nauš] +-4)+ aruvastam upariy [Dāraya]vau[m] xšā-5)yaθiyam + + + + +

2. θātiy D[ārayava]uš x[šā-6)ya]θiya vašnā Auramazd[āhā] + + + + kar[tam] + + 7)[ma]iy tya + daršam + + + + + + + Au[ramazdā] + + + + + + + daršam + + + +

Dar. NRc.

1)Gaubruva Pātišuvariš Dāra-2)yavahauš xšāyaθiyahyā arštibara

Dar. NRd.

1)Aspacanā vaθ'abara[1] Dārayavahauš xš-2)āyaθiyahyā išuvām[2] dāraya^n tā[3]

Dar. NRe.

Iyam[4] Maciyā

INSCRIPTIONS OF SUSA

Dar. Sus. a.

1)[Adam Dārayavauš XŠ vazarka XŠ XŠyā]nā[m 2)XŠ dahyūnām Viš]tāspahyā puθ'a Ha-3)[xāmanišiya θā]tiy Dārayavauš XŠ 4)+ + + + + + + + + + + + + + + ava akunavam tya 5)+ + + + + + + + + + + + n$_{am}^{h\,ta}$yā fraš$_{am}^{ta}$ y(?)adayāmaiy[5]

Dar. Sus. b.

1)[Adam Dārayava-2)uš xšāyaθiya 3)vazarka xš]ā[ya-4)θiya xš]-āyaθi-5)[yānām] xšāya-6)[θiya] dahyūnā-7)[m xšā]yaθiya 8)[ahyā]-yāy[6] 9)[būmiy]ā V'[št]ā-10)[spahy]ā puθ'a 11)[Haxāma]nišiya

Art. Sus. a.

1)Θātiy Artaxšaθ'ā XŠ vazarka XŠ XŠyānām XŠ DAHyūnām XŠ ahyāyā BŪMIyā Dārayavaušahyā[7] XŠhyā puθ'a D-2)āravavaušahyā Artaxšaθ'āhyā XŠhyā puθ'a Artaxšaθ'ahyā Xšayārca-

---

[1] va^n θ'abara, Justi.
[2] išuvām, Bartholomae. išunām, WB.
[3] dārayatā, Foy. dāsyamā, Justi.
[4] im*y* — imaiy, Bartholomae.
[5] θadayāmaiy, Weissbach. y(?)adayāmaiy, Tolman.
[6] [ahyā]yāy [būmiy]ā, Foy; stone-cutter's blunder for ahyāyā.
[7] dārayavauš-hyā, artaxšaθ'ā-hyā, etc., Marquart.

son of Xerxes the king; Xerxes (was) the son of Darius the king; Darius was the son of Hystaspes, the Achaemenide; this apadâna Darius, my ancestor made; [later under Artaxerxes my grandfather it was burned; By the grace of Ahura Mazda, Anâhita and Mithra I built this apadâna; may Ahura Mazda, Anâhita and Mithra protect me].[1]

Art. Sus. b.

On pedestal of column, now in Louvre.

I (am) Artaxerxes, the great king, king of kings,[2] the king, the son of Darius the king.

Art. Sus. c.

On stone fragment, now in Louvre.

+ + + + the Achaemenide. Says Artaxerxes the great king, king of kings, king of countries, king of this earth: this dwelling and this + + + + stone window-cornice? + + + +

INSCRIPTIONS OF SUEZ

Memorial of completion of canal from Nile to Red Sea; on stele found near Shalûf et-Terrâbeh at the 133d kilometer of Suez Canal.

Sz. a.

Between two standing figures.

Darius.

Sz. b.

Persian at right of the figures; at left Elamite and Babylonian.

Darius the great king, [king of kings, king of countries, king of] this great [earth], the son [of Hystaspes], the Achaemenide.

---

[1] Supplied from Elam. version; cf. Foy, Die Neuelamische Inschrift, Art. Sus. a, WZKM, 19, 277 ff.

[2] In 1895 I copied the original and my notes show XŠyānā for XŠyānām

hyā XŠhyā puθ^ra Xšayārcahyā Dāra-3)yavaušahyā XŠhyā puθ^ra Dārayavaušahyā Vištāspahyā puθ^ra Haxamān[i]šiya¹ imam apadāna Dārayavauš apanyākama ak-4)unaš ab(i)ypara [u]pā Arta- [xšaθ^rām nyā]kam² + + + + [An(ā)]h(i)ta[hyā u]tā [M¹]θra[hyā] + + + + dā + + + m + a + + + AURAMAZDĀ A-5)n(ā)h(i)ta ut[ā M¹]θra + + + + + + +

Art. Sus. b.

Adam Artaxšaθ^rā XŠ vazarka XŠ XŠyānā XŠ Dārayavauš XŠhyā puθ^ra

Art. Sus. c.

+ +
1)[Hax]āmaniši[ya θātiy Artaxšaθ^rā] 2)xšāyaθiya va[zarka xšāyaθiya x]-3)šāyaθiyanām xšāya[θiya dahyūn]-4)ām xšāyaθiya ahyāyā [būmiyā i]-5)mām hadiš utā imām + + + + 6)canām³ tya aθa^ngainām ta + + + + 7)+ + + + + + + Au[ramazdā] + + + +

INSCRIPTIONS OF SUEZ

Sz. a.

D[ā]ra[ya]vau[š]

Sz. b.

1)[Dāra]yavauš XŠ vazarka 2)[XŠ XŠyānām XŠ dahy-3)ūnām XŠ ahyā]yā 4)[būmiyā vazarkā]yā 5)[Vištāspahyā] pu-6)[θ^ra] Haxā[maniši]ya

Sz. c.

1. 1)[Baga] vazarka Auramazdā hya avam asmānam adā hya imām bū-2)mim⁴ adā hya [mar]tiyam ad[ā] h[ya š]iyātim adā martiyahy-3)ā hya Dārayavaum XŠyam akunauš⁴ hya D[ā]rayavahauš XŠyahyā xšaθ^ra-4)m frābara tya vazarkam tya [uvaspam u]mar[ti]yam

2. adam Dārayavauš 5)XŠ vazarka XŠ XŠyānām XŠ dahyūnām v[ispazan]ānām⁴ [XŠ] ahyāy-6)ā⁴ būmiyā vazarkāyā dūraiy apiy Vištās[pahyā⁴ p]uθ^ra Ha-7)xāmanišiya

---

¹ thus written for haxāmanišiya.

² abyapara [u]pā arta[xšaθ^rām nyā]kam [+ + + vašnā AURAMADĀha An(ā)]h(i)ta[hyā u]tā [M(i)]θra[hyā imam apa]dā[na ada]m a[kunā] AURAMAZDĀ An(ā)h(i)ta ut[ā] M(i)θra [mām pātuv hacā gastā utā imam tya akunā], Foy. I would rather supply [vaya]m a[kunaumā?] [utāmaiy xšaθ^ram].

³ [usta]canām — ustašanām, Foy.

⁴ so Daressy, Révision des Textes de la Stèle de Chalouf.

Sz. c.

The Persian with Elamite and Babylonian (latter obliterated) covers the remaining space; on other side hieroglyphics, not bearing however, on Persian text.

1. A great [god is] Ahura Mazda who created yonder heaven, who created this earth, who created man, who created welfare for man, who made Darius king, who gave the kingdom to Darius, which (is) great, which possesses good horses (and) good men.

2. I (am) Darius the great king, king of kings, king of countries possessing all people, [king] of this great earth far and wide, son of Hystaspes, the Achaemenide.

3. Says Darius the king: I am a Persian; from Persia I seized Egypt; I commanded to dig this canal from the Nile by name a river which flows in Egypt, to the sea which goes from Persia; afterwards this canal [was dug] thus as I commanded, and [ships] passed[1] from Egypt by this canal to Persia as was my [will].

INSCRIPTION OF KERMAN
Dar. Kr.

On three sides of small tetragonal pyramid; Persian, Elamite, Babylonian.

I am Darius, the great king, king of kings, king of countries, king of this earth, son of Hystaspes, the Achaemenide.

INSCRIPTIONS OF ELVEND
Dar. Elv.

On steep rock in niche to left; Persian, Elamite, Babylonian.

1. A great god (is) Ahura Mazda who created this earth, who created yonder heaven, who created man, who created welfare for man, who made Darius king, one king of many, one lord of many.

---

[1] āyaⁿtā; for transfer to them. conjugation cf. New Pers. āya$d$ < ā + *ayatiy. Cf. Horn. NS, 19, 2.

3. θātiy Dāra[ya]vauš XŠ ada[m P]ārsa ami[y hac]ā Pā-8)[rs]ā Mudrāyam agarbāyam¹ adam ni[yaš]tāyam imām [yuviyā]-9)m¹ kaⁿtanaiy hacā¹ Pirāva nāma rauta tya Mudrāyaiy danu[vatiy² ab]-10)iy draya³ tya hacā Pārsā aitiy pa[sāva]⁴ iyam yuviyā [akāniy]⁵ 11)ava[θā ya]θā⁶ adam niyaštāyam ut[ā] ₊ ₊ ₊ ₊ ₊⁷ āyaⁿtā¹ hacā [Mudrā]-12)yā ta ₊ ₊ ₊ m⁸ yuviyām [a]biy¹ Pār[sa]m [avaθ]ā yaθā mā[m kāma āha]⁹

INSCRIPTION OF KERMAN

1)Adam Dārayavauš x-2)šāyaθiya vazarka x-3)šāyaθiya xšāya-θ-4)iyānām xšāyaθ-5)iya dahyūnām xš-6)āyaθiya ahyāyā 7)būmi-yā Vištā-8)spahyā puθʳa Haxā-9)manišiya

INSCRIPTIONS OF ELVEND

Dar. Elv.

1. 1)Baga vazarka Auramazdā 2)hya imām būmim 3)adā hya avam asmā-4)nam adā hya martiya-5)m adā hya šiyāti-6)m adā martiyahyā 7)hya Dārayavaum xšāya-8)θiyam akunauš aiva-9)m parūnām xšāyaθ-10)iyam aivam parūnām 11)framātāram

2. adam 12)Dārayavauš xšāyaθi-13)ya vazarka xšāyaθiya 14)xšāyaθiyānām xš-15)āyaθiya dahyūnām pa-16)ruzanānām xšā-yaθ-17)iya ahyāyā būmiy-18)ā vazarkāyā dūraiy 19)apiy Vištās-pahy-20)ā puθʳa Haxāmanišiya

Xerx. Elv.

1. 1)Baga vazarka Auramazdā 2)hya maθišta bagānām 3)hya imām būmim ad-4)ā hya avam asmānam 5)adā hya martiyam ad-6)ā hya šiyātim adā 7)martiyahyā hya Xša-8)yāršām xšāyaθi-yam 9)akunauš aivam parūn-10)ām xšāyaθiyam aivam 11)parū-nām framātāram

---

¹ so Daressy, Révision des Textes de la Stèle de Chalouf.
² danu[taiy], cf. Bartholomae, Altiran. Wb. 683.
³ daraya, ed. wrongly.
⁴ aitiy pasāva, Bartholomae. aitiy iyam yuviyā, ed.
⁵ The supplement akāniy seems quite certain; cf. Daressy.
⁶ avaθā yaθā, Bartholomae. ava ₊ ₊, Daressy. pasāva, ed.
⁷ nāviyā, WBⁿ., a very doubtful supplement and hardly justified from the use of the word in Bh. I, 18; I would rather read *nāva, *ships*; cf. Skt. nāvas.
⁸ ta[ra imā]m, WBⁿ.
⁹ mā[m kāma āha], WBⁿ.

2. I (am) Darius the great king, king of kings, king of countries possessing many kinds of people, king of this great earth far and wide, the son of Hystaspes, the Achaemenide.

Xerx. Elv.

On same rock in niche to right; Persian, Elamite, Babylonian.

1. A great god (is) Ahura Mazda who (is) greatest of the gods, who created this earth, who created yonder heaven, who created man, who created welfare for man, who made Xerxes king, one king of many, one lord of many.

2. I (am) Xerxes the great king, king of kings, king of countries possessing many kinds of people, king of this great earth far and wide, the son of Darius the king, the Achaemenide.

INSCRIPTION OF VAN
Xerx. Van

On niche in perpendicular rock of citadel; Persian, Elamite, Babylonian.

1. A great god (is) Ahura Mazda who (is) the greatest of the gods, who created this earth, who created yonder heaven, who created man, who created welfare for man, who made Xerxes king, one king of many, one lord of many.

2. I (am) Xerxes the great king, king of kings, king of countries possessing many kinds of people, king of this great earth far and wide, the son of Darius the king, the Achaemenide.

3. Says Xerxes the king: Darius the king, who (was) my father, he by the grace of Ahura Mazda did much which (was) beautiful and he commanded to dig out this place where he did not make an inscription written; afterwards I commanded to write this inscription; [let Ahura Mazda] protect [me with the gods, and my kingdom and what (has been) done by me].

2. 12)adam Xšayāršā xšā-13)yaθiya vazarka xšāyaθi-14)ya xšāyaθiyānām xš-15)āyaθiya dahyūnām par-16)uzanānām xšāyaθiya 17)ahiyāyā būmiyā va-18)zarkāyā dūraiy apiy 19)Dārayavahauš xšāyaθiya-20)hyā puθ^ra Haxāmanišiya

INSCRIPTION OF VAN

1. 1)Baga vazarka Auramazdā hya maθi-2)šta bagānām hya imām būm-3)im adā hya avam asmānam 4)adā hya martiyam adā hya 5)šiyātim adā martiyahyā 6)hya Xšayāršām xšāyaθiyam 7)akunauš aivam parūnām x-8)šāyaθiyam aivam parūnām 9)framātāram

2. adam Xšayāršā 10)xšāyaθiya vazarka xšāyaθiya 11)xšāyaθiyānām xšāyaθiya da-12)hyūnām paruv zanānām xš-13)āyaθiya ahyāyā būmiyā va-14zarkāyā dūraiy apiy Dāraya-15)vahauš xšāyaθiyahyā puθ^ra Ha-16)xāmanišiya

3. θātiy Xšayāršā 17)xšāyaθiya Dārayavauš xšāya-18)θiya hya manā pitā hauv va-19)šnā Auramazdāha vasiy tya 20)naibam akunauš utā ima st-21)ānam hauv niyaštāya ka^ntanaiy 22)yanaiy[1] dipim naiy nipišt-23)ām akunauš pasāva adam ni-24)yaštāyam imām dipim nip-25)ištanaiy [mām Auramazdā p]ā-26)tū[v hadā bagaibiš utāmai-27)y xšaθ^ram utā tyamaiy kartam]

INSCRIPTION OF HAMADAN
Art. Ham.

1)Θātiy Artaxšaθ^rā XŠ vazarka XŠ [XŠyānām XŠ DAHyūnām XŠ ah]-2)yāyā BŪMIyā Dārayavašahyā[2] XŠhyā [puθ^ra Dārayavašahyā Artaxšaθra]-3)hyā XŠhyā puθ^ra Artaxšaθrahyā[3] X[šayāršahyā XŠhyā puθ^ra Xšayār]-4)šahyā Dārayavašahyā XŠhyā pu[θ^ra Dārayavašahyā Vištāspahyā puθ^ra] 5)Haxāmanišiya imam apadāna vašn[ā AURAMAZDĀhā An(ā)h(i)tahyā utā M^1trahyā akunā m]-6)ām[4] AURAMAZDĀ An(ā)h(i)ta utā M^1tra mā[m utāmaiy xšaθ^ram[5] ut]-7)ā imam tya akunā mā[6] + + + + +

---

[1] yana naiy, Bollensen.
[2] dārayava[u]šahyā, Tolman.
[3] artaxšaθ^rahyā, Bartholomae, but the copy I made of the original shows traces of θ^ra.
[4] [akun]ām, Foy.
[5] [utāmaiy xšaθ^ram], Tolman. [hacā gastā], WB.
[6] akunaumā(?) Tolman. akunavam, Bartholomae. See voc.

INSCRIPTION OF HAMADAN
Art. Ham.
On moldings of pedestals, now in British Museum; Persian, Elamite, Babylonian.

Says Artaxerxes, the great king, king [of kings, king of countries, king] of this earth, [son] of Darius the king: [Darius] was the son of Artaxerxes the king; Artaxerxes (was) [the son of] Xerxes [the king]; Xerxes (was) the son of Darius the king; [Darius (was) the son of Hystaspes], the Achaemenide; this apadâna by the grace [of Ahura Mazda, Anâhita and Mithra we (?) made]; let Ahura Mazda, Anâhita and Mithra [protect] me [and my kingdom] and this which we (?) have done.

INSCRIPTION OF MURGHAB
On monolith, above winged figure clad in long garments, repeated on other pillars; Persian, Elamite, Babylonian.

I (am) Cyrus the king, the Achaemenide.[1]

SEAL INSCRIPTIONS
Dar. Seal
On small cylinder in British Museum; the king in chariot attacking lion; Persian, Elamite, Babylonian.

I (am) Darius the king.

Seal Inscr. a.
Arsaces by name, [the son] of Athiyâbaushna.

---

[1] Cf. Herzfeld's Pasargadae, Klio, 1908; Hoffmann-Kutschke, Philol. Nov., Nov. 1907.

INSCRIPTION OF MURGHAB
1)Adam Kūruš xšāya-2)θiya Haxāmanišiya

SEAL INSCRIPTIONS
Dar. Seal
Adam Dārayavauš XŠ

Seal Inscr. a.
1)Arša-2)ka n-3)āma 4)Aθi-5)yāba-6)ušna-7)hya[1] 8)[puθ^{r}a]

Seal Inscr. b.
1)Hadaxaya[2] 2)+ + + + + + + + + 3)θadaθa ⊥ +

Seal Inscr. c.
Vašdāsaka[3]

Seal Inscr. d.
Vahyav'šdāpāya[4]

Seal Inscr. e.
1)m^a Xa-2)ršā-3)dašyā[5]

WEIGHT INSCRIPTION
1)ll karšā 2)adam Dāra-3)yavauš xš-4)āyaθiya va-5)zarka Viš-6)tāspahyā 7)puθ^{r}a Hax-8)āmanišiya

VASE INSCRIPTIONS
Xerx. Vases
Xšayāršā XŠ vazarka

Art. Vases
Artaxšaθ^{r}ā XŠ vazarka

The Venice Vase reads ardaxcašca, see voc.; the Berlin Vase has simply xšāyaθiya after the name of the king.

---
[1] āθiyābaušnahya, Bartholomae.
[2] hadaxya, WB.
[3] vašdā saka, WB.
[4] vahyav[i]šdā pāya, WB.
[5] xišyāršā, Justi.

Seal Inscr. b.
Hadakhaya (?).

Seal Inscr. c.
Vashdâsaka (?).

Seal Inscr. d.
Vahyavishdāpāya (?).

Seal Inscr. e.
Seal. Xerxes (?).

WEIGHT INSCRIPTION

Dar. Weight Inscr.

Green basalt; British Museum; Persian, Elamite, Babylonian.

2 Karsha-weight. I (am) Darius, the great king, the son of Hystaspes, the Achaemenide.

VASE INSCRIPTIONS

Xerx. Vases

On several alabaster specimens (London, Paris, Philadelphia); Persian, Elamite, Babylonian, and Hieroglyphics.

Xerxes the great king.

Art. Vases

Now in Philadelphia, Berlin, Venice; the Venice Vase is of porphyry; Persian, Elamite, Babylonian, and Hieroglyphics.

Artaxerxes the great king.

FRAGMENTS OF VASES FOUND AT SUSA
(trilingual)

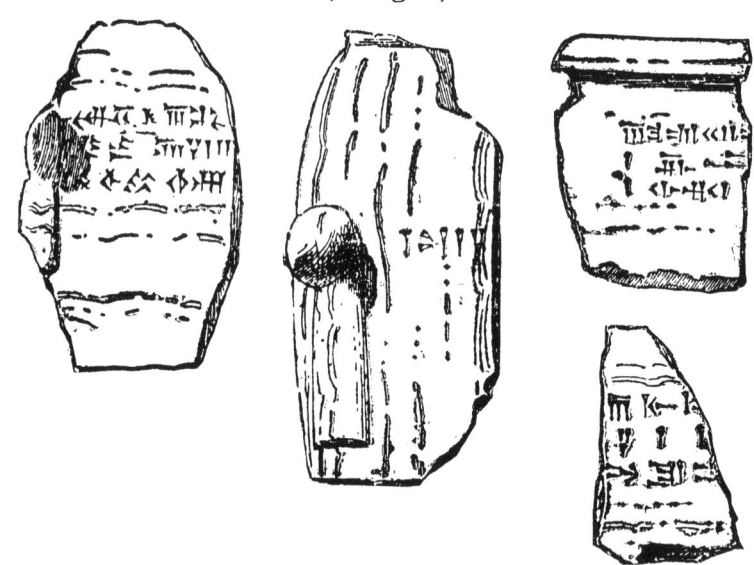

J. de Morgan, Délégation en Perse, Vol. 1, p. 130.

xšayārš[ā], *Xerxes*

artax[šaθ^rā], *Artaxerxes*

[xš]āyaθ[iya], *king*

(58)

ANCIENT PERSIAN LEXICON

A, Ā

ā, 1)Verbal prefix, *to, unto;* e. g. āya^{n}tā = ā + aya^{n}tā (them. to i), Dar. Sz. c. 3; cf. New Pers. āyaδ < ā + *ayatiy. Note Turfan MSS. â-gad (better than agad, Müller). 2)Postpos. prep. with loc., *in, on, by;* e. g., gāθavā, *in place,* dastayā, *at hand,* arbairāyā, *in Arbela,* drayahyā, *by the sea.* Cf. Jackson, Av. Gram. 736; Schulze, KZ, 29, 264; Brugmann, Grundr²., 619; Bartholomae, Grundr. d. iran. Philol., 217–9. In Av. also with acc., abl., gen., dat.; e. g. Av. x^{v}afāδa, Skt. svapnād ā; Av. ahurāi ā, Skt. asurāya. Av. ā, Skt. ā.

a- (before consonants; an- before vowels), neg. prefix; a-xšata, *inviolate, unhurt,* a-nāmaka, (*month*) *of the nameless* (*god*), an-āhita, *without blemish.* I. E. *n̥-, *n̥n-, Av. a-, an- (Middle Pers. a-, an-), Skt. a-, an-, Gr. α-, ἀν-, Lat. in- (for en-), Goth. un-; Gr. νᾱ-, νη- (I. E. *n̥); cf. Schulze, KZ, 27, 606.

a, demon. pron. *this.* Gen. sg. f. ahyāyā (written [ahyā]yāy by stone-cutter's blunder in Dar. Sus. b.), ahiyāyā. Loc. sg. f. ahyāyā, ahiyāyā. In both gen. and loc. the stem a has been increased by hy (from gen. sg. ?), to which is added an ending analogous to that of nouns. Cf. Bartholomae, Grundr. 239, 2; Foy, KZ, 35, 9. I. E. *o-, Av. a, Skt. a, Gr. ἑ-ί, Cret. ἥ.

aita, demon. pron. *this.* Acc. sg. n. aita. I. E. *eito, YAv. aēta (Turfan MSS. 'êd), Skt. eta.

aina[ira] (Elam. ainaira; Bab. a-ni-ri-'), m. name of a Babylonian, father of Nidintu-Bêl. The word is clear in Elam. and Bab. texts. KT record space for about two characters. Gen. sg. aina[ira]hyā, Bh. 1. 16.

aiva, num. *one.* Acc. sg. m. aivam. I. E. oiu̯o, Av. aēva (Middle Pers. ēv, New Pers. yak < *aivaka, cf. Horn, NS, 19, 4.), Gr. οἶος, Cypr. οἶϝος.

autiyāra (Elam. autiyaruš; Bab. u-ti-ia-a-ri), m. name of a district in Armenia. Nom. sg. autiyāra.

aura, m. *god.* Instr. sg. aurā, Dar. Pers. e, 3. šiyātiš axšatā hauvciy aurā nirasātiy; cf. Foy, KZ, 37, 561. Gen. sg. (with mazdāh), aurahya mazdāha; cf. Jackson, Zoroaster, 171; Tolman, PAPA, 33, 68. Av. ahura, Skt. asura.

auramazdāh (Elam. uramašta; Bab. u-ra-ma-az-da), m. name of the supreme god, *Ahura Mazda.* Nom. sg. auramazdā. Acc. sg. auramazdām. In the mutilated passage, Bh. 4. l. 44, auramazd^a + + + + + rtaiyiya, KT plainly record d^a, thus making impossible the supplement auramazdiya of WB, which otherwise might receive some support from the Elam. ankirir ^{an}uramašta-ra, *I state as a follower of Ahura Mazda.* I have proposed the supplement auramazd[ām upāva]rtaiy (Vdt. Stud. 1, 31), regarding + + + + rtaiyiya as dittography for + + + + rtaiy (cf. tyanā manā, Bh. 1, 8), and translating, *I turn unto Ahura Mazda* (i. e. *I appeal to him*). For this meaning of upa + ā + vart in Skt., cf. MBh. 5, 1679 and examples quoted in PWb. KT give space for four or five characters in the lacuna. See other proposed supplements s. v. + + + + rtaiyiya. For former discussions of the passage cf. Foy, KZ, 37, 539, (ibid. 35, 44), ZDMG, 52, 565; Gray, JAOS, 23, 61; Fr. Müller, WZKM, 1, 59. Gen. sg. auramazdāha (frequently written auramazdāhā in Dar. Pers. d, e, NR; Xerx. Pers. a). aura (q. v.) + mazdāh, *the lord knowing all*, Av. mazdāh, name of supreme god (with and without ahura), Ar. *ma(n)δdhā-; cf. Bartholomae, BB, 13, 80. Phl. ōhrmazd, New Pers. hormizd; cf. Horn, NS, 37, 21.

axšata, adj. *unhurt, inviolate, undisturbed.* Nom. sg. f. axšatā, Dar. Pers. e, 3. hyā duvaiš[ta]m šiyūtiš axšatā, *prosperity for a long time undisturbed.* Thumb (Tolman, O. P. Inscr. 148, n) regarded the preceding hyā as 3 sg. opt. of ah. For Bartholomae's view see s. v. hyā. a(neg.) + xšata, ppl. of xšan, Skt. kṣan, Gr. κτείνω; cf. Kretschmer, KZ, 31, 428.

āgar[tar], m. supplement which I proposed (Vdt. Stud. 1, 9) for ag^{a}r^a + +, KT, who record space for two characters. I take the word as nom. ag. of ā + *gar, *to wake* (YAv. gar, Skt. gṛ), *a* *watcher, wakeful, zealous.* This meaning fits the Bab. pi-it-ku̇-du, *watchful.* Weissbach (ZDMG, 61, 725) makes the same conjecture; "Ich vermute eine Ableitung von der Wurzel gar, *wach sein* + ā." He writes me under date of May 19, 1908; "Ich freue mich dass wir hinsichtlich agara ₊ ₊, 1. 21, und [biy]ā, 4. 69, einer Ansicht sind." Bartholomae, WZKM, 22, 72, compares Skt. gūrta, Av. āgrəmaitiš, translating *willig, willfährig, folgsam.* The emendation daušta of ed. is impossible. [akka kannaš], *who was friendly,* of Weissbach and KT can hardly be the correct supplement for the corresponding Elam. Should we, however, restore the verb kanne, its form would be kanneš, aor. 3 sg., not kannaš. Nom. sg. āgar[tā]. Note Turfan MSS. vigarānêd.

aⁿtar, prep. with acc. *within, among, in.* Bh. 4. 3. aⁿtar imā hamaranā. Bh. 2. 13. [aⁿta]r didām frāhaⁿjam. Av. antarə (Turfan MSS. 'andar), Skt. antar.

atiy, verbal prefix, *beyond, across, past.* I. E. *eti, YAv. aiti (Turfan MSS. 'ad, 'êd), Skt. ati.

aθaⁿgaina or āθaⁿgaina, adj. *of stone.* Nom. sg. m. aθaⁿgaina, Dar. Pers. c. ardastāna aθaⁿgaina. Acc. sg. f. aθaⁿgaināk, Art. Sus. c; aθaⁿganām for aθaⁿgainām, Art. Pers. a, b, 3. YAv. asənga (New Pers. sang, Horn, NS, 38, 2). Cf. KZ. 39, 69.

aθahavaja, a doubtful word read by KT in Bh. 4. l. 90. Hoffmann-Kutschke would connect with pepraka of Elam. Bh. L. l. 8.

aθiy, thus to be read in place of a[b]iy of WB¹ in Bh. 1. l. 91. This old reading is confirmed by KT, who remark; "The reading of the sign θ is certain." aθiy bābiru[m yaθā naiy up]āyam, *when I had not come to Babylon.*

aθiyābaušna, m. name of the father of Arsaces. Gen. sg. aθiyābaušnahya. *aθiyā, *true* (cf. hašiya, q. v.) + *baušna, fr. buj, *to free,* YAv. buj (Middle Pers. bōxtan); cf. ZDMG, 51, 248. Bartholomae reads āθiyābaušna, but against his etymology cf. Justi, IF, 17, Anz. 106, who gives the meaning of the compound, *wahrhaftige Erlösung habend.*

aθurā (Elam. aššura; Bab. aš-šur; Gr. 'Ασσυρία), f. *Assyria.* Nom. sg. aθurā. Loc. sg. aθurāyā; cf. Bartholomae, Grundr. 413.

aθ^rina or āθ^rina (Elam. aššina; Bab. a-ši-na), m. name of a Susian rebel. Nom. sg. āθ^rina. Acc. sg. āθ^rinam. The Persian name is quite likely a transcription of the Elam.; cf. Foy, KZ, 37, 498. Justi, on the other hand, suggested a possible connection with Av. ātar (New Pers. āδar), *fire;* cf. YAv. ātərə-dāta, *fire-given*, Bartholomae, Altiran. Wb., 324.

āθ^riyādiya (Elam. aššiyatiyaš; Bab. kislimu, ninth month), n. name of a Persian month, Nov.-Dec. Gen. sg. āθ^riyādiyahya (sic KT, not āθ^riyādiyahyā of the ed.; cf. Bartholomae, Grundr. 412, n. 1). *ātar, *fire*, Av. ātar (Turfan MSS. 'adûr, New Pers. āδar) + *yādiya, *worship*, fr. yad (q. v.).

ada, adv. *then.* GAv. adā, YAv. aδa, Skt. adha. a + da; cf. Jackson, Av. Gr. 729; Whitney, Skt. Gr. 1103.

adakaiy, adv. *then.* ada + kaiy, loc. sg. to I. E. *ko, Gr. ποι; cf. Thumb, KZ, 33, 22. Bartholomae (Grundr. 218, 3) reads ada-kīy, instr. sg., Skt. kim in mākīm, Lat. quī in atquī. Note Turfan MSS. 'êg.

[[ād]āta, adj. *noble.* Nom. pl. m. [ād]ātā, emendation (Andreas-Hüsing) in Bh. 1. 7, for which Bab. [mār]-bânûti gave some support, is now impossible because of clear record of [ā]mātā in KT; also Jackson's conjecture (JAOS, 24, 89) in Bh. 4. 1. 51 in place of [y]ātā of KT and [yāt]ā of ed. The old reading [y]ātā āha^n, *as long as they lived*, seems more in accord with Elam. and Bab. versions. Jackson's view would, of course, connect the word with YAv. āzāta (New Pers. āzād).]

adam, pers. pron. *I.* Nom. sg. adam, Av. azəm (Turfan MSS. 'az), Skt. aham. Acc. sg. mām, Av. mam, Skt. mām, Abl. sg. ma, GAv. mat, Skt. mat, Gen. sg. manā, maiy, YAv. mana, mē, GAv. mōi, Skt. mana, me. Nom. pl. vayam, Av. vaēm, Skt. vayam. Gen. pl. amāxam, YAv. ahmākəm, Skt. asmākam.

adiy, prep. with loc. *in.* Bh. 4. 14. ufraštādiy parsā. Cf. Bartholomae, IF, 12, 110. Skt. adhi. Cf. Turfan MSS. 'adiyâvar.

adukaniša (thus read for adukani of ed.; cf. KT, 35. Elam. atukannaš), f. name of a Persian month, Oct.-Nov., Oppert; June-July, Foy; May-June, Justi. Gen. sg. aduka[ni]šahya, Bh. 2. 12. **kan**, *to dig* (q. v.), *Graben*, Ausstechen der Bewässerungskanäle, Bartholomae, Altiran. Wb., 61.

ana, demon. pron. *this.* Instr. sg. anā, Dar. Pers. e. hadā anā pārsā kārā. Av. ana, Skt. ana.

anā, prep. with instr. *along, throughout.* Xerx. Pers. a. anā pārsā. YAv. ana, Gr. ἀνά.

anāmaka (Elam. anamakkaš; Bab. ṭebêtu, tenth month), adj. name of a Persian month, Dec.-Jan. Gen. sg. anāmakahya (Bartholomae, Grundr. 412, n. 1). a + nāmaka, Skt. anāmaka; *Monat des namenlosen*, d. i. des höchsten Gottes, Bartholomae, Altiran. Wb.; cf. Justi, ZDMG, 51, 248.

anāhita, name of a goddess; written in text anᵃhᵃtᵃ, Art. Sus. a; Art. Ham. YAv. an-āhita, *spotless;* cf. Wilhelm, ZDMG, 40, 105; Foy, KZ, 35, 63; Tolman, PAPA, 33, 69.

aniya, adj. 1)*other, another.* Nom. sg. m. aniya. Acc. sg. m. aniyam. Nom. pl. m. aniyā, aniyāha (thus read in Bh. 4. 1. 63 and probably in l. 61; "From the traces which exist the form aniyāha is more probable than aniyā" KT). Nom. pl. f. aniyā. Loc. pl. f. aniyāuvā. 2)*the one—the other.* Acc. sg. m. aniyam, Bh. 1. 18. aniyam ušabārim akunavam, *one part I put on camels.* Gen. sg. m. aniyahyā, Bh. 1. 18. aniyahyā asam frānayam, *for the other I brought horses.* 3)*strange, hostile, an enemy.* Nom. sg. m. aniya, Bh. 1. 19. aniya āpiyā [āhyat]ā (Kern, [aharat]ā, Oppert, KT). Instr. sg. m. aniyanā, Dar. Pers. d. hacā aniyanā (Jackson, JAOS, 27, 191). 4)with ciy, Nom. sg. n. aniyašciy. Av. anya (Turfan MSS. 'anī, Middle Pers. an, Oss. inna, Pāz. han), Skt. anya.

anuv, prep. with instr. (according to reading ufrātᵘuvā, KT, in Bh. 1. 19); otherwise Bartholomae, WZKM, 22, 71. *along, after.* Av. anu, Skt. anu.

anušiya, adj. *devoted to, ally, follower.* Nom. pl. m. anušiyā. anuv (q. v.) + Ar. suffix ṭia.

apa, verbal prefix, *from, away.* YAv. **apa,** Skt. **apa,** Gr. ἀπό.

apatara, adj. Acc. sg. n. as adv. **apataram,** *away from, outside of, elsewhere.* **apa**(q. v.) + comp. suffix **tara.** Skt. **apataram.**

apadāna, n. *palace.* Acc. sg. **apadāna,** Art. Ham. **imam apadāna.** Cf. Skt. **apadhā,** *concealment;* **apa** (q. v.) + ²**dā** (q. v.).

apanyāka, m. *ancestor.* Nom. sg. **apanyāka** (with encl. **ma,** abl. or = **maiy;** cf. Foy, KZ, 35, 59), Art. Sus. a. **imam apadāna dārayavauš apanyākama akunaš.** **apa** (q. v.) + **nyāka** (Phl. **nyāk**).

apara, adj. Acc. sg. n. as adv. **aparam,** *afterwards.* The Bab. **ša be-la-a ar-ki-ia,** *who shalt rule after me,* leads Bartholomae to suggest **apara-ma,** *posterior me,* in Bh. 4. 5, 14, 19, **hya apar^{a}m^a āhy.** Comp. of **apa,** Av. **apara,** Skt. **apara.**

āpī, f. *water.* Nom. sg. **āpiš,** Bh. 1. 19. **āpišim** (i. e., **āpiš-šim;** cf. KZ, 35, 36; ibid. 40, 134) **parābara;** as loc. Pedersen, KZ, 40, 134, *es riss ihn fort im wasser.* Loc. sg. **āpiyā,** Bh. 1. 19. **aniya āpiyā [āhyat]ā** (Kern; [**aharat]ā,** Oppert, KT). Av. **āp** (Turfan MSS. 'ab, 'āp, New Pers. **āb,** Gīl. **ōv,** Afγ. **ōba,** Geiger, SA, 4), Skt. nom. pl. **āpas.**

apiy, adv. *on, upon, thereto, still.* **dūraiy apiy,** *far and wide.* Probably **apiy** is to be read in Bh. 4, l. 46. **[ap]imaiy aniyašciy vasiy kartam,** *still much else was done by me* (cf. KT, 68), thus setting aside Gray's theory (**avā** as abl. sg.). Av. **aipi,** Skt. **api,** Gr. ἐπί.

abiy, prep. with acc. *to, against.* GAv. **aibī.** YAv. **aiwi,** Skt. **abhi.**

abicariš. The reading **abācariš** with which the critics have operated, Spiegel, Darmesteter (Étud. Iran. 2. 130), Justi (IF, 17, Anz. 105), is superseded. "My inference from the absence of a note is that the text stands as first given by Rawlinson, i. e., **abicariš.**" Jackson, JAOS, 24, 85. The word is thus recorded by KT who translate *pasture-lands.* The Elam. and Bab. give no assistance. Some of the various proposed meanings are: *Weideplätze* (Spiegel), cf. New Pers. **carīdan,** *to pasture; Hilfsmittel* (WB); *commerce* (Tolman, O. P. Inscr. 121); *i pascoli* (Rugarli);

en sauveur (Oppert); *servitium = servos* (Gray, AJP, 21, 17); *Weide* (Bartholomae, Altiran. Wb., 89).

ab(i)ypara, an uncertain word in Art. Sus. a; according to Foy abyapara [u]pā, *later under (Artaxerxes)*.

abiš, adv. *thereby*. Bh. 1. 18. abiš nāviyā āha. Cf. abiy, Brugmann, KZ, 27, 417 vs. Schmidt, Pluralb. 352; Foy, ZDMG, 54, 371; Pedersen, KZ, 40, 129, *on opposite side;* Bartholomae, Zum Altiran. Wb., suggests possibly abi-ša (abl.).

ama, pron. stem, Av. ahma; see adam.

amuθa, see muθ.

ayadaiy, see yad.

āyadana, n. *sanctuary, place of worship*. Acc. pl. āyadanā. Elam. ᵃⁿziyan ᵃⁿnappanna; Bab. bitàti ša ilâni. ā + *yadana, fr. yad (q. v.). āyadanā (Bh. 1. 14) can hardly be the temples of foreign gods; cf. Tolman, PAPA, 33, 70 against the view of Foy, KZ, 35, 23.

āyasatā, for āyastā of ed. and KT; see yam.

ar (Inchoative pres. rasa-, Bartholomae, Grundr., 135), *to set in motion, go, come, arrive*. Pret. 1 sg. arasam. Av. ar (Turfan MSS. 'avar, New Pers. rasaδ), Skt. r̥.

—— with prefix parā, *come to, arrive*. Pret. 1 sg. parārasam. 3 sg. parārasa.

—— with prefix niy, *come down, descend*. Pres. subj. 3 sg. nirasātiy.

araika (or arika, cf. Bartholomae, Altiran. Wb., 189.), adj. *hostile*. Nom. sg. m. araika.

arabāya (Elam. arpaya; Bab. a-ra-bi; Gr. Ἀραβία), m. *Arabia*. Nom. sg. arabāya.

arakadri (Elam. arakkatarriš; Bab. a-ra-ka-ad-ri-'), m. name of a mountain. Nom. sg. arakadriš. Perhaps *ara, *mountain* + *kadrī, *ravine*. Against the reading and etymology of Foy and Bartholomae, cf. Justi, IF, 17, Anz. 106. Note also Bartholomae, Zum Altiran. Wb., 116.

arxa (or **araxa**, Elam. arakka; Bab. a-ra-ḫu), m. name of an Armenian rebel. Nom. sg. arxa. Acc. sg. arxam.

ariya, adj. *Aryan*. Nom. sg. ariya. Members of compound separated, ariya c[i]θ^ra, *of Aryan lineage*, Dar. NR. a. l. 14. YAv. airya (New Pers. ērān, Horn, NS, 103), Skt. ārya.

ariyāramna (wrongly ed., ariyārāmna; cf. KT, 2. Elam. arriyaramna; Bab. ar-ia-ra-am-na-'; Gr. Ἀριαράμνης), m. *Ariaramnes*, name of the great-grandfather of Darius. Nom. sg. ariyāramna. Gen. sg. ariyāramnahyā. ariyā (nom. pl., q. v.; otherwise Foy, KZ, 35, 9) + *ramna, fr. *ram, *to be* or *cause to be at peace*, YAv. ram, Skt. ram.

aruvastam? Dar. NR. b. aruvastam upariy [dāraya]vau[m] xšāyaθiyam.

artaxšaθ^{r}a (Elam. irtakšašša; Bab. artakšassu; Gr. Ἀρταξέρξης; cf. Lycian ärtaχssirazahä on Xanthos stele), m. *Artaxerxes*. 1)*Artaxerxes* I. Gen. sg. artaxšaθ^{r}ahyā, artaxšaθ^{r}āhyā (written artaxšaθrahyā in Art. Ham. See Tolman, Reexamination of Columns, PAPA, 36, 33), artaxšaθ^{r}ā (for gen. sg.), Art. Pers. a, b. dārayavauš artaxšaθ^{r}ā xšāyaθiya puθ^{r}a artaxšaθ^{r}ā xšayāršā xšāyaθiya puθ^{r}a; cf. Marquart, ZDMG, 49, 665; Thumb, KZ, 32, 130; Foy, KZ, 35, 55. 2)*Artaxerxes* II. For nom. sg. artaxšaθ^{r}ā, Art. Sus. a. θātiy artaxšaθ^{r}ā XŠ vazarka; also Art. Pers. a, b, 2; Sus. b; cf. Foy, KZ, 35, 57. For gen. sg. artaxšaθ^{r}ā, Art. Pers. a, b. adam artaxšaθ^{r}ā xšāyaθiya puθ^{r}a. 3)*Artaxerxes* III. For nom. sg. artaxšaθ^{r}ā, Art. Pers. a, b, 2, 3, 4. θātiy artaxšaθ^{r}ā. For acc. sg. artaxšaθ^{r}ā, Art. Pers. a, b, 1. hya mām artaxšaθ^{r}ā xšāyaθiya akunauš. 4)*Artaxerxes* I(?), II(?), III(?), cf. Weissbach, Iran. Gr. II, 60, 18; Longpérier, RA, 2, 446; Foy, KZ, 35, 58. Nom. sg. ardaxcašc(?)a, Vase of Artaxerxes (Venice). This is the reading of the editions and generally accepted (cf. Foy, KZ, 37, 565; Bartholomae, Altiran. Wb., 192), šc being regarded as a phonetic representation of θ^r (Elam. šš; Bab. ts). The vase, however, as far as I can infer from the photographs which I have seen, clearly gives **ardaxcašda**, showing an uncut space between dᵃ and the mutilated word-divider. Either we must suppose that the engraver omitted the small horizontal wedge which differentiated cᵃ and dᵃ, or we must accept the reading ardaxcašda. *arta, *law*, Av. arəta + xšaθʳa, *kingdom* (q. v.).

artavardiya (Elam. irtumartiya; Bab. ar-ta-mar-zi-ia), m. name of one of the generals of Darius. Nom. sg. artavardiya. Acc. sg. artavardiyam. *arta, *law*, Av. arəta + *vard, *to increase*, Av. varəd (New Pers. bālīdan), Skt. vr̥dh.

ardaxcašc(?)a, see artaxšaθʳa.

ardastāna, m. *window-cornice* (?). Nom. sg. ardastāna, Dar. Pers. c. ardastāna aθaⁿgaina dārayavahauš XŠhyā viθiyā karta. *arda, *half*, YAv. arəda + stāna, YAv. -stana (New Pers. stān), Skt. sthāna; cf. Bartholomae, Altiran. Wb., 193. Foy, KZ, 35, 48. connects the first member of the compound with Av. arəzō, *bright*, Skt. r̥jra.

ardumaniš (Elam. [artumanniš]; Bab. a-ar-di-ma-ni-iš), m. name of one of the allies of Darius against Gaumāta. Nom. sg. ar[duma]n[iš]. *ardu, *right*, GAv.ərəzu, Skt. r̥ju + *maniš, *mind*, Av. manah, Skt. manas.

arbairā (Elam. arpera; Bab. ar-ba-'il), f. *Arbela*. Loc. sg. arbairāyā.

armina (Elam. arminiya; Bab. u-ra-aš-ṭu; Gr. 'Αρμενία), m. *Armenia*. Nom. sg. armina. Acc. sg. arminam. Loc. sg. arminaiy.

arminiya, adj. as subs. 1)*Armenian*. 2)*Armenia*. Nom. sg. m. arminiya. Loc. sg. m. arminiyaiy (thus read in Bh. 2. ll. 34, 39, 44 in place of armaniyaiy of ed., and to be supplied in Bh. 2. ll. 48, 63; cf. KT, 29). Written armⁱniyaiy in Bh. 2. ll. 34, 39, 44.

aršaka, m. *Arsaces*. Nom. sg. aršaka. *aršan, *man*, YAv. aršan, Gr. ἄρσην + suffix ka.

aršādā (Elam. iršata), f. name of a fortress. Nom. sg. aršādā. Cf. Justi, IF, 17, Anz. 106.

aršāma (Elam. iršama; Gr. 'Αρσάμης), m. *Arsames*, name of the grandfather of Darius. Nom. sg. aršāma. Gen. sg. aršāmahyā. *aršan, *man, hero* (cf. aršaka) + *ama, *might*, YAv. ama.

arštā (for arštatā; "the sign is quite clearly r and not b on the rock" KT), f. *Rectitude*. Acc. sg. arštām, Bh. 4. 13. upariy arštām upariy + + + +; Elam. šutur ukku hupa git, *I ruled in accordance with the ordinance;* Bab. ina di-na-a-tu a-si-ig-gu, *in accordance with the laws I governed.* The old reading of Rawlinson abaštam was nearer correct than the later abištam, as Jackson (JAOS, 24, 91) and KT clearly indicate the absence of i in the word. arštā was first conjectured by Foy (KZ, 35, 45) and later confirmed by Jackson's reëxamination of the Behistan Rock. We cannot, however, accept Foy's further conjecture āpariyāyam, *ich verehrte die aufrichtigkeit*, as Jackson and KT record the presence of the second upariy on the stone; cf. Tolman (Vdt. Stud. 1, 32). The emended reading has an important bearing on the religion of the Achaemenidan kings: cf. Jackson, JAOS, 21, 169; Foy, ZDMG, 54, 341; Wilhelm, ibid. 40, 105; Tolman, PAPA, 33, 67. Weissbach (ZDMG, 61, 733) would emend the Bab. u-ša-as-gu-u. YAv. arštāt, *goddess of rectitude*, fr. aršta, *upright*.

aršti, f. *spear*. Nom. sg. arštiš. YAv. aršti, Skt. r̥šti.

arštibara, m. *spear-bearer*. Nom. sg. arštibara. aršti (q. v.) + *bara, fr. bar (q. v.).

ava, demon. pron. *that*. Acc. sg. m. avam. Gen. sg. m. avahyā. Acc. sg. n. ava, avaš-ciy. Nom. pl. m. avaiy. Nom. pl. f. avā, NRa. 4. As acc. pl. m. avaiy, Bh. 2. 13. avaiy —— frāhaⁿjam. Gen. pl. m. avaišām (cf. Turfan MSS. 'ovêšân). I. E. oṷo, Av. ava (New Pers. ō, Kurd. af).

ava, verbal prefix, *down*, e. g. ava + jan, *to strike down*. Av. ava (Middle Pers. ō), Skt. ava.

avā, adv. *thus*. Correlative to yaθā, Bh. 4. 1. 51. avā naiy astiy kartam yaθā, reading confirmed by KT. Cf. Tolman, Vdt. Stud. 1, 32.

avākanam, a reading confirmed by KT in Bh. 1. 18. maškāuvā avākanam, *I placed (my army) on floats of skins;* cf. Tolman, Vdt.

Stud. 1, 15. Pedersen, KZ, 40, 133, translates, *Ich setzte das heer auf*. The attempted emendation **avakarnam**, fr. **kart**, *to cut, divide*, is superseded.

avajam, Bh. 2. 13, 14. **utāšaiy [u]cašma avajam (a-vajam** or **a-va**ⁿ**jam**, Bartholomae), *I put out his eyes*. Cf. KZ, 37, 554. Jackson (JAOS, 24, 88) remarks: "The sight is destroyed by means of a red-hot iron brought near the ball. This latter observation may throw some additional light on the meaning of **avajam**. The reading of this word is beyond question." See **ucašma**. The sense of both Elam. and Bab. version is as given above.

avaθā, adv. 1)*thus*, 2)*then*. Bh. 4. 10. **nūram** (Jackson, JAOS, 24, 90; KT, 69) **θuvām varnavātam tya manā kartam avaθā sā + + + d + + + ādiy**, *let it now convince thee what has been done by me, so + + +.* In Dar. NRa. 4 Stolze's photograph shows [avad]ā or [avaθ]ā where Foy, KZ, 35, 51 reads [ava]dā. Bartholomae, by reference to Ménant and Daressy (Recueil de trav.) reads **avaθā yaθā** for **pa[s]āva** of ed. in l. 11 of Dar. Sz. c, 3. YAv. **avaθa**.

avaθāstā pari[ba]rā, *thus preserve them* (i. e. the sculptures), reading of KT for **avā avaiy parikarā** of ed. in Bh. 4. l. 72. See **bar**. Hoffmann-Kutschke would take the first word as **avaθā štā**, *stand thou* (as I stand with subdued rebels before me).

avadā, adv. 1)*there*, 2)*thither*, 3)**hacā avadaša** (i. e. **avadā + ša**, abl. sg. pron.; cf. Bartholomae, BB, 14, 247. Foy, KZ, 35, 29, on the other hand compares Lat. **sed**, e. g., sed fraude), *therefrom, thence*. [a]**vadā** for [a]**dā**[**raya**] of ed. is to be read in Bh. 2. l. 29, followed by a lacuna affording, as KT record, "scarcely room for more than two signs. The traces of the last sign seem to be those of nᵃ or hᵃ." Can we supply **āha**, *there he did not abide* ? Cf. Tolman, Vdt. Stud. 1, 18. YAv. **avaδa** (Turfan MSS. 'ōōd, Bal. **ōdā**).

avaparā, adv. *there along, there before*. Read thus in Bh. 2. l. 72 for **avadā** of ed.; cf. KT, 35. Bh. 3, 12. **aršādā nāmā didā** [**ha**]**rauvatiyā avaparā atiyāiš** (Bartholomae, Grundr. 360). KT plainly record the reading **avaparā**, thus setting aside Foy's conjecture **avadaparā**. **ava** (acc. sg. n.) + *****parā**, *before*, Av. **para**, Skt. **purā**.

avast[ā]ya[m], reading of KT in Bh. 4. l. 91, in which Weissbach (ZDMG, 61, 730) sees a possible reference to the Avesta.

āvahana, n. *dwelling place.* Nom. sg. **āvahanam.** Skt. **vasana.** ā + *vah, *to dwell*, YAv. **vah,** Skt. **vas.**

avahya, *to ask aid, implore.* Denominative of *avah, Av. **avah;** cf. Skt. **avasya.**

—— with prefix **patiy,** *seek for help, supplicate.* Mid. pret. 1 sg. **patiyāvahyaiy,** Bh. 1. 13. **adam auramazdām patiyāvahyaiy,** *I prayed Ahura Mazda for help.* "The true reading of the radical part of the word is —vahyaiy (—v^{n}h^{a}y^{a}iy^a, with hy, not y) as is plainly shown in a photograph which I took of it when I examined the Behistan Rock in 1903. The verb patiyāvahyaiy is therefore naturally to be connected, as a denominative, with Av. avah-, avahya-, *aid, assistance, support,* cf. Bartholomae, Altiran. Wb., 179, and see especially Friedrich Müller in WZKM, 1, 122, and Tolman, OP. Insc. p. 167; and it is precisely the Iranian equivalent of the Sanskrit denominative avasya-, *seek for aid, take refuge with,* in Rig Veda, I, 116. 23 (avasyate, dat. pres. ptcpl.)." Jackson, JAOS, 27, 190. KT confirm Jackson's reading thus removing all possible connection with the root van (Bartholomae, ZDMG, 48, 156; Foy, KZ, 37, 518). For Bartholomae's later view, see Zum Altiran. Wb., 217. The same scholar writes me in a personal letter: "Die Turfanhandschriften bieten **padvahīd, padvahām, padvahišn,** u. s. w, alle im Sinn des lat. *supplicari.*"

avahyarādiy, adv. *for this reason, therefore.* **avahya** (for avah**yāyā,** loc. sg. f.; cf. Bartholomae, Grundr. 239, 2) + *rādiy, loc. sg. *cause,* New Pers. **rā**; cf. Justi, IF, 17, Anz. 91.

av^{a}h^a[r $_{+ +}$] thus read in place of av[ārada] of ed. in Bh. 2. l. 94. a[va]m kāra av^{a}h^a[r $_{+ +}$], *the people forsook him.* The Elam. version makes the sense certain. The Bab. is wanting. KT record: "The traces of the sign following h are probably those of r. There is room for one more sign in this word." In Vdt. Stud. 1, 22, I suggested the supplement **avahar[ja],** Skt. **avas̥r̥jat,** (*the people*) *cast off allegiance to him,* which seems quite certain when we compare Turfan MSS. hêrz. Weissbach (ZDMG, 61, 726) suggests **avahar[ta],** part. perf. to *har, Skt. **sar,** *weggelaufen seiend.*

asa, m. *horse.* Acc. sg. **asam** (in collective sense), Bh. 1. 18. **aniyahyā asam frānayam,** *for the rest I brought horses.* This is plainly the reading of the stone. Jackson records: "The reading **aŝm₊₊** of Spiegel, Kossowicz, and Tolman, or **taŝma[kam]** of Fr. Müller, WZKM, 1, 222, and **as[pā]** of Weissbach and Bang, though the latter were on the right track, must be abandoned. The word is simply **asam,** *horse.*" KT confirm Jackson's reading. The conclusion of Gray (AJP, 21, 7) concerning a double representation by sp and s of Iranian sp is hereby shown to be correct; cf. Horn, Grundr. d. neupers. Etym., 160, 749. See s. v. **aspa.**

asagarta (Elam. **aŝŝakartiya;** Bab. **sa-ga-ar-ta-a-a**), m. *Sagartia.* Nom. sg. **asagarta.** Acc. sg. **asagartam.** Loc. sg. **asagartaiy.** Against Bartholomae's etymology cf. Justi, IF, 17, Anz. 114, **asa** (q. v.) + *garta, Skt. **garta,** *wagon.* Note also Bartholomae, Zum Altiran. Wb., 120.

asagartiya, adj. *Sagartian.* Nom. sg. m. **asagartiya.**

asabāri (thus read since Jackson's and KT's confirmation of **asa** against Bartholomae's **asbārī** for **aspabāri,** Altiran. Wb., 219; Hübschmann, ZDMG, 36, 133; Justi, IF, 17, Anz. 114; Pedersen, KZ, 40, 133), adj. *mounted on horses, horsemen.* Instr. pl. **asabāribiŝ.** New Pers. **suvār.** **asa** (q. v.) + **bāri,** fr. **bar** (q. v.).

[**aspa,** in composition, *horse.* YAv. **aspa** (New Pers. **asp,** Afγ. **aspā,** f., Oss. **afsa,** Kurd. **hasp,** Socin, SK, 9), Skt. **açva**].

aspacanah, name of Persian, *Aspathines.* Nom. sg. **aspacanā,** Dar. NRd. ***aspa** (q. v.) + ***canah,** n., *desire,* YAv. **cinah,** Skt. **canas.**

asman, m. 1)*stone,* 2)*firmament, heaven.* Acc. sg. **asmānam** (written **asmānām** in Art. Pers. **a, b**). YAv. **asman** (Turfan MSS. 'asmân, New Pers. **āsmān,** Gab. **asbān**), Skt. **açman.** Cf. KZ, 39, 69; Wackernagel, Ai. Gram. 71.

aŝnaiy, a doubtful word in Bh. 2. 4. **adam aŝnaiy āham abiy uvajam.** The Elam. renders **kanna enni git.** WB and KT translate both Persian and Elam., *I was friendly with Susiana.* I think it doubtful if Elam. **kanna** means *friendly*, for it is not likely that [**akka kannaš**] is the correct supplement for the Elam. corresponding to Persian ag^{a}r^a $_+$ $_+$, Bh. 1, 8; cf. Tolman, Vdt. Stud. 1, 9. Bartholomae (Altiran. Wb., 264) regards **ašnaiy** as loc. sg. to **ašna**, *march*, i. e., *I was on the march to Susiana.* The Elam. passage is discussed by Foy (KZ, 35, 37), who favors the interpretation, *auf dem marsche.* The Bab. gives no assistance. Cf. Bartholomae, Grundr. 1, 31; Foy, ZDMG, 52, 567.

azdā, adv. *known* (Bartholomae, IF, 9, 279; nom. sg. **azdā** Johansson, IF, 2, 28). Bh. 1. 10. **kārahy[ā naiy] azdā abava,** *it was not known to the people.* GAv. **azdā** (Middle Pers. **azd,** Afy. **zda,** Geiger, SA, 7), Skt. **addhā.**

[**ah** (text, $_+$ $_+$ $_+$ $_+$ ā), *to throw.* Pass. indic. pret. 3 sg. [**āhyat**]ā, Bh. 1. 19. **aniya āpi[y]ā [āhyat]ā,** *the enemy* (Foy, *the other part*) *were driven into the water.* Rugarli, *il nemico fu gettato nell' acqua.* Cf. Kern, ZDMG, 23, 239; Foy, KZ, 37, 554. Bartholomae, AF, 1, 61, first suggested **ahadatā** (**had** = Skt. **sah**), but later (Altiran. Wb., 279) favors Kern's reading. WB, [a]ha^n[jat]ā (ha^{n}j = Skt. **sañj**); Oppert (Le peuple — des Mèdes, 169 [a]ha[ra]tā (har = Skt. **sar**) which Gray favors in AJP, 21, 22, and which KT supply, remarking: "There is room for this restoration on the rock;" they translate the Elam., *I drove them into the river.* The Bab. gives no assistance. YAv. **ah**, Skt. **as.**]

ah (Pres. **ah-, h-,** Bartholomae, Grundr. 122), *to be.* Act. indic. pres. 1 sg. **amiy.** 3 sg. **astiy.** 1 pl. **amahy.** 3 pl. **ha^{n}tiy.** Pret. 1 sg. **āham.** 3 sg. **āha.** 3 pl. **āha^n.** Subj. 2 sg. **āhy** (for a^{h}ahiy. Wrongly read in cd. and KT, **ahy.** The subjunctive is certain as seen in such a phrase as **tuvam kā hya aparam imām dipi[m] patiparsāhy,** *thou whosoever shalt hereafter read this inscription;* cf. Tolman, Vdt. Stud. 1, 30). 3 sg. **ahatiy.** Mid. pret. 3 pl. **āha^{n}tā** (written **āha^{n}ta** in Bh. 3. ll. 49, 51). Av. **ah**, Skt. **as.**

I, Ī

i (Pres. **ai-, i-,** Bartholomae, Grundr. 122), *to go.* Indic. pres. 3 sg. **aitiy.** Aor. 3 sg. **aiš^a** (read **aiš** or **aiša** with thematic vowel). Av. **i** (New Pers. **āyaδ**), Skt. **i.**

—— with prefix ā, *come.* Pret. 3 pl. āya^{n}tā (thematic), Dar. Sz. c. 3.

—— with prefix atiy, *go beyond, go along.* Aor. 3 sg. atiyāiš^a (see āiš^a).

—— with prefix abiy(?) or upa(?), *go unto, arrive.* Pret. 1 sg. [abiy]āyam (Foy, ZDMG, 54, 363), [up]āyam (WB, KT), Bh. 1. 19. aθiy (sic; cf. KT, 19) bābiru[m yaθā naiy up]āyam.

—— with prefix upariy(?). In upariy[āyam], Bh. 4. 13, upariy is clearly seen on the stone (Jackson and KT); āyam, however, is very doubtful. "Instead of āyam naiy, it looks more like a long word ending in h^{a}iy or j^{a}iy—the former h^{a}iy is, however, better, and it seems so to be clear," JAOS, 24, 93. KT read without comment + + + + naiy. The obliquely meeting wedges initial in the cuneiform sign for h, which alone differentiate it from that for n, may of course be in the preceding lacuna. In Vdt. Stud. 1, 32, I proposed the rather desperate supplement upariy [axšayaiy] naiy; see xši. Weissbach (ZDMG, 61, 729) reads upariy arštām upariy[āyam], *nach dem Gesetze habe ich geherrscht.* Jackson's and KT's confirmation of upariy makes impossible Foy's conjecture āpariyāyam, KZ, 35, 45. For Rawlinson's upariy mām Jackson suggests the meaning *beyond measure.*

   with prefix nij (Bartholomae, Grundr. 269, 2, n. 1), *go forth.* Pret. 1 sg. nijāyam.

—— with prefix patiy, *to come unto, be one's possession.* Aor. 3 pl. patiyāiša^n (with thematic vowel, Bartholomae, Grundr. 329, 360).

—— with prefix parā, *go forth, proceed.* Impv. pres. 2 sg. paraidiy. Pret. 2 pl. (Injunctive, Bartholomae, Grundr. 166), paraitā. Part. nom. pl. paraitā.

—— ap^{a}riy^{a}ay^a of ed. and KT (Bh. 1. 8) is to be read āpariyāya' for a^{h}apariyāya^n; see hapariya.

idā, adv. *here.* YAv. iδa, Skt. iha.

ima, demon. pron. *this*. Acc. sg. m. **imam**. Acc. sg. n. **ima** (KT record auramazdām[aiy] ima for auramazdā manā of ed. in Bh. 1. l. 25). Acc. sg. f. **imām**. Nom. acc. pl. m. **imaiy** (Bartholomae, Grundr. 240). Acc. pl. n. **imā**. Nom. acc. pl. f. **imā**. Gen. pl. m. **imaišām** (thus read for imišam of KT; cf. Weissbach, ZDMG, 61, 730), Bh. 4. 87. tyām imaišām martiyānām taumām [ubart]ā[m] par-[ibar]ā, *die Nachkommenschaft dieser Männer behüte wohl*, Weissbach (op. cit.), who observes that ideogram GUL, *family*, is to be supplied before appa (m)ruh(id) appi ir kuktaš of Elam. version, while in Bab. there is preserved a trace of ziru before sabe. Av. ima (Turfan MSS. 'im, New Pers. im-), Skt. ima. Note Turfan MSS. 'imešân < imaišām.

imaniš (Elam. ummanniš; Bab. im-ma-ni-e-šu), m. name assumed by Martiya in his insurrection in Susiana. Bh. 2. 3; 4. 2; f.

iyam (*ī-am, Bartholomae, Grundr. 236), demon. pron. *this*. Nom. sg. m. iyam. In Dar. NRe. iyam maciyā, Bartholomae suggests the emendation im^{a}y^n (imaiy). Nom. sg. f. iyam. In Bh. 4. 1. 90, the form according to KT seems to be written iya; "This would be certain if the reading of the division wedge before i were clear upon the rock;" cf. Bartholomae, WZKM, 22, 66. Skt. ayam, m., iyam, f., GAv. ayǝm, m.

i + + ā (text as confirmed by KT who record space for two signs in the middle of the word. i[zar]ā, Tolman, in place of [iz]i[tuš] of the ed. which the Elam. izzila, wrongly read before izzitu, makes impossible; cf. Vdt. Stud. 1, 20), f. name of a district in Assyria. Nom. sg. i[zar]ā, Bh. 2. 10. i[zar]ā nāmā dahyāuš aθurāyā. Weissbach (ZDMG, 61, 726) proposes i[zal]ā.

iš, *to put in motion, send*. Av. iš, Skt. iṣ.

—— with prefix **frā**, *send forth*. Caus. pret. 1 sg. frāišayam. 3 sg. frāišaya.

išunām, reading of WB in Dar. NRd. išunām dāraya^{n}tā, *Pfeilbewahrer*. Bartholomae, išuvām dāraya^{n}tā. Hoffmann-Kutschke, Iran. denānām dārayantā = Elam. tenim kuktikra, *Träger der Gesetzestafeln*, Or. Lit. Ztg., Sept., 1906. Old reading isuvām dāsayamā, cf. Justi, ZDMG, 50, 663; Gray, AJP, 21, 2; Foy, ZDMG, 55, 514.

U, Ū

u (before vowels uv), adv. (in composition), *good, well*, e. g. ufraštam, *well punished*, umartiya, *poss. good men*, uvaspa, *poss. good horses*. Av. hu, Skt. su, Gr. ὑ-γιής, *well living* (cf. βίος; Brugmann, Gr. Gram.³ 98, 2).

[ukarta]m, (₊ ₊ ₊ ₊ m, KT.), a mutilated word in Bh. 4. l. 76. From the traces of wedges given by KT I proposed (AJP, under date of Feb. 1908) the reading [ukarta]m kunautuv, *may he make it well done* (i. e. successful), which corresponds closely with the Elam. aiak kutta appa huttanti huhpe ᵃⁿuramašta azzašne, *and whatsoever thou doest, this may Ahura Mazda cause to succeed*. In case the word-divider is mutilated (which is quite likely), the obliquely-meeting wedges suggest initial u. The two small horizontals (if the second be slightly lower) may be the sign for k, while the three parallel horizontals are probably what remains of r. vazarkam (Oppert, Foy) is also possible, but the word certainly did not begin with m, as Rawlinson supposed (mazānam, WB¹; maθitam, Bartholomae).

[u]cᵃšᵃmᵃ, *eye*. Acc. sg. [u]cᵃšᵃmᵃ, Bh. 2. 13, 14. utāšaiy [u]cᵃšᵃmᵃ avajam, *and I put out his eyes*. KT regard the sign š as quite clear and c as fairly certain, while the first sign appears as u. Jackson, however, feels less certain; "The obliterated word yielded no new results. The internal letter looks more like an h than it does like an š, but the likeness between the two letters in the cuneiform character leads easily to misapprehension" (JAOS, 24, 88). Weissbach (ZDMG, 61, 726) proposes the reading ucašma, = hu-cašma, comparing the Av. hu-xšnaoθra. Jackson would interpret KT's reading as word-divider + cašma. Note Turfan MSS. cašm.

utā, conj. *and*. The tendency of vašnā auramazdāha to begin the clause places that phrase before utā in Bh. 2. 1; 4. 8; but Bartholomae's proposed emendation [utā]maiy (Bh. 4. l. 46) based on this principle is now set aside by KT's reading [ap]imaiy. Correl. with cā, Bh. 1. 14. adam kāram gāθavā avāstāyam pārsam[c]ā mādam[c]ā utā aniyā dahyāva. utā — utā, *both — and*, Bh. 1. 12. adīnā kaⁿbūjiyam utā pārsam utā mādam utā aniyā dahyāva. YAv. uta (Turfan MSS. 'ûd), Skt. uta.

utāna (Elam. huttana; Bab. u-mi-it-ta-na-'; Gr. 'Οτάνης), m. *Otanes*, name of one of the allies of Darius against Gaumāta. Nom. sg. [u]tā[na].

ud, us, adv. *up, forth,* e. g. udapatatā, Bh. 2. 5, et passim; ustašanā, Art. Pers. 1. 3. Av. us (Middle Pers. uz, New Pers. zi; cf. Horn, Grundr. d. neupers. Etym. 143), Skt. ud.

upā, 1)adv. *unto, to.* Bh. 1. 19. aθiy (sic) bābiru[m yaθā naiy up]āyam (WB; KT). 2)prep. with acc. *to, by.* Bh. 3. 6. kāram pārsam utā mādam frāišayam hya upā mām āha. Av. upa, Skt. upa. Cf. Jud. Pers. awāz < upācā.

upadara^n ma (Oppert, Le peuple—des Mèdes; Gray, AJP, 21, 19. Elam. ukpa + + ranma), m. name of the father of Āθ^r ina, Bh. 1. 16. Gen. sg. upadara^n mahya. upadarma, *der Ordnung* (cf. Skt. dharma) *untertan,* Bartholomae, Altiran. Wb., 390. Cf. Hūsing, Ir. En. 14, 38.

upariy, prep. with acc. *above, over.* upariy arštām upariy + + + + (Jackson; KT), Bh. 4. 13. YAv. upairi (New Pers., Kurd. bar), Skt. upari.

upastā, f. *help, aid.* Acc. sg. upastām. YAv. upastā; upa + stā (q. v.).

ufrašta (thus read in Bh. 4. 1. 38; cf. KT, 66: elsewhere written ufrasta), part. pass., *well punished.* Bartholomae formerly read ufrasata, part. with gerundive meaning, Whitney, Skt. Gr. 1176, e., but has just recently changed his view (WZKM, 22, 75), owing to the corrected reading ufrašta. For interchange of s and š note the Turfan manuscripts (F. W. K. Müller, SBAW, 1904, I; II, 1907). Acc. sg. m. ufraštam (ufrastam). u + frasta, fr. fras, *to ask, examine, punish,* Av. fras (New Pers. pursad), Skt. pr̥chati.

ufrašti (thus read in Bh. 4. 1. 69 in place of ahifrašti of ed.; cf. KT, 73), f. *severe punishment.* Loc. sg. ufraštā + adiy (q. v.). u + frašti, GAv. ferašti, fr. fras; inchoative pres. parsa (q. v.).

ufrātu (Elam. upra[tu]; Bab. purattu; Gr. Εὐφράτης), m. *Euphrates.* ufrāt^n uvā (thus written on the stone in Bh. 1. 1. 92 in place of ufrātauvā of ed.; cf. KT, 19. Bartholomae (WZKM. 22, 71) regards the case as gen. sg. with anuv (cf. schol. to Pāṇini, 2. 1. 16, gaṅgāyā anu). In Vdt. Stud. 1, 16, I cite this form as a possible instance of anuv with instr. sg. According to Justi, IF, 17, Anz. 116, u (q. v.) + *frāta, *fire* (cf. Arm. hrat), *dem das heilige Feuer gut oder gnädig ist*. It seems more probable, however, that the last element of the compound is a foreign word. Bartholomae favors a "Volksetymologie."

ubarta, part. pass., *well esteemed*. Bartholomae formerly favored ubarata, part. with gerundive meaning, but has now returned to the older view; see s. v. ufrašta. Acc. sg. ubartam. u + bar (q. v.).

umartiya, adj. *possessing good men*. Nom. sg. f. umartiyā. Nom. sg. n. umartiyam. u + martiya (q. v.).

u[yam]ā (supplied from Elam. uiyama), f. name of a fortress in Armenia. The reading u[hy]āma of ed. is impossible; cf. KT, 30. Nom. sg. u[yam]ā, Bh. 2. 9.

uvāipašiya, n. *own possession* (Elam. tuman-e). Acc. sg. uvāipašiyam, Bh. 1. 12. hauv āyasatā uvāipašiyam akutā, *he seized (the power and) made it his own possession*. KT give the traditional translation, *he did according to his will*, which is impossible as the meaning is clear from both Elam. (see above) and Bab. $_{+\,+}$ ti a-na ša ra-ma-ni-šu ut-te-ir, *he took it for himself;* cf. Tolman, Vdt. Stud. 1, 11. YAv. x^{v}aēpaiθya, *own*, *uvāi, Av. x^{v}aē- (as dat. to x^{v}a, Skt. sva) + *pašiya, Av. *paiθya, fr. *paiti, *selbst* (Bartholomae) *gehörig* (Foy; *das, worüber man herr ist*).

uvaxštra (Elam. makištarra; Bab. u-ma-ku-iš-tar; Gr. Κυαξάρης), m. *Cyaxares;* cf. Tolman and Stevenson, Hdt. and Empires of the East, 68. Gen. sg. uvaxštrahyā, uvaxštrahya. u + *vaxštra, fr. *vaxš, *grow*, Av. vaxš (Middle Pers. vaxšītan), Skt. vakṣ. Justi (Iran. Namenbuch, 140), retains the old reading uvaxšatara, regarding it a comparative of u + vaxša, *growth*.

uvaja (Elam. alpirti; Bab. e-lam-mat), m. *Susiana*. Nom. sg. uvaja. Acc. sg. uvajam. Loc. sg. uvajaiy. Hübschmann, Pers. Stud. 214, (h)uvža; Foy, KZ, 35, 62, comparing Skt. aja translates *ziegenreich;* cf. KZ, 37, 542.

uvajiya, adj. *Susian.* Nom. sg. uvajiya. Nom. pl. uvajiyā. Instr. pl. uvajiyaibiš, Bh. 5. l. 10, [hamaranam a]kuna[uš hadā] uvajiyaibiš, (*Gobryas*) *waged battle with the Susians.*

uvādaicaya (Elam. mateziš ₊ ₊), m. name of a Persian town. Nom. sg. uvādaicaya.

uvāmaršiyu, adj. *dying by one's own hand.* Nom. sg. uvāmaršiyuš, Bh. 1. 11. pasāva ka^nbūjiya uvāmaršiyuš amariyatā, *afterwards Cambyses died by his own hand*, i. e. by suicide or by accident; cf. Hdt. 3, 62. "As he was leaping on his horse the blade of his sword struck his thigh." See Marquart, Philol. Suppl. 6, 621. *uva, Av. x^va, Skt. sva + *maršiyu, Av. mərəθyu, Skt. mṛtyu, fr. mar (q. v.).

uvārazm¡i (Elam. marašmiya; Bab. ḫu-ma-ri-iz-mu), f. *Chorasmia.* Nom. sg. uvārazmiš. Cf. Y.Av. x^vāirizəm, Bartholomae, Grundr. 402, n. 2. Ir. -zmi-, Skt. jmas, Gr. χαμαί, Foy, KZ, 35, 1, 23; Justi, IF, 17, Anz. 113, *Schoen-land.*

uvārazm¡iya, adj. Nom. sg. m. uvārazm¡iya in collective sense, *Chorasmia.* Bh. 1. 6; Dar. Pers. e. 2.

uvaspa, adj. *possessing good horses.* Nom. sg. f. uvaspā. Nom. sg. n. [uvaspam], Dar. Sz. c. 1. u + aspa (q. v.).

ustašanā, f. *staircase, Bauwerk* (WB), *Treppe* (Bartholomae). Acc. sg. ustašanām, Art. Pers. a, b, 3. imam ustašanām aθa^nganām mām upā mām kartā. Foy (KZ, 35, 60) reads ustacanām (= ustašanām, cf. xšayārcahyā, Art. Sus. a, 1) in Art. Sus. c. imām ₊ ₊ ₊ ₊ ₊ ₊ canām tya aθa^ngainām. us (see ud) + *tašanā, fr. *taš, *cut, fashion*, Av. taš, Skt. takṣ.

ušabāri (Jackson; "An examination and rëexamination of the rock proves the certainty of this reading." KT; "The reading of the signs uša is certain"), adj. Jackson suggests *borne by oxen*(?), Av. uxšan, Skt. ukṣan. Bartholomae's uštrabāri, *mounted on camels*, possible on the theory that the stone-cutter failed to write t^ᵃr^ᵃ, agrees with the sense of the Elam. version; cf. Tolman, Vdt. Stud. 1, 15. Weissbach (ZDMG, 61, 725) suggests uša as a "Nebenform" to uštra. The numerous conjectures, several of which seemed plausible before this confirmation of Oppert's reading, must now be set aside, e. g. ašabārī (Müller, WZKM, 1, 220), maišabārī (ibid. 11, 252), īšubārī (Gray, AJP, 21, 20) etc.; cf. the literature in KZ, 38, 259. Acc. sg. m. ušabārim, Bh. 1. 18. aniyam ušabārim akunavam aniyahyā asam frānayam, *the one (part of my army) I put on camels; for the other I brought horses.*

uška, adj. *dry;* n. *dry land, mainland.* Gen. sg. n. uškahyā, Dar. Pers. e. 2. yaunā tyaiy uškahyā. YAv. huška (New Pers. xušk, Afγ. vuc).

uzma, adj. *what is up from the earth;* n. *stake, pile.* Loc. sg. uzmayā (i. e.—ai + postpos. ā) with patiy. Bh. 2. 13. uzmayāpatiy akunavam, *I crucified him.* ud (q. v.) + *zam, *earth* (Turfan MSS. zamîg); cf. Bartholomae, Grundr. 219, 2; Foy, KZ, 37, 529; Wackernagel, Ai. Gram. 72. Nearly the exact equivalent appears in the Turfan MSS. qarênd dârôbadag (Bartholomae; dârûbadag, Müller), *they will crucify;* qarênd < kar; dârô, cf. New Pers. dār, *wood;* bad < patiy.

K

kā, particle giving to preceding tuvam, *thou,* an indefinite force. Bab. man-nu at ta šarru ša be-la-a ar-ki-ia = Pers. tuvam [kā] xšāya[θ]iya hya aparam āhy, Bh. 4. 19, *thou whosoever shalt be king hereafter.* Cf. Gray (JAOS, 23, 60) who rejects Kern's view in Caland, Synt. der Pron. 47, and regards kā as correspondent to the Doric κά (I. E. qā) with a generalizing power.

ka, 1) interrog. pronoun, *who?* 2) indef. with ciy, *any.* Nom. sg. m. kašciy. Acc. sg. n. cišciy. Cf. Bartholomae, Grundr. 415. Av. ka (New Pers. ki, Oss. k'a), Skt. ka. Note Turfan MSS. ke.

kaufa, m. *hill, mountain.* Nom. sg. kaufa. YAv. kaofa (Phl. kōf, New Pers. kōh).

katpatuka (Elam. katpatukaš; Bab. ka-at-pa-tuk-ka; Gr. Καππαδοκία), m. *Cappadocia.* Nom. sg. katpatuka.

kan, *to dig, chisel out.* Pres. inf. **ka**ⁿ**tanaiy.** The ed. supply **akāniy** (Aor. pass. 3 sg.) in the mutilated portion of Dar. Sz. c. 3. **iyam yuviyā** [**akāniy**]. YAv. **kan** (New Pers. **kandan**), Skt. **khan**.

—— with prefix **niy**, *obliterate, cause to be forgotten.* Pres. impv. 3 sg. **nika**ⁿ**tuv**.

—— with prefix **viy** (thus I read in Bh. 4, ll. 71, 73, 77 against KT's **visan-**; cf. Tolman, Vdt. Stud. 1, 34. The question involves simply the absence of a medial wedge in the cuneiform sign. Jackson in all these places records the **k** as fairly clear. So too the Elam. **sari** points to the certainty of the reading—**kan-**; cf. Weissbach, ZDMG, 61, 729), *destroy.* Pres. subj. 2 sg. **vikanāhy**, Bh. 4. ll. 71, 73. **vikanāh(i)diš**, Bh. 4. l. 77. Pret. 3 sg. **viyaka**ⁿ, Bh. 1. 14.

kaⁿ**pada** (**ka**ⁿ**pa**ⁿ**da**, Foy, KZ, 37, 531. Elam. **kampantaš**), m. name of a district in Media. Nom. sg. **ka**ⁿ**pada**. Cf. Hüsing, Ir. En. 38.

kāpišakāni (Elam. **kappiššakaniš**), f. name of a fortress in Arachosia. Nom. sg. **kāpišakāniš**.

kaⁿ**būjiya** (Elam. **kanpuziya**; Bab. **kam-bu-zi-ia**; Gr. Καμβύσης), m. *Cambyses.* Nom. sg. **ka**ⁿ**būjiya**. Acc. sg. **ka**ⁿ**būjiyam**. Gen. sg. **ka**ⁿ**būjiyahyā**. Abl. sg. **ka**ⁿ**būjiyā**, Bh. 1. 11. **kāra haruva hamiθ'iya abava hacā ka**ⁿ**būjiyā**, *the whole people became confederate from Cambyses.* **ka**ⁿ**bū** + **jiyā**, *mit Sehnen aus* —?, Bartholomae, Altiran. Wb., 437. **kam**, Skt. **kam** + **buj**, Skt. **bhuj**, *glückgeniessende*, Foy, KZ, 35, 62. Cf. KZ, 37, 543; Justi, Iran. Namenbuch, 490.

kāma, m. *desire, wish.* Nom. sg. **kāma**, Bh. 4. 4. **yaθā mām kāma**, *as was my will.* Av. **kāma**.

kamna, adj. *few.* Nom. sg. n. **kamnam**, Bh. 2. 6. **kāra pārsa u[tā m]āda hya upā mām āha hauv kamnam āha**, *the Persian and the Median army, which was by me, this was small.* For a like use of the neuter we can compare [t]**ya ciyakaram a**[**vā dahy**]**ā**[**va**], Dar. NRa. 4. Foy (KZ, 35, 38) would read **kamnama** regarding the word as a superl. formation. I suggested (Vdt. Stud. 1, 18) the possible reading **kamnama** (i. e. **kamna**, nom. sg. m. + **ma** = **maiy**), though the objections to assuming ma = maiy cannot be denied; cf. apanyākama, Art. Sus. a. The Elam. version shows no pronoun here. Instr. pl. kamnaibiš. YAv. kamna (New Pers. kam).

kar (Pres. kunau-, Bartholomae, Grundr. 131; Wackernagel, Ai. Gram. 29), *to do, make.* Act. pres. subj. 2 sg. kunavāhy. Impv. 3 sg. kunautuv (wrongly transliterated kunutuv by KT in Bh. 4. 16, for n^a, not n^u, plainly appears in the cuneiform text). Pret. indic. 1 sg. akunavam. 3 sg. akunauš (akunaš is written in Art. Sus. a. 4; cf. Foy, KZ, 37, 540). 1 pl. akunaumā?, Art. Hamadan, l. 7 (akunā mā is written on the stone). I examined in 1905 these Moldings of Columns from Ecbatana and noted clearly the presence of the word-divider. We cannot doubt that we are dealing with a stone-cutter's blunder. I proposed (PAPA, 36, 32) the epigraphical emendation akunaumā, involving the joining at right angles of the first perpendicular wedge with the horizontal above in the cuneiform sign for ā and the raising of the oblique word-divider to a horizontal position above the two remaining perpendicular strokes. The restored form would be the first person plural of the nu class, built, however, against the rule on the strong stem, as illustrated by akunava^n, akunava^{n}tā. The Persian akumā (Ir. akr-mā) is, of course, outside this class. The same form I would supply in the lacuna of l. 5, where I spoke of a possible reference to the combined work of Achaemenidan kings. Bartholomae (Altiran. Wb., 444) emends akunavam. Cf. Foy, KZ, 37, 540. 3 pl. akunava^n. Aor. 1 pl. akumā (Bartholomae Grundr. 290, n. 1. In Bh. 1. l. 90 Jackson records that akumā "though defaced, is still legible" (JAOS, 24, 88) against KT's [ak]umā). Perf. opt. 3 sg. caxriyā. Inf. cartanaiy (Fr. Müller's connection of the form with root cai, *go,* is very improbable, since the Elam. renders by the same verb, hutta, which elsewhere translates the Persian kar). Mid. pret. 3 pl. akunava^{n}tā, akunavaya^{n}tā (Bartholomae, BB, 12, 68, for akunavyatā of ed.; cf. KZ, 39, 153). Aor. 3 sg. akutā (Skt. akr̥ta). Pass. pret. 3 pl. akariya^{n}tā (Bartholomae) where KT record the old reading asariyatā. In Vdt. Stud. 1, 23, I adopted Bartholomae's conjecture because 1) a small horizontal wedge is all that differentiates s and k, and 2) Jackson regards k as quite certain (JAOS, 24, 89). Weissbach, writing at about the same date, likewise is of this opinion, since the Elam. word (pela) renders Persian kar of the phrase, uzmayāpatiy—kar—, in Bh. 2. 76, 91; 3. 52. Both the Elam. ((m)u šera) and Bab. (anaku tēme altakan) versions of the passage point to an imperative, *I decreed, saying, let them*, etc.; but there is probably not an exact correspondence here, since we have no evidence of a final m in the word. Part. nom. n. kartam (kartā is written in the loose syntax of Art. Pers. a, b, 3, 4). Av. kar (Turfan MSS. qėrd, qar, New Pers. kardan, Gīl. kudan), Skt. k̥r.

kāra, m. 1)*the people*. 2)*army*. Nom. sg. kāra. Acc. sg. kāram. Gen. sg. kārahyā (in addition to its recorded occurrences [k]ārahyā is to be read for udapatatā of the ed. in Bh. 3. 1. 80; cf. KT, 56). New Pers. kār-zār, *battle-field*, Bartholomae, Altiran. Wb., 465.

karka, m. name of a people, Nom. pl. karkā.

karša, m. name of a Persian weight. Nom. du. karšā. Dar. Weight Inscr. II karšā adam dārayavauš——, *a two karsha weight. I am Darius*, etc. Gray (JAOS, 20, 55) determines the value of this weight (2573 grains Troy = 15.5 Ind. karsas; one Persian karša = 7.75 Ind. karsa. Gray's 7.25 Ind. karsa is certainly a 'Druckfehler'). Skt. karsa (s. v. karsa in PWb). Cf. Weissbach, ZDMG, 61, 402, "2 karšū (bez. 2 kuršam, ⅓ mana)."

kuganakā (Elam. kukkannakan; Bab. ku-gu-na-ak-ka), f. name of a Persian (according to Elam. version) town. Nom. sg. kuganakā, Bh. 2. 3. kuganakā nā[ma vardanam pārsaiy].

ku^nduru (anaptyxis for ku^ndru, Bartholomae, Grundr. 300, 6. Elam. kuntarruš; Bab. ku-un-du-ur), m. name of a Median town. Nom. sg. ku^nd^uruš.

kūru (Elam. kuraš; Bab. ku-ra-aš; Gr. Κῦρος), m. *Cyrus*. Nom. sg. kūruš. I fail to see any valid reason why the small inscription of Murghab, adam kūruš xšāyaθiya haxāmanišiya, should not be assigned to the reign of Cyrus the Great; cf. Herzfeld, Pasargadā, Klio, Beitr. z. alt. Gesch., 8, 1908; Hoffmann-Kutschke, Phil. Nov. 1907; Foy, ZDMG, 54, 361. Many scholars influenced by the fact that the documents of Cyrus are written in Babylonian, and by Weissbach's interpretation of a doubtful passage in the Elam. Bh. L. that Darius was the first to inscribe in the Persian tongue (zaumin ⁿuramašta-na (m)u (det)tuppime tale-ikki hutta arriya-ma) put this in the time of Cyrus the Younger. Sayce goes to the extreme of assigning it to a Persian satrap, the brother of Xerxes, called Achaemenes by Ktesias. For the place of Cyrus in Achaemenidan dynasty, see Cyrus Cylinder, 20 (where Teispes is recorded as the common ancestor with Darius line; cf. Tolman and Stevenson, Hdt. and Empires of East, 73 ff.). Nom. sg. kūruš, Cyrus Inscr. Gen. sg. kūrauš, Bh. 1. 10. kaⁿbūjiya nāma kūrauš puθʳa, *Cambyses by name the son of Cyrus.* Bh. 1. 11. adam bardiya amiy hya kūrauš puθʳa, *I am Smerdis the son of Cyrus*, et passim.

kušiya, m. name of a people. Nom. pl. kušīyā, Dar. NRa. 3.

X

xaršādašyā? Of the fifth character only the two perpendicular wedges are visible, which can represent i as well as d. Justi taking signs in order 15678234 reads xišyāršā, Bab. form of name of Xerxes. Seal Inscr. e. m xaršādašyā. Cf. Ménant, Archives des missions scientifiques, 3, 418; Justi, Iran. Namenbuch, 173; IF, 17, Anz. 112; Foy, KZ, 37, 566; Bartholomae, Zum Altiran. Wb., 163. See xšayāršan.

xš see xšāyaθiya.

xšaθrita (Elam. šattarrita; Bab. ḥa-ša-at-ri-it-ti), m. name assumed by Phraortes, the Median pretender. Nom. sg. xšaθrita. Cf. Tolman and Stevenson, Hdt. and Empires of East, 60.

xšaθʳa, n. *lordship, kingdom.* Nom. acc. sg. xšaθʳam. Av. xšaθra (New Pers. šahr), Skt. kṣatra, fr. xši (q. v.). I would supply [utāmaiy xšaθʳam] for [hacā gastā] of WB in Art. Ham. l. 6. See Tolman, PAPA, 36, 33.

xšaθʳapāvan, m. *satrap.* Nom. sg. xšaθʳapāvā. xšaθʳa (q. v.) + pāvan, fr. pā (q. v.). Cf. Lenschau, Leipz. Stud. 12, 137.

xšap, f. *night.* Gen. sg. ? xšapa (cf. Skt. kṣapas——usras, *night and day*, RV. 6. 52, 15; 7, 15, 8), against the view which now generally regards xšapa as acc. sg. after the analogy of the following neutr. rauca. Bh. 1. 7. xšapavā raucapativā, *either by night or day.* YAv. xšap (New Pers. šab, Bal. šap, Geiger, SB, 3, Afγ. špa, Kurd. šav, Oss. axšav), Skt. kṣap. It might be added that Bartholomae (Grundr. 219) formerly regarded the form as instr. sg. comparing Skt. kṣapā, but has now abandoned this view in favor of the acc. sg.; cf. Altiran. Wb., 547; Delbrück, Vgl. Syntax, 1, 124; 3, 105.

xšāyaθiya (written as ideogram in Dar. Pers. b, c; Sus. a; Sz. b, c; Seal Inscr.; Xerx. Pers. ca, cb; Vase Inscr.; Art. Sus. a, b; Hamadan; Vase Inscr.), m. *king.* Nom. sg. xšāyaθiya. Acc. sg. xšāyaθiyam. Gen. sg. xšāyaθiyahyā. For gen. sg. xšāyaθiya in Art. Pers. a, b, 2. Nom. pl. xšāyaθiyā. Gen. pl. xšāyaθiyānām (written xšāyaθiyanām in Art. Pers. a, b, 2; and xšāyaθiyānā in Art. Sus. b, which blunder of the stone-cutter I was able to attest by an examination of the original which I made in 1895). The royal title xšāyaθiya xšāyaθiyānām (New Pers. šāhanšāh for šāhānšāh), *king of kings,* in Dar. Pers. a. and Xerx. Pers. e. was the first expression translated, but not then transliterated, from the cuneiform. This was done by Grotefend who later read in part the two inscriptions; (1)*Darius, the great king, king of kings + + + + son of Hystaspes.* (2)*Xerxes, the great king, king of kings + + + + son of Darius, the king.* See the interesting account in Rogers, History of Babylonia and Assyria, Vol. I, 1–84. Bartholomae (Altiran. Wb.) recognizes a survival of the adjectival meaning in Bh. 1. 3. hyā amāxam taumā xšāya[θiyā ā]ha, i. e. *our family was royal* rather than *our family were kings.* For attributive gen. in the oft-recurring phraseology, cf. Delbrück, Vgl. Syntax, 3, 102. Phl. New Pers. šāh; fr. xši (q. v.).

xšayāršan (Elam. kšeršša; Bab. ḫi-ši-'-ar-ši, Gr. Ξέρξης), m. *Xerxes.* Nom. sg. xšayāršā. Acc. sg. xšayāršām (Bartholomae, Grundr. 213, 2). Gen. sg. xšayāršahyā (Hamadan. "The common xšayāršahyā instead of xšayārcahyā must be read in l. 3. That the correct spelling appears here as in the inscriptions of Xerxes at Persepolis, Elvend, and Van, is shown by the unmistakable occurrence of —šahyā at the beginning of l. 4." Tolman, Rēexamination of the Inscription of Art. II on Moldings of Columns from Ecbatana, PAPA, 36, 32.) In Art. Sus. a, written xšayārcahyā. For gen. sg. xšayāršā, in Art. Pers. a, b. 2. Justi, Iran. Namenbuch (cf. IF, 17, Anz. 111) would identify xaršādasyā (q.v.), Seal Inscr. e, with xšayāršā. *xšaya, *king*, Av. xšaya, Skt. kṣaya + *aršan, *man*, YAv. aršan, Skt. r̥sabha, Gr. ἄρσην.

xši (Pres. xšaya-, Bartholomae, Grundr. 123), *to rule*. Av. xši (New Pers. šāyad), Skt. kṣi.

—— with prefix patiy, *hold lordship over*. Mid. pret. 1 sg. patiyaxšayaiy, Dar. NRa. 3. adamšām patiyaxšayaiy. This reading is clearly shown in Stolze's photograph, Pers. II, 109 (cf. Foy, KZ, 35, 49), thus setting aside patiyaxšaiy of ed. and all former theories connecting it with axš, see.

—— with prefix upariy(?), *rule*. Mid. pret. 1 sg. upariy[axšayaiy], a bold supplement which I suggested (Vdt. Stud. 1, 33) in Bh. 4. 1. 65, upariy arštām upariy[axšayaiy] naiy, *with rectitude* [*I ruled*], as corresponding to Elam. šutur ukku hupa git, *I ruled in accordance with the ordinances;* Bab. ina di-na-a-tu a-si-ig-gu, *in accordance with the laws I governed*. Does the supplement answer in any way to the lithograph of Rawlinson, who on the weathered surface of the rock may have confounded the signs for yᵃiyᵃnᵃ with those for yᵃ + + tᵃhᵃ? KT do not remark on the space in the lacuna, but Jackson says: "It looks like a long word ending in hᵃiy." Weissbach (ZDMG, 61, 729) favors the old reading upariy[āyam].

xšnā, *to know*. Inchoative pres. subj. 2 sg. xšnāsāhy. Dar. NRa. 4, xšnās[āh(i)diš]. 3. sg. xšnāsātiy. Av. xšnā (Turfan MSS. ʾišnāsêd, New Pers. šināsad), Skt. jñā.

G

gaiθā, f. *personal property*. KT translate Persian and Elam. *herds*. The Bab. word is wanting. Darmesteter, *les fermes;* Rugarli, *le campagne;* WB, *die Herden*, Bartholomae, *fahrende Habe;* Justi (IF, 17, Anz. 108), *Gehöfte*. Acc. sg. gaiθām, Bh, 1. 14. Av. gaēθā, *life, subsistence, world* (New Pers. gēhān, *world*), fr. ji, *live*, Skt. jī-va-ti. For meaning (as well as etymology) cf. βί-ος, *life, livelihood* (βίοτος); cf. Tolman, Vdt. Stud. 1, 13.

gaubruva (Elam. gauparma; Bab. gu-ba-ru-'; Gr. Γωβρύας), m. *Gobryas*, ally of Darius against the pretender Gaumāta. Nom. sg. gaubruva. According to Justi (IF, 17, Anz. 111) *gau, *cattle* + *baruva, Skt. bharu, *lord*, *Rinder besitzend*. Otherwise Foy, ZDMG, 54, 360. Cf. Tolman and Stevenson, Hdt. and Empires of East, 87, n. 4.

gaumāta (Elam. gaumatta; Bab. gu-ma-a-tu), m. the Median pretender who assumed the name of Smerdis. Nom. sg. gaumāta. Acc. sg. gaumātam. The popular version, followed by Hdt. III, 61-64, which designated the conspirator by the name "Smerdis" was doubtless based on a *vaticinium post eventum* showing an ambiguity in the oracular vision as well as a personal negligence in Cambyses' failure to fathom its true meaning. Cf. Tolman and Stevenson, Hdt. and Empires of East, 86-88; Nöldeke, Aufsätze z. pers. Gesch. 30; Müller, Ztschr. f. Assyriologie, 9, 112.

gauša, m. *ear*. Acc. du. gaušā. YAv. gaoša (New Pers. gōš, Oss. γos, Kurd. gūh), Skt. ghoṣa, *sound;* fr. guš, *hear*.

gāθu, m. 1)*place*. 2)*throne*. Acc. sg. gāθum. Dar. NRa. 4. [tya]i[y manā] gāθum baraⁿtiy, *who bear my throne*. Loc. sg, (with postpos ā), gāθavā, Bh. 1. 14. adamšim gāθavā avāstāyam, *I settled it in its place*. KT's gāθvā should be read gāθavā; cf. Bartholomae, BB, 13, 69; KZ, 30, 540. Av. gātu (Turfan MSS. gâh, New Pers. gâh, Afγ. γāl'ai), Skt. gātu.

gaⁿdāra (Bab. pa-ar-u-pa-ra-e-sa-an-na), m. name of a region. Nom. sg. gaⁿdāra.

gaⁿdutava (thus read according to KT in place of Justi's emendation gaⁿdumava. Elam. kantuma + + +), m. name of a district in Arachosia. Nom. sg. gaⁿdutava, Bh. 3. 11. Hoffmann-Kutschke writes me (May 17, 1908) that he still favors gaⁿdumava on the ground of a possible error in KT's record; "gaⁿdumava nach elam. kantuma-[ma] selbst verständlich." Justi's etymology (ZDMG, 51, 240) connecting gaⁿdumava with YAv. gantuma, *wheat*, is possible only on the supposition of a local change of the surd to sonant after the nasal; cf. Foy, KZ, 37, 518.

gam (Pres. jam-, Bartholomae, Grundr. 122), *to go*. Av. **gam** (Turfan MSS. pra-gâmêd, New Pers. āmadan), Skt. **gam**.

—— with prefix ā, *come.* Pres. opt. 3 sg. ājamīyā (= Skt. gamyāt, Wackernagel, Ai. Gram. 8; I. E. g̥mm-ie̯-t).

—— with prefix parā, *go forth.* Part. nom. sg. f. parāgmatā.

—— with prefix ham, *come together, assemble.* Part. nom. pl. m. haⁿgmatā. KT have followed WB's hagamatā (even in their exception haⁿgmatā in Bh. 3. 11). In all places the word is better read haⁿgmatā; cf. Foy, KZ, 37, 511.

garmapada, (Elam. karmapattaš), m. name of a Persian month. KT favor the identification of Garmapada with Tammuz (June-July); July-Aug. (Justi); March-Apr. (Oppert). See s. v. māh. Gen. sg. garmapadahya (in place of garmapadahyā of ed.). *garma, *heat*, Skt. gharma, Av. garəma, *warm* (New Pers. garm, Oss. γarm) + *pada, *step, station*, Skt. pada, YAv. paδa (New Pers. pai); fr. *pad, *go*, YAv. pad, Skt. pad. For date of Gaumāta's assumption of royal power see s. v. θard.

gasta, adj. *repugnant, adverse.* Nom. sg. f. gastā, Dar. NRa. 6. hauvtaiy gastā mā θadaya, *may it* (i. e., the law of Ahura Mazda) *not seem to thee repugnant.* New Pers. gast. Thumb (Tolman, OP. Inscr. 147, n 3) returned to Kern's interpretation (ZDMG, 23, 222) respecting gasta as connected with Skt. gad, *speak*, and the hyā of the preceding phrase as the opt. 3 sg. of ah, translating; *Lass dir die lehre des Auramazda gesagt sein.* That this view is incorrect is shown by the Elam. visnika (Weissbach) and the Bab. bi-i-ši, both of which signify *evil, hostile;* cf. Hübschmann; *er soll dir nicht übel erscheinen.*

gud, *to conceal.* YAv. guz, Skt. guh.

—— with prefix apa, *hide away, conceal.* Caus. pres. subj. 2 sg. apagaudayāhy. Pret. 2 sg. (Injunctive) apagaudaya, Bh. 4. 10. avaθā sā + + + + ādiy mā apagaudaya, *thus + + + + conceal thou not.*

gub (Pres. gauba-, Bartholomae, Grundr. 123), *to speak.* Mid. 1)*to call one's self, take the name of.* 2)*to declare allegiance to.* Mid. indic. pres. 3. sg. gaubataiy, Bh. 3. 10. kāram hya dārayavahauš xšāyaθiyahyā gaubataiy, *the army which declares allegiance to Darius the king.* Pret. 3 sg. agaubatā, Bh. 3, 10. hauv vahyazdāta hya

bardiya agaubatā (written **agaur ͨ tā** by stone-cutter's blunder; cf. KT, 51), *that Vahyazdata who has assumed the name of Smerdis*. 3 pl. [**aga**]**u**[**ba**ⁿ]**tā**, Bh. 2. 16. Subj. pres. 3 sg. **gaubātaiy**. Middle Pers. **gōwet**, New Pers. **gōyad**; cf. Bartholomae, Altiran. Wb., 482.

grab (Pres. **garb-ā-ya-**, Skt. **g̥rbh-ā-ya-**; cf. Kretschmer, KZ, 31, 403), *to seize*. Act. pret. 1 sg. **agarbāyam**. 3 sg. **agarbāya**. 3 pl. **agarbāya**ⁿ. Mid. pret. 3 sg. **agarbāyatā**.

—— with prefix **ā**, *seize*. Part. pass. nom. sg. m. **āgarbīta** (so Bartholomae, WZKM, 22, 65, who compares Skt. **āg̥rbhita**), thus read for **agarbāyatā** of ed. in Bh. 2. 1. 73, **fravartiš āgarbīta anayatā**, *Phraortes seized was led*. KT's view that we have here the passive form, 3 sg., is not likely. Av. **grab**, Skt. **grabh**.

C

cā, encl. conj. *and*. Av. **cā** (Middle Pers. **ca**), Skt. **ca**.

[Word-divider + **cašma**, *eye*. Jackson's reading for **uc ͣ š ͣ m ͣ** in Bh. 2. 13, 14].

ciⁿ**cixri** (Elam. **zinzakriš**; Bab. **ši-in-ša-aḫ-ri-iš**), m. name of the father of Martiya. Gen. sg. **ci**ⁿ**cixrāiš**.

citā, adv. *so long*, Bh. 2. 9, 11; with **yātā**, *until*. Wrongly supplied in the ed. in Bh. 2. 1. 28; cf. KT, 26. **ci** (cf. **ka**) + **ta** (cf. -τα in 'ἔπειτα).

ciθra, n. *seed, lineage;* second member of the compound in **ariya c**[**i**]**θ**ʳ**a**, *of Aryan lineage;* see **ariya**. Av. **ciθra** (New Pers. **cihr**), Skt. **citra**.

ciθʳ**a**ⁿ**taxma** (Elam. **ziššantakma**; Bab. **ši-it-ra-an-taḫ-ma**), m. name of a Sagartian rebel. Nom. sg. **ciθ**ʳ**a**ⁿ**taxma**. Instr. sg. **ciθ**ʳ**a**ⁿ**tax-mā**. **ciθ**ʳ**a** (q. v.) + *****taxma**, *brave*, Av. **taxma** (New Pers. **tahm**)

ciy, encl. pcl. 1)makes indefinite the interr. pron., e. g., **kašciy**, *any one*, **cišciy**, *anything;* 2)emphasizes slightly the word to which it is joined, e. g., Bh. 1. 14. **yaθā** [**par**]**uvam**[**ci**]**y**, *just as it was before*.

Cf. Delbrück, Vgl. Syntax, 3, 49. YAv. cit, GAv. cīṯ (Middle Pers. ci, New Pers. cih, Oss. ci, Kurd. cī), Skt. cit; Acc. n. of ka with palatalization.

ciyakara, adj. *how many, restricted in number*. Nom. sg, n. ciyakaram, Dar. NRa. 4. Cf. Foy, KZ, 35, 47; Bartholomae, Altiran. Wb., 597. *ciya (cf. ka), Skt. kiyant + *kara, fr. kar (q. v.). ciya^n of ed. is better read ciya- (for ciyat).

c^{a}iš^{a}p^{a}i, read cišpi (Elam. zišpiš; Bab. ši-iš-pi-iš) or caišpi (Gr. Τεΐσπης), m. *Teispes*, common ancestor of Cyrus (Cyrus Cylinder, 20) and Darius (Bh. 1. 2; Bh. a). Cf. Prášek, Forsch. z. Gesch. d. Altert. 3, 24, vs. the extreme view of Winckler, Or. Litt. Ztg. 1898, 43; Tolman and Stevenson, Hdt. and Empires of East, 73–78. Nom. sg. cišpiš, Bh. a (omitted in Bh. 1. 2; KT record that there is room for this restoration on the eroded surface of the rock). Gen. sg. cišpāiš, Bh. 1. 2.

J

jatar (nom. ag.), m. *smiter, slayer*. Nom. sg. jatā, Bh. 4. 11. auramazdātay jatā bīyā, *may Ahura Mazda be thy slayer*, i. e. may he slay thee; cf. the so-called Skt. Periphrastic Future, Whitney, Skt. Gram. 942-4. jatā can also be read ja^{n}tā; cf. Bartholomae, IF, 4. 128. For this curse upon the would-be destroyer of the royal memorial, note phraseology of Inscr. of Ašur-nâṣir-pal (Schrader, Keilinschriftliche Bibliothek, Vol. I. 122), ašur bilu rabu-u ilu aš-šu-ru-u bil ši-ma-a-ti s[i-m]a-ti-šu li-ru-ur ip-ši-ti-šu lu-na[k-ki]-ir, *Ashur the great Lord, the Assyrian God, Lord of Fate, may he curse the fate of him (who destroys this monument) and annihilate his works*. Cf. Bang, Mélanges de Harlez, 11; Tolman, PAPA, 33, 70. YAv. jantar (Middle Pers. žatār), Skt. hantar; fr. jan (q. v.).

jad (Pres. jadiya-, Bartholomae, Grundr. 147) *to pray*. Pres. 1 sg. jadiyāmiy, Dar. NRa. 5. aita adam auramazdām jadiyāmiy, *this I beg of Ahura Mazda*. Dar. Pers. d. 3. yānam (Jackson, JAOS, 27, 191) jadiyāmiy (The m of jadiyāmiy, though hardly legible in Stolze's photograph, is attested by Jackson as "quite clear on

the stone" and should now be removed from brackets in the ed.).
YAv. jad (Turfan MSS. nīzāy(and).

jan (Pres. jan-, ja-, Bartholomae, Grundr. 122), *to smite, slay.*
Indic. pret. 1 sg. ajanam, Bh. 4. 2. adamšim ajanam, *I waged these
(battles)*; wrongly KT, *I overthrew nine kings.* 3 sg. aja^n. Injunctive, 2 pl. j^{n}t^{n}a (jatā or ja^{n}tā). Pres. impv. 2 sg. jadiy. Av.
jan (New Pers. zanad, Kurd. zanin), Skt. han.

—— with prefix **ava**, *smite down, slay.* Part. nom. sg. avajata.
This reading recorded by KT in Bh. 1. l. 32, sets aside Bartholomae's conjecture avājata and confirms Rawlinson's lithograph
av^a $_{letter}^{no}$ j^{n}t^n. KT's cuneiform text shows no space between v^n and
j^a; cf. Tolman, Vdt. Stud. 1, 10.

—— with prefix **ava + ā**, *smite down, destroy.* Indic. pret. 1
sg. avājanam. 3 sg. avāja^n. 3 pl. avājana^n (with thematic vowel;
cf. Skt. ahanan, Whitney, RVf. 202). Opt. 3 sg. avājaniyā; cf.
Wackernagel, Ai. Gram. 8.

—— with prefix **patiy**, *wage (battle) against, fight.* Mid. pret.
3 sg. patiyajatā, Dar. NRa. 4.

—— with prefix **frā**, *cut off.* Pret. 1 sg. frājanam.

ji (I. E. gei-, Pres. jī-va-, Bartholomae, Grundr. 141; cf. Skt.
jī-va-ti), *to live.* Subj. 2 sg. jīvā, Bh. 4. 10. dargam jīvā, *mayest
thou live long.* Av. jivaiti (New Pers. zinda, Kurd. zīn), Skt. jīvati.

jiyamna (thus read for jiyamana of KT; cf. Weissbach, ZDMG,
61, 726. KT's record supersedes the various emendations of
iyamanam of ed.) adj. *waning, growing old*, as subs. *completion,
end.* Acc. sg. jiyamnam, Bh. 2, l. 62. θūravāharahya māhyā jiyamnam patiy, *at end of the month Thūravāhara;* or as Bartholomae
(WZKM, 22, 9) puts it, *mensem senescentem versus.* Elam. version renders, *at the end of the month Turmar;* Bab. *on the thirtieth day of the month Iyyar.* Cf. Tolman, Vdt. Stud. 1, 20.
YAv. jyamna, fr. jyā, *grow weak.*

jīva, adj. *living.* Gen. sg. jīvahyā. Av. jva, Skt. jīva; fr. jī
(q. v.).

T

taiy (encl. I. E. t(u)ei, t(u)oi, Bartholomae, Stud. 1. 114). See **tuvam**.

taumā, f. *family.* Nom. sg. **taumā**. Gen. sg. **taumāyā**. Foy (KZ, 35, 6) connects the word with YAv. **taoxman** (New Pers. **tuxm**), Skt. **tokman**, but such etymology becomes somewhat uncertain when we remark the retention of Ir. x in -taxma (ciθʳaⁿtaxma), Av. **taxma** (New Pers. **tahm**). Jackson's identification (JAOS, 20, 57) of the festival of Xerxes' birthday (Hdt. 9. 110; Περσιστὶ μὲν τυκτά, κατὰ δὲ τὴν Ἑλλήνων γλῶσσαν τέλεον) with Iranian root **tuk** holds good for YAv. **taoxman**, but we are not certain of the comparison which he gives with Persian **taumā**. It would be easy for the Greeks, of course, to confound the foreign word with τυκτά and render it by τέλεον.

[**tauman** (Foy, KZ, 35, 47; cf. Bang, ZDMG, 43, 533; Reichelt, KZ, 39, 74; Bartholomae, Altiran. Wb., 613) n. *power, might.* Nom. sg. **taumā**, Bh. 4. 16, 17; 5. 3, 6, yāvā taumā ahatiy, *as long as will be possible.* Foy renders the corresponding Elam. word, **patta**, *possibility*; cf. Tolman, Vdt. Stud. 1. 34. Hoffmann-Kutschke writes me: "Es kann doch nicht bedeuten, *du bewahre, so lange deine Familie lebt;* man kann doch nur schützen, so lange man selbst lebt. Übrigens steht in Elamischen nicht das Ideogramm GUL, *Familie.*" *tu, *be strong*, Av. **tu**, Skt. **tu**.]

takabara, adj. a word of doubtful meaning and characterizing the Ionians in Dar. NRa. 3. Nom. pl. m. **takabarā**. WB retain the old interpretation, *welche geflochtenes Haar tragen.* Cf. Foy, KZ, 35, 63 and later KZ, 37, 545. Bartholomae rejects on philological grounds the attempted connection with Arm. tʻagavor, *Krone tragend.* Could the word signify *swift-* (YAv. **tak**, *hasten*, Skt. **tak**) *riding* or *sea-faring* (YAv. **taka**, *water-course* + **bara**, cf. **asabāri**)?

taxmaspāda (Elam. **takmašpata**), m. name of one of the commanders of Darius. Nom. sg. **taxmaspāda**. **taxma**, *brave*, Av. **taxma** (New Pers. **tahm**) + *spāda, *army*, GAv. **spāda**, YAv. **spāδa** (New Pers. **sipāh**, Horn, NS, 42, 3).

taxš (Pres. taxša-, Bartholomae, Grundr. 123), *to be active*. Foy regards the root as a *kompromissbildung* between *taš (Skt. takṣ, Av. taš in tašan) and *tvaxš (Skt. tvakṣ, Av. θwāxš).

—— with prefix **ham**, *work together, cöoperate, work*. Pret. 1 sg. hamataxsaiy. 3 sg. hamataxšatā. 3 pl. hamataxša^ntā.

tacara, *palace*. Acc. sg. tacaram, Dar. Pers. a. New Pers. tazar. Cf. Horn, NS, 31, 2; Foy, KZ, 37, 546.

tar, *to cross over*. Av. tar, Skt. tr̥.

—— with prefix **fra**, *depart from, abandon*. The old reading of Rawlinson fratarta, Bh. 3. 5, part. nom. sg. is confirmed by KT. Foy (KZ, 35, 43) first suggested frarixta, but later (KZ, 37, 556) returns to the reading fratarta; cf. Hoffmann-Kutschke, Or. Litt. Ztg. Nov. 1905; Tolman, Vdt. Stud. 1, 24.

—— with prefix **viy**, pres. taraya- (Bartholomae, Grundr. 145), *put across, cross*. Pret. 1 sg. viyatarayam (confirmed by KT), Bh. 5. 4. 1 pl. viyatarayāmā (confirmed by KT's cuneiform text; KT's transliteration has the old reading viyatarayāma which Bartholomae, Grundr. 109, regarded as pret. with pres. ending; cf. Skt. apaçyāmas), Bh. 1. 18.

taradraya, adv. *across the sea*. *tara, *beyond*, YAv. tarō (New Pers. tar), Skt. tiras + drayah (q. v.).

tāravā (Bab. ta-ar-ma-'), f. name of a Persian town. Nom. sg. tāravā (confirmed by KT); cf. Foy, KZ, 37, 515.

tarsa-, inchoative stem (Ir. tr̥s‘-a- for tr̥s-sx‘-a-, Bartholomae, Grundr. 135), *to fear;* with **hacā** followed by instr. or abl. Pres. 3 sg. tarsatiy, Dar. Pers. d. 2. hacā aniyanā naiy tarsatiy, *it fears no enemy*. Pret. 1 sg. (Injunctive) tarsam, Dar. Pers. e. 3. hacā aniyanā mā [ta]rsam, *no foe will I fear*. 3 sg. atarsa, Bh. 1. 13. kārašim hacā darsma^n (Bartholomae) atarsa kāram vasiy avājaniyā hya paranam bardiyam adānā, *the people feared his tyranny;* (*they feared*) *he would slay in great numbers the people who had formerly known Smerdis*. Bartholomae is doubtless right in regarding the opt. clause as the object of atarsa; cf. Tolman, Vdt. Stud. 1,

11. Otherwise Foy, KZ, 37, 548. Gray, AJP, 21, 15, renders, *the people were mightily afraid of him.* "*He would be killing at will the people.*" KT entirely miss the force of the opt. in their translation, *the people feared him exceedingly*, (*for*) *he slew many*. 3 pl. atarsaⁿ. YAv. tərəsaiti (Turfan MSS. tersâd, Oss. t'arsun, Kurd. tirsin, New Pers. tarsīdan), Skt. trasati, Gr. τρέειν (for τρέσ-ειν; cf. L. Meyer, Gr. Etym. 809).

tigra (Elam. tikra), m. name of a fortress in Armenia. Nom. sg. tigra.

[tigra, a supplement of Foy in Bh. 5. l. 22, [xaudā]m tigrām baraⁿ-tayᵃ, (*gegen die Saken welche*) *den Helmspitz tragen* (cf. tigraxauda) in place of ₊ ₊ tigrām baratya of ed. and KT. Hoffmann-Kutschke writes me: "Es wohnen doch keine Saken am Tigris." KT's cuneiform text records tigrām; their transliteration, tigram. Which is the reading on the stone? Foy's emendation is impossible since KT attest the certainty of the preceding sakām.]

tigrā (Elam. tikra; Bab. di-ig-lat), f. *Tigris*. Acc. sg. tigrām. Kossowicz's quotation from Eust. ad Dionys. perieg. 5, 984, Τίγρις ταχύς ὡς βέλος. Μῆδοι γὰρ Τίγριν καλοῦσι τὸ τόξευμα, shows only a popular association of the word with YAv. tiγri, *arrow* (New Pers. tīr), but it is of no etymological value. Cf. Hübschmann, IF, 16, 421. Note θὴρ ποταμὸς in Theophanes, 52, 23 (cf. New Pers. tīr) "mit volksetymologischer Umänderung," Horn, NS, 19, 6.

tigraxauda, adj. *with pointed cap*, epithet of Scythians. Nom. pl. tigraxaudā. Cf. Hdt. 7. 64, Σάκαι δὲ οἱ Σκύθαι περὶ μὲν τῇσι κεφαλῇσι κυρβασίας ἐς ὀξὺ ἀπηγμένας ὀρθὰς εἶχον πεπηγυίας. So the ninth standing figure opposite Darius on the Behistan rock (over which is written iyam skuⁿxa hya saka, *this is Skunkha the Scythian*) is represented wearing this national head-dress. *tigra, *pointed*, YAv. tiγra (New Pers. tēz) + xauda-, *hat*, YAv. xaoδa- (Oss. xodä).

₊ ₊ ₊ tᵘnᵘvᵃtᵃmᵃ, the reading of KT in Bh. 4. l. 65 who remark; "Space for division sign and two characters. It is possible that the break may be restored mām stunuvatam, *those that praise me*." Jackson recorded manᵘuvᵃtᵃmᵃ (q. v.). Weissbach (ZDMG, 61, 729) suggests a derivation from tanu, **weak**, and translates, *dem Armen*. The Bab. apparently renders the word by **muš-ki-nu**. See s. v. **šakaurim** and **man^uuv^at^am^a**.

tuvam (I. E. tu, tū; cf. Wackernagel, Das Dehnungsg. 5), pron. 2 pers. *thou*. Nom. sg. tuvam. Acc. sg. θuvām. Gen. sg. taiy (encl., written tay in Bh. 4. 11). Skt. tvam, GAv. tvə̄m, YAv. tūm (New Pers. tu).

tya (I. E. tio, tiā. Ir. tia which should become according to phonetic laws *θia, Pers. *šiya, is probably due to the analogy of the demon. ta; Bartholomae, Grundr. 416, n.), originally a demon. pron., but generally used as a relative. Cf. hya. 1)The demon. meaning is seen in the following: ^a)hadā kārā nipadi[y] t[ya]iy ašiyava, *he went in pursuit of them with his army*, Bh. 3. 12. This reading is confirmed by KT, thus making impossible Bartholomae's conjecture avaiy (Stud. 2. 68); cf. Tolman, Vdt. Stud. 1. 26. ^b)introducing a phrase characterizing the preceding noun like the Gr. article (Tolman, OP. Inscr. 42): paθim tyām rāstām mā avarada, *depart not from the true way*, Dar. NRa. 6; xšaθ^ram tya bābirauv, *the royal power at Babylon*, Bh. 1. 16; kāram tyam mādam, *that Median army*, Bh. 2. 6. etc. Cf. Delbrück, Vgl. Syntax, 3, 313. 2)Rel. pron. *who, which*. Acc. sg. m. tyam. Acc. sg. f. tyām. Acc. sg. n. tya. Nom. acc. pl. m. tyaiy (Bartholomae, Grundr. 240). Nom. acc. pl. f. tyā. Nom. acc. pl. n. tyā (written on rock tyanā), Bh. 1. 8. imā dahyāva tyā manā dātā āpariyāya^n, *these lands respected my laws;* cf. Bartholomae, Altiran. Wb. 659; Foy, KZ, 37, 501. The reading of the stone tyanā (confirmed by KT) was regarded as dittography by Benfey (Pers. Keilinschr. 9) as early as the year 1847, who remarked: "Es ist aber wohl Fehler des Steinmetz, welcher zuerst auf das gleich folgende manā abirrte." Gen. pl. m. tyaišām. For. gen. pl. f. tyaišām, Dar. Pers. e. dahyūnām tyaišām parūnām. Skt. tya, Turfan MSS. 'i. Note article on Persian relative in Delbrück, Vgl. Syntax, 3, 311.

tya (acc. sg. n. to tya), conj. 1)*that*. Bh. 1. 10. azdā abava tya bardiya avajata (sic), *it was (not) known that Smerdis was murdered*. 2)*because*. Bh. 4. 4. drauga di[š hamiθ^riy]ā akunauš tya imaiy kāram adurujiyaša^n, *Deceit made them rebellious, because those deceived the people*. Cf. Delbrück, Vgl. Syntax, 3, 327.

Θ

θāigarci (Elam. saikurrizis; Bab. simânu), m. name of a Persian month. The Bab. indicates agreement with Sivan (third month) i. e. May–June; April–May (Justi); May–June (Oppert). See s. v. māh. Gen. sg. *θāigarcais*.

θᵃkᵃtᵃa, written *θᵃkᵃtᵃmᵃ* in Bh. 3. 1. The generally accepted opinion, until the reading *θᵃkᵃtᵃmᵃ* was attested, regarded *θakatā* as loc. sg. *in completed course.* In Vdt. Stud. 1. 23, I shared the view of KT that *θᵃkᵃtᵃmᵃ* was simply a stone-cutter's blunder. Bartholomae writes me concerning this: "Das *θakatam* 'a blunder' sei für 'ta glaube ich nicht. Bh. 3. 1, ist die einzige Stelle da es sich um nur einen Tag des Monats handelt." The same scholar (WZKM, 22, 90) now takes *θakatā* (nom. pl.) and *θakatam* (n. sg.) as adjectival predicates either of a part. fut. pass. or part. pres. act. *θakaⁿtā, θakaⁿtam*. In every passage save Bh. 3. 1, the instr. pl. is used as subject of the following āhaⁿ, a use of the case occasional in YAv. (Schmidt, Pluralbld. 98; Jackson, Av. Gr. 229; Bartholomae, AF, 2, 104; Caland, GGA, 401 for year 1893; Tolman, Vdt. Stud. 1. 10). Bh. 1. 13. bāgayādais māhyā 10 raucabis *θakatā* āhaⁿ, *in the month of Bāgayādi ten days were coming to the end;* et passim. In Bh. 3. 1, we appear to have a nom. sg. as subject of āha (cf. Gray, AJP, 21, 10); garmapadahya māhyā 1 rauca *θakatam* āha, *in the month of Garmapada one day was completing its course.* *θak, YAv. sak, (of time) *to pass* (to completion).

θatagu (Elam. sattakus; Bab. sa-at-ta-gu-u), *Sattagydia.* Nom. sg. *θatagus.* **θata, hundred,* YAv. sata (New Pers., Kurd. sad, Oss. sada), Skt. çata + **gāu, cattle,* Av. gāu (New Pers. gāv, Kās. gó, Kurd. gā), Skt. gāu. Cf. Fick, BB, 41, 343.

θaⁿd (Pres. *θadaya*, a for I. E. n; Bartholomae, Grundr. 145), *to seem.* Pres. subj. 3 sg. *θadayā*? (Bartholomae, ZDMG, 46, 295), Bh. 4. 8. avahyā paruv *θa[dayā]*, *should seem to him much.* KT read *θā[dutiy]* remarking that the restoration is not certain. *θadᵃ₊₊*, however, seems certain in Jackson's examination. Pret. 3 sg. (Injunctive) *θadaya*, Dar. NRa. 6. hauvtaiy gastā mā *θadaya, may it not seem repugnant to thee.* *θadayāmiy* is read in Dar. Sus. a. by WB, where I have suggested y(?)adayāmaiy. YAv. sand (Middle Pers. sahēt, Turfan MSS. hûnisandêft), Skt. chand.

*θ*ada*θ*a, uncertain word in Seal Inscr. b. hadaxaya ₊ ₊ ₊ ₊ *θ*ada*θ*a.

*θ*ard, f. *year*. Gen. sg. *θ*arda; hamahyāyā *θ*arda, *in the same year*, (connecting *θ*ard with YAv. sarəd, Turfan MSS. sâr). The meaning *in the same way* (YAv. sarəda) was favored by the Elam. pelki-ma without the determinative (an). The interpretation seems now certain through Bab. ideogram MU-AN-NA, *year* (which KT, however, render adverbially, *always;* cf. šattišam, *yearly, always*): cf. Weissbach, ZDMG, 61, 724. In a personal letter Weissbach several months later writes me concerning his interpretation as follows: "Meine Deutung hamahyāyā *θ*arda, *in einem und demselben Jahre* halte ich für absolut sicher. So sagt Darius. Eine andere Frage ist nun aber, ob seine Angabe ganz wörtlich zu verstehen sei und diese Frage muss ich verneinen. Offenbar liegt die Sache so, dass die Empörungen alle in einem und demselben Jahre ausgebrochen sind; aber zu ihrer Bewältigung hat er einer etwas längeren Zeit bedurft. Die Chronologie der Bisutun-Inschrift bietet noch jetzt gewisse Schwierigkeiten; aber über einige Grundwahrheiten kann man schon jetzt nicht mehr im Zweifel sein. Gaumāta erhob sich am 14. Viyakhna = 14. Addaru des 7. Jahres des Kambyses, also am 10. März 522 v. Chr. Er ergriff die Herrschaft am 9. Garmapada. Für mich kann dieser Monat nur dem Nisannu gleichgesetzt. 9. Garmapada also = 3. April 522 v. Chr. Am 10. Bāgayādiš fiel Gaumāta und Darius wurde König. Nun solt Gaumāta 7 Monate regiert haben, also ist der Bāgayādiš entweder der VII Monat oder der VIII Monat, je nachdem man entweder von Gaumātas Erhebung oder von seiner Ergreifung der Herrschaft ausrechnen will. Tertium non dafür. Folglich ist Darius—mit einer Fehlergrenze von 1 Tag—entweder am 28. Sept. oder am 27. Oct. 522 König geworden. Die Rebellionen sind demnach alle in dem Jahr 522//⌃ ausgebrochen und zum grossen Teil auch noch in diesem Jahr niedergeschlagen worden." Acc. sg. *θ*ardam, Bh. 5. 1; cf. Weissbach, ZDMG, 61, 731.

*θ*ah (Pres. *θ*aha-> *θ*ā-, Bartholomae, Grundr. 123; 270, c, *6)*, *to declare, speak, say*. Act. ind. pres. 3 sg. *θ*ātiy. Pret. 1 sg. a*θ*aham. 3 sg. a*θ*aha. Subj. pres. 2 sg. *θ*āhy (< *θ*ahāhy). Pass. pres. 1 pl. (with act. ending, Bartholomae, Grundr. 325) *θ*ahyāmahy. a*θ*ⁿhᵃyᵃ (read a*θ*ahya, pass. pret. 3 sg. with act. ending,

Bartholomae, Altiran. Wb., 1579 or aθahy, pass. aor. 3 sg.; cf. Skt. çaṅsi, Tolman, OP. Inscr. 50; Bartholomae, Grundr. 154). Inf. θastanaiy. Av. sah, Skt. çaṅs. Cf. Fick, BB, 41, 343.

θuxra (Elam. tukkurra; Bab. su-uh-ra-'), m. name of the father of Otanes. Gen. sg. θuxrahyā. Probably connected with *θuxra, *bright*, Av. suxra (New Pers., Oss. surx, Afγ. sur, Kurd. sōr, Socin, SK, 31), Skt. çukra; cf. Foy, KZ, 35, 20.

θūravāhara (Elam. turmar; Bab. airu), n. name of a Persian month. The Bab. indicates agreement with Iyyar (third month) i. e. April–May. March–April (Justi); April–May (Oppert). Gen. sg. θūravāharahya (Bartholomae, Grundr. 412, n). *θūra, *vigorous* + *vāhara, *spring time*, New Pers. bahār; cf. Skt. vāsara (Hillebrandt, Ved. Myth. 1, 26).

θuvām (I. E. tue-, Av. θwam, Skt. tvām). See tuvam.

Θ^r

θ^ri, *to lean.* YAv. sri, Skt. çri.

—— with prefix niy (Pres. θ^rāray-, Bartholomae, Grundr. 128), *to restore.* Pret. 1 sg. niyaθ^rārayam, Bh. 1. 14. āyadanā —— adam niyaθ^rārayam, *I restored the places of worship.* āyadanā is better taken thus than with the preceding akunavam (WB, 15; Bartholomae, Altiran. Wb., 1638; KT, 13; Tolman, Vdt. Stud. 1, 13). Otherwise AJP, 21, 16; ZDMG, 54, 373. KT ignore avaθā adaṇ. akunavam altogether in their translation.

θ^ritīya, num. ordinal, *third.* Acc. sg. f. θ^r[itīyām] (Weissbach, θ^ritiyam), Bh. 5. 1. Acc. sg. n. (as adv.) θ^ritīyam, *for the third time*, Bh. 2. 9. Skt. tṛtīya (Whitney, Skt. Gr. 243), YAv. θritya (Middle Pers. sitīkar).

D

1) dā (I. E. pres. *di-dō-mi, *di-d-mes; Persian pres. sg. dadā-, Bartholomae, Grundr. 126), *to give.* Impv. 3 sg. dadātuv, Dar.

Pers. d. 3. ai[tamai]y [au]ramazdā dadātu[v], *this let Ahura Mazda grant me.* Av. dā (Turfan MSS. diyâd, New Pers. dihaδ, Oss. dädt'un, Hübschmann, Oss. Sprache, 96), Skt. dā.

2)dā (I. E. pres. *dhi-dhĕ-mi, *dhi-dh-mes; Skt. pres. da-dhā-mi, da-dh-mas), *to put, make, create.* Pret. 3 sg. adadā (Skt. adadhāt), Dar. Pers. d. 1. hauv dārayavaum xšāyaθiyam adadā, *he made Darius king.* Aor. 3 sg. adā (Skt. adhāt), Dar. Elvend, 1. hya imām būmim adā, *who created this earth.* Av. dā, Skt. dhā.

daiy, reading of KT in Bh. 5. l. 11. See marda.

[dauš, duš?, *to take pleasure in, esteem.* The form on which Bartholomae, AF, 2, 30, based the occurrence of this verb is dauštā (Bh. 4. 14) which he regarded as an s- aor. mid. 2 sg. KT record avaiy mā dauštā + + + ā. In Vdt. Stud. 1, 33 I supplied [bīy]ā (opt. 2 sg), cf. θuvām dauštā bīyā (Bh. 4. 1. 55). Weissbach makes same supplement (ZDMG, 61, 729) and Bartholomae (WZKM, 22, 88) is now inclined to abandon his former view. The Elam. word corresponding here to the Persian is kannenti, fut. 2 sg, while the same verb (kanešne, prec. 3 sg.) renders the Persian dauštā bīyā in Bh. 3. ll. 55, 75, 86; cf. Tolman, op. cit. 33].

dauštar, m. *friend.* Nom. sg. dauštā. With acc. θuvām dauštā bīyā, *may he be a friend to thee,* Bh. 4. 10, et passim. New Pers. dōst; fr. *duš, *to esteem, take delight in,* YAv. zuš, Skt. juṣ.

dāta, n. *law.* Nom. sg. dātam. Acc. pl. dātā, Bh. 1. 8. tyā manā dātā āpariyāyaⁿ, *they respected my laws* (written on the stone tyanā manā dātā. See tya). Av. dāta; fr. 2)dā (q. v.). Cf. Turfan MSS. dâdîst.

dᵃ? tⁿsᵃ?, a doubtful reading of KT in Bh. 4. 1. 72. Hoffmann-Kutschke suggests the emendation yāvā tava ahy, *so lange du mächtig bist* (Phil. Nov. 3, 105).

dātuhya (Elam. tattu[hi]ya; Bab. za-'-tu-'-a), m. name of the father of Megabyzus. Gen. sg. [dātu]hyahyā. Cf. KZ, 39, 153.

dādarši (Elam. tataršiš; Bab. da-da-ar-šu), m. name of 1)a Persian satrap (xšaθʳapāvan); 2)an Armenian subject. Nom. sg. dādaršiš.

The word is clearly written in Bh. 2. 1. 29 and should be removed from brackets in ed.; cf. KT, 27. Acc. sg. dādaršim. Redup. theme (intens.) of darš (q. v.).

dan (Pres. dānā-, Bartholomae, Grundr. 132), *to know.* Pret. 3 sg. adānā. Av. zan (Turfan MSS. dânêm, New Pers. dānaδ), Skt. jānāti. Cf. KZ, 39, 157; Wackernagel, Ai. Gram. 76.

dan (Pres. danu-, Bartholomae, Grundr. 131), *to flow.* Pres. 3 sg. $d^a n^u u$ + + + + (Dar. Sz. c. 3) which may be read danu[taiy], cf. Bartholomae, Altiran. Wb., 683; Keller, KZ, 39, 175, or danu-[vatiy], cf. Skt. dhanvati, Whitney, Skt. Gr. 716. New Pers. danīdan, Skt. dhan.

dar (Caus. pres. dāraya-, Bartholomae, Grundr. 151), 1)*to hold*, 2)*hold a position, halt.* Pres. 1 sg. dārayamiy. Pret. 3 sg. adāraya. In Dar. NRa. 3, Foy (KZ, 37, 560) would restore the form adāraya in place of adāriy. s- aor. 1 sg. adaršiy (Bartholomae, Grundr. 156) or adaršaiy (with thematic vowel), Dar. Pers. e. 2. Aor. (pass.) 3 sg. adāriy, Bh. 2. 13, 15. Av. dar (Turfan MSS. dârêd, New Pers. dāraδ), Skt. dhr̥.

—— with prefix ham, *obtain.* Mid. pret. 1 sg. hamadārayaiy, Bh. 1. 9. yātā ima xšaθ^ram ha[ma]dārayai[y], *until I obtained this kingdom.* This reading is attested by KT, and supersedes [ad]āry of ed. and the various attempts at emendation; cf. Tolman, Vdt. Stud. 1, 9.

dārayaⁿtā, reading of WB in Dar. NRd., *Pfeilbewahrer* (išunām; išuvām, Bartholomae). Cf. ZDMG, 50, 663; AJP, 21, 2; Foy, ZDMG, 55, 509; Hoffmann-Kutschke, Or. Litt. Ztg. Sept. 1906 (denānām dārayaⁿtā); Justi, dāsyamā (dāsya + man).

dārayavau (Elam. tariyamauš; Bab. da-ri-ia-muš; Gr. Δαρεῖος for *Δαρειαῖος, cf. Keiper, Sem. Phil., Erlangen, 1, 253; Aesch. Pers. Δαρειάν, 662), m. 1)*Darius* I. Nom. sg. dārayavauš. Acc. sg. dārayavaum. Gen. sg. dārayavahauš (dārayavaušahyā in Art. Sus. a). For gen. sg. dārayavauš (Art. Pers. a, b, 2). 2)*Darius* II. Gen. sg. dārayavaušahyā (Art. Sus. a, 1; in Art. Hamadan, dārayava(u)šahyā, Tolman, PAPA, 36, 32). For gen. sg. dārayavauš (Art. Sus. b; Art. Pers. a, b, 2). Darius I, after the death of Cambyses, ascends the throne by virtue of his kinship to the royal race (see s. v. cⁱšᵃpᵃi). Political tradition has colored the popular version of Hdt. III, 85–7 (cf. Schöll, Die Anfänge einer politischen Litteratur bei den Griechen) respecting the counsel of the allies and the stratagem of Darius' groom. Cf. Duncker, Gesch. d. Altert. 4⁵, 388; Marquart, Philol. Suppl. 6, 588; Winckler, Untersuchungen z. altorient. Gesch., 126; Nöldeke, Aufsätze z. pers. Gesch., 15; Tolman and Stevenson, Hdt. and Empires of East, 86. dāraya-, pres. part. to dar, + *vahu, Skt. vasu, *good*, as. n. sg. *wealth.*

dargam, adj. *long.* GAv. darəga, YAv. darəya (Oss. dary, Bal. drag, Afy. lārya, Geiger, SA, 2).

darš (Pres. daršnu-, Bartholomae, Grundr. 131), *to dare.* Pret. 3 sg. adaršnauš. Skt. dhr̥ṣ.

daršam, adv. *mightily, much;* cf. darš.

daršman, n. *boldness, tyranny, despotism.* Abl. sg. (with hacā) daršmaⁿ, Bartholomae's conjecture for daršam of ed. in Bh. 1. 13, kārašim hacā daršmaⁿ atarsa, *the people feared his tyranny;* cf. Tolman, Vdt. Stud. 1, 11. darš (q. v.).

dasta, m. *hand.* Loc. sg. (with postpos. ā) dastayā. Av. zasta (New Pers. dast), Skt. hasta.

dahyu, f. *province, district, land.* Nom. sg. dahyāuš. Acc. sg. dahyāum (DAHyum in Art. Pers. a, b, 4). Loc. sg. (with postpos. ā) dahyāuvā. Nom. pl. dahyāva. Gen. pl. dahyūnām. Loc. pl. (with postpos. ā) dahyušuvā. Av. dahyu (Middle Pers. dēh, New Pers. dih, *town*, Horn, NS, 42, 1), Skt. dasyu, used as the title of the demons.

di, demon. pron. (most often encl.), *it, them.* Acc. sg. f. dim, Dar. NRa. 4. pasāvadim (i. e. imām būmim) manā frābara, *he gave it to me.* Acc. pl. m. diš, Bh. 4. 4. imaiy kāram adurujīyašaⁿ pasāva di[š auramaz]dā manā dastayā akunauš, *these deceived the people; afterwards Ahura Mazda put them* (i. e. the people; cf. Elam. version) *into my hand.* Acc. pl. f. diš (Bh. 4. 1. 34), m. (Bh. 4. 16, 17). YAv. di.

dī (Pres. dīdī-, Bartholomae, Grundr. 126), *to see*. Impv. 2 sg. dīdiy (haplography for dīdīdiy; cf. Bartholomae, Altiran. Wb., 725), Dar. NRa. 4. Av. dī (Turfan MSS. dīd, New Pers. dīdan), Skt. dhī.

dī (Pres. dīnā-, Bartholomae, Grundr. 132), *to injure, deprive one* (acc.) *of something* (acc.), *take* (acc.) *from one* (acc.). Pret. 1 sg. adīnam, Bh. 1. 13. xšaθʳamšim adam adīnam, *I took the kingdom from him.* 3 sg. adīnā. Part. acc. sg. m. dītam, Bh. 1. 13. avam gaumātam tyam magum xšaθʳam dītam caxriyā, *could make Gaumāta the Magian deprived of the kingdom.* YAv. zī (Middle Pers. zīnītan), Skt. jī.

didā, f. *stronghold*. Nom. sg. didā. Acc. sg. didām. New Pers. diz; cf. YAv. diz, *heap up.*

dipi, f. *inscription*. Acc. sg. dipim. Loc. sg. d[i]p[iy]ā, Bh. 4. 8. New Pers. dibīr. Cf. Assyr. duppu, Elam. tuppi; Jensen, ZA, 6, 172; Foy, ZDMG, 50, 128; Pedersen, KZ, 40, 190. According to Hüsing's interpretation of the Elam. (Bh. L.) Darius declares that he made inscriptions on bricks, halat, and leather, SU.

dubāla, m. name of a district in Babylonia, Nom. sg. dubāla.

dūraiy, adv. *far*. In Dar. NRa. l. 44, dūraiy for dū[ra]y is clearly to be read. With apiy written dūraiy apiy, Xerx. Pers. a. 2; dūraiapiy, Dar. NRa. 2 (so Stolze's photograph, Pers. II, 109); dūrayapiy, ibid. (so Stolze's photograph). Loc. sg. of *dūra, *far*, Av. *dūra (New Pers., Kurd. dūr, Gab. dur), Skt. dūra.

duruj (Pres. durujiya-, Bartholomae, Grundr. 148), *to lie, deceive.* Pret. 3 sg. adurujiya. 3 pl. (with s of sigmatic aor.) adurujiyaša[n], Schmidt, KZ, 27, 326; Bartholomae, Grundr. 309, II: as an s-aor, Fr. Müller, WZKM, 7, 253; Foy (KZ, 35, 30) regarded the –ša as encl. (cf. Lat. se-) "weg," translating *sie logen weg;* cf. ZDMG, 52, 597. Part. acc. n. sg. duruxtam, Bh. 4. 7. ima hašiyam naiy duruxtam adam akuna[vam], *I did this as something true not pretended.* For Oppert's duruxtam in Bh. 4. 1. 43, [drauj]īyāhy (see draujīya) is better to be supplied. adurujiya, occurring in Bh. Inscr. over twenty times, clearly represents each rebel as a follower of the Druj, *the Lie*, the personification of Evil (cf. Tolman, PAPA,

33, 69), for it is the Druj which is the source of rebellion; drauga dī[š hamiθʳiy]ā akunauš, *the Lie made them rebellious*, Bh. 4. 4. YAv. druj (Middle Pers. družītan), Skt. druh.

duruva, adj. *sound, secure.* Nom. sg. f. duruvā, Bh. 4. 5. YAv. drva, Skt. dhruva.

duvaištam, adv. *very long.* Dar. Pers. e. 3. Acc. sg. n. of superl. *duvaišta, cf. dūraiy; Bartholomae, Altiran. Wb., 763; IF, 12. 127.

duvara (duvar, transf. to a- decl.; cf. Skt. dvāra, Whitney, Skt. Gr. 399), m. *door.* Loc. sg. (with postpos. ā) duvarayā, *at (my) door*, Bh. 2. 13, 14. YAv. dvar (New Pers. dar, Oss. dvar), Skt. dvār.

duvarθi, m. *portico, colonnade.* Acc. sg. duvarθim, Xerx. Pers. a. 3. Bartholomae suggests haplography for duvar-varθi.

duvitāparanam (Tolman, Vdt. Stud. 1, 8. *duvitā, *long*, GAv. daibitā, Skt. dvitā, against Geldner, Ved. Stud. 3. 1; cf. Gray, JAOS, 23, 63, + paranam, *before, antehac*, q. v.), adv. *long aforetime.* Bartholomae writes me under date of May 13, 1908, that he takes paranam as I have suggested above, but concerning the first member of the compound he adds: "duvitā ist das mpp. dīt, alter. Das Ganze scheint mir danach zu bedeuten, *cum altero prior, alter cum altero, post alterum.* Das elamische šamak-mar bedeutet *ex* (= mar) *ordine*, franz. *de suite.*" KT read duvitāparnam, *in two lines*, which is supported by Weissbach (ZDMG, 61, 725) who connects parnam with Skt. parṇa, *wing.* Hoffmann-Kutschke (Phil. Nov. 3, 103), whose treatment of the compound defies philological laws, remarks: "parnam jedoch entspricht lat. plenus, germ. fulna (sic), *voll*, und steht für palna." These views, of course, are in accord with Oppert's early interpretation, *en deux branches*, which seems not only at variance with the Elam. šamak-mar, but to lack historical support; cf. Tolman and Stevenson, Hdt. and Empires of East, 74. The old reading duvitātaranam with which critics have operated is superseded. KT record: "The reading p in place of t is certain."

duvitīya, adj. *second.* Nom. sg. duvitīya (cf. Bartholomae, Altiran. Wb., duvitīya-ma for duvitīyam of ed. and KT), Bh. 3. 5.

hauv duvitīyama udapatatā pārsaiy, *he was the second to rise against me in Persia.* Acc. sg. n. (as adv.) duvitīyam, *for a second time*, Bh. 3. 13, et passim. GAv. daibitya, YAv. bitya (New Pers. dīgar), Skt. dvitīya.

dušiyāra (dušiyār, transf. to a- decl.), n. *bad harvest, scarcity, famine.* Nom. sg. dušiyāram, Dar. Pers. d. 3. "There is some space between the i and the y, due apparently to an original defect in the stone before it was lettered." Jackson, JAOS, 27, 191. Abl. sg. dušiyārā, Dar. Pers. d. 3. "The u is not clear but can be made out." Jackson, JAOS, 27, 191. duš, *ill*, Av. duš (New Pers. duš), Skt. dus + *yār, *year*, YAv. yār. Note Turfan MSS. dûsyâriy.

drauga, m. *the Lie.* Nom. sg. drauga. Abl. sg. (with hacā) draugā, Bh. 4. 5; Dar. Pers. d. 3. Ahura Mazda, as guardian of Truth and Avenger of Deceit, is opposed to that force embodied in the Lie. Hdt. testifies to the Persian veneration of truth and abomination of deceit; αἴσχιστον δὲ αὐτοῖσι τὸ ψεύδεσθαι νενόμισται, I. 138; παιδεύουσι δὲ τοὺς παῖδας—τρία μοῦνα ἱππεύειν καὶ τοξεύειν καὶ ἀληθίζεσθαι, I. 136. The Druj (drauga) is certainly a personification of Evil (cf. Jackson, Grundr. d. iran. Philol. II, 630). It is the Druj which is the source of rebellion, Bh. 4. 4. The prayer of Darius is that his country may be saved from the Druj, Pers. d. 3. He warns his successor to guard against the Druj and to punish the liar, Bh. 4. 5. It was because Darius was not under the influence of the Druj that he became the favorite of Ahura Mazda, Bh. 4. 13. Morality is to walk in the path of Truth, NRa. 6. This personification of the Avestan Druj in the Persian drauga, found, as we should expect, no correspondence in the Babylonian thought (cf. Gray, JAOS, 21, 181). How strikingly is this seen in the contrast between drauga dahyauvā vasiy abava, *the Druj (Lie) dominated the province* and the lame Babylonian version par-sa-a-tu ina mâtâti lu ma-du i-mi-du, *in the lands lies became numerous*, Bh. 1. 10. Tolman in PAPA, 33, 69. In Bh. 4. 4. drauga di[š hamiθ^riy]ā akunauš, KT ignore entirely this personification in their translation, *lies made them revolt.* Cf. Wilhelm, ZDMG, 40, 105; Bang, ZDMG, 43, 533; Foy, KZ, 35, 69; Horn, Beilage zur Allg. Ztg. 1895; Jackson-Gray, JAOS, 21, 170. YAv. draoga (Phl. drōg, New Pers. duroy), Skt. drogha; fr. duruj (i. e. druj.).

draujana, adj. *deceiving, false, a follower of the Druj*, cf. drauga and Turfan MSS. drōzaniy. Nom. sg. draujana, Bh. 4. 5, 13, 14. Jackson and KT record the legibility of draujana in Bh. 4. 1. 68. YAv. draojina-; fr. duruj (i. e. druj).

draujīya (denom. pres. to *drauja, *lie;* Bartholomae, Grundr. 152), *to regard as a lie.* Pres. subj. 2 sg. [drauj]īyāhy, cf. Rawlinson, JRAS, 12. This form (cf. Bartholomae, Altiran. Wb., 769) is best read in Bh. 4. 6. KT give [duruj]iyāhy, but the context as well as the Elam. shows a meaning impossible for this verb. Cf. Tolman, Vdt. Stud. 1, 30.

drayah, n. *sea.* Acc. sg. draya, Dar. Sz. c. 3; thus read also in Bh. 5. 1. 23, abiy draya in place of darayam of ed. The absence of final m, as recorded by KT, gives the regular form and supersedes the theory that the word is here a transfer to the a- declension; cf. Tolman, Vdt. Stud. 1, 36. Loc. sg. (with postpos. ā) drayahyā. YAv. zrayah (Middle Pers. zray, New Pers. zirih), Skt. jrayas, *an expanse.* Cf. Fick, BB, 41, 343.

N

naiba, adj. *beautiful*, Nom. sg. f. naibā, Dar. Pers. d. 2. Nom. sg. n. naibam, Xerx. Pers. a. 3. Acc. sg. n. naibam, Xerx. Van. 3. Phl. nēv, New Pers. nēv, *brave, good.*

naiy, adv. *not;* written nai with enclitics maiy and šim. YAv. naē- cf. Delbrück, Vgl. Syntax, 2, 524. Otherwise Bartholomae, Altiran. Wb., 1073.

nadi^ntabaira (Elam. nititpel; Bab. ni-din-tu-(ilu)bêl), m. *Nidintu-Bêl*, name of a Babylonian rebel. Nom. sg. nadi^ntabaira. Acc. sg. nadi^ntabairam. Gen. sg. nadi^ntabairahyā. Cf. Duncker, Gesch. d. Altert. 4^5, 472.

napāt, m. *grandson.* Nom. sg. napā (reformation with ā; cf. Bartholomae, Grundr. 397, n.), Bh. 1. 1; Bh. a. 1. Av. napāt (New Pers. nava), Skt. napāt.

nabukudracara (Elam. napkuturruzir; Bab. nabù-kudurri-usur), m. *Nebuchadrezar*, the assumed name of the rebels Nidintu-Bêl and Arkha. Nom. sg. nabukudracara. Cf. Justi, ZDMG, 51, 236; Weissbach, Grundr. d. iran. Philol. 2, 55.

nabunaita (Elam. napuneta; Bab. nabù-na'id), m. *Nabonidus*, name of the last king of the new Babylonian empire (cf. Nabû-na'id-Cyrus Chronicles); written in Hdt. *Labynetos*, cf. Tolman and Stevenson, Hdt. and Empires of East, 81-6. Gen. sg. nabunaitahyā, Bh. 1. 16, nabunaitahya (Bartholomae, Grundr. 412, n; thus to be read in Bh. 3. 14; 4. 2; Bh. d; Bh. i. cf. KT, 56).

nāman, n. *name*. n^{a}am^a, *by name*, written n^{a}am^{a}a with fem. noun. The following are some of the theories respecting this latter form. J. Schmidt (Pluralbld. 82) regarded it as forming the second member of a bahuvrîhi-compound (Whitney, Skt. Gr. 1293) with a fem. formation in *-ōn, e. g. yutiyā nāmā dahyāuš, *a region possessing the name of Yutiyā*. Thumb (KZ, 32, 132) would derive nāmā from *nōmn̥ comparing gāθu<g$\bar{m}$tu. Foy (KZ, 35, 11) at first suggested a transition to the fem. of a sandhi-form *nāman < nōmn̥n; cf. later IF, 12, 172 and note various theories there cited. Bartholomae (Grundr. 403, II) proposed a possible distinction of case nāmā (acc. sg.) and nāma^n (loc. sg.), but has later shifted his position, taking both forms as loc. sg. and transcribing nāma^n and nāmā^n. Can we regard n^{a}am^{a}a as scriptio plena influenced by fem.? Cf. gen. sg. -h^{a}y^{a}a < Ar. -sia, often written h^{a}y^a when immediately preceding the noun on which it depends. Tolman in Vdt. Stud. 1, 12. Av. nāman (New Pers. nām, Oss. non, Afγ. num, Bal. nām), Skt. nāman.

navama, adj. *ninth*. Nom. sg. navama, Bh. 1. 4; Bh. a. 4. Skt. navama, YAv. nāuma (Jackson, Av. Gr. 64).

nāviyā, Bh. 1. 18. The word is generally regarded as nom. f. of an abstract formation from nāv, *ship*, and as signifying *a collection of ships, fleet;* so Kern (ZDMG, 23, 237), Müller (WZKM, 11, 252), Gray (AJP, 21, 19), Bartholomae (Altiran. Wb., 1065). The old interpretation (*bei den Schiffen*, WB), defended by Foy (ZDMG, 54, 371) regards the form as loc. sg. of nāv with postpos. ā; so Pedersen, KZ, 40, 129, *on opposite side (the enemy) was on shipboard*. Skt. nāv, *ship*, New Pers. nāv.

nas, see **viyanā[sa]ya**.

nāh, m. *nose.* Acc. sg. **nāham**, Bh. 2. 13, 14. YAv. **nāh**, Skt. **nās**.

niy, verbal prefix, *down.* e. g., Xerx. Van. 3, **nipištanaiy**. Av. **nī** (New Pers. **ni-**), Skt. **ni**.

nī (Pres. **naya**, Bartholomae, Grundr. 123), *to lead.* Act. pret. 3 sg. **anaya**, Bh. 2. 14. Mid. pret. 3 sg. (with passive sense) **anayatā**, Bh. 1. 17. Av. **nī** (Middle Pers. **nītan**), Skt. **nī**.

—— with prefix **fra(?)**, *lead forth, bring forward.* Pret. 1 sg. **frānayam**, Bh. 1. 18. **aniyahyā asam frānayam**, *for the rest I brought forward horses.* KT state that the reading **frānayam** is probable from the traces on the rock. Jackson (JAOS, 24, 87) feels less certain respecting the prefix. "I appended a further note that the appearance of the word suggested rather **[up]ānayam** or **[uz]ānayam**, but such a restoration is quite uncertain, though I tried my best to assure it by examining the weathered stone again and again."

nij, verbal prefix, *away.* Bh. 2. 12, **nijāyam**; see **i**. Av. **niš**, Skt. **niṣ-**.

nipadiy, adv. *in pursuit of, close after.* Read **nipadiy** for **tyaipatiy** of ed. in Bh. 2. 1. 72 (cf. KT, 36), **adam kāram frāišayam nipadiy**, *I sent forth my army in pursuit.* The word hardly means *on foot* as given by KT and ed. Both Elam. and Bab. versions give no warrant for this older interpretation of the word. Bh. 3. 12. **hadā kārā nipadi[y] t[ya]iy ašiyava**, *he went with his army close on the heels of these.* Cf. Tolman, Vdt. Stud. 1. 26. Probably loc. sg. of **niy** + **pad**, *foot;* cf. Bartholomae, Altiran. Wb., 1083, who happily compares Lesb. Boeot. πεδ-ά (instr. sg. to πούς). To this might be added Lat. **pedisequus**, *following one's steps.*

niyašādayam, see **had**.

nisāya (Elam. **niššaya**; Bab. **ni-is-sa-a-a**), m. name of a Median district. Nom. sg. **nisāya**, Bh. 1. 13. **niy** + ***sāya**; fr. ***sī**, *lie,* YAv. **si** (Middle Pers. **nisītan**), Skt. **çī**.

nūram (Jackson and KT record the absence of a lacuna before the word in Bh. 4. 10), adv. *now.* Av. nūrəm (Oss. nur, New Pers. nun).

nyāka, m. *grandfather*, supplied in Art. Sus. a. arta[xšaθrām nyākam], *Artaxerxes my grandfather.* YAv. nyāka.

P

pā (Pres. pā-, Bartholomae, Grundr. 122), *to protect, sustain.* Act. impv. 2 sg. pādiy. 3 sg. pātuv. Part. nom. sg. m. pāta. Av. pā (New Pers. pāyaδ), Skt. pā.

—— with prefix patiy (Pres. paya-, Bartholomae, Grundr. 148), *guard oneself* (mid.) *against* (abl. with hacā). Impv. 2 sg. patipayauvā, Bh. 4. 5.

paišiyāuvādā (pišiyāuvādā, Bartholomae, Altiran. Wb., 908. Bab. pi-ši-'-ḫu-ma-du), f. name of a district. Acc. sg. paišiyāuvādām, Bh. 3. 7. Abl. sg. (with hacā) paišiyāuvādāyā, Bh. 1. 11. According to Justi (IF, 17, Anz. 107) *Pasargada*, paišiya, fr. piš (q. v.) + *uvādā, Skt. svadhā, *abode; Ort der Schriften*, i. e., depository of the archives and sacred books. Cf. Oppert, La. langue—des Mèdes, 110.

pat (Pres. pata-, Bartholomae, Grundr. 123), *to fly, fall.* YAv. pat (New Pers. uftādan), Skt. pat.

—— with prefix ud, *rise up, rebel.* Mid. pret. 3 sg. udapatatā.

patiy, prep. postpos. 1) with acc. *during, throughout, at;* cf. Foy. WZKM, 14, 291. Bh. 2. 11. θuravāharahya māhyā jiyamnam (q. v.) patiy, *at the end of the month Thūravāhara.* Bh. 1. 7. xšapavā raucapativā, *by night or day.* 2) with instr. *at*, Bh. 3. 5. hya viθāpatiy, *which was at the palace.* 3) with loc. *in, at*, Bh. 2. 13, et passim. uzmayāpatiy akunavam, *I crucified.* Av. paiti (Turfan MSS. pad, New Pers. paδ-).

patiy, adv. *on the other hand, moreover, again, once more.* Bh. 2. 9, et passim. patiy θritīyam ha[m]iθr[iyā] hangmatā, *again for the third time the confederates assembled.* Postpos., not always with the adversative force which Foy gives it. Xerx. Pers. a. 3. **tyapatiy kartam**, *moreover what work;* Elam. **appa šarak huttukka.** Dar. NRa. 4. **yadipatiy** (sic, cf. Stolze's Phot., Persepolis II, 109) **maniyā[ha]y** (cf. Stolze's Phot.), *furthermore if thou thinkest*, where again the Elam. has **šarak** for Persian **patiy**. On the ground that **šarak** also renders **patiy** above, Foy argues that they are identical. Bartholomae, on the other hand, still adheres to the old view that **patiy** in the last two passages cited is an enclitic particle with indefinite force and has no etymological connection with **patiy**, the prep. and adv.

patikara, m. *picture, likeness.* Acc. sg. **patikaram.** Acc. pl. **patikarā.** **patiy** + **kar** (q. v.). Cf. New Pers. **paikar,** Horn, NS, 26.

patigrabanā (Elam. **pattikrappana**), f. name of a Parthian town. Nom. sg. **patigrabanā.** **patiy** + **grab** (q. v.).

patipada, adj. *in its own place.* Acc. sg. n. **patipadam,** Bh. 1. 14. **ava adam patipadam akunavam,** *I put it in place* (i. e. *restored it*). **patiy** + **pada (thematic), *foot.* Av. **pad** (Phl. **pāī,** Turfan MSS. **pād,** New Pers. **pāi,** Afγ. **pal**), Skt. **pad.**

patiš, prep. with acc. *against, towards.* Cf. **patiy**; for final **š** of **patiš** see Brugmann, KZ, 27, 417 vs. Schmidt, Pluralbld. 352.

pātišuvari, adj. *a Patischorian.* Nom. sg. m. **pātišuvariš,** Dar. NRc. Cf. Horn, KZ, 38, 290.

paθi, f. *way, path.* Acc. sg. **paθim,** Dar. NRa. 6. **paθim tyām rāstām mā avarada,** *depart not from the true way.* Cf. Av. **paθā** (Oss. **fändäg**) Skt. **panthan.**

pāya, the second word in Seal Inscr. d. **vahyav'šdā pāya** according to WB.

parā, prep. postpos. with acc. e. g. **avaparā,** *there before,* Bh. 3. 12. This reading confirmed by KT sets aside Foy's conjecture **avadaparā,** *davor.* Av. **para,** Skt. **purā.**

para, adj. *after,* e. g. **hyāparam** (adv.), *thereafter,* Bh. 3. 7. **hyā** (abl. sg.) + **param** (acc. sg. n.). Av. **para-,** Skt. **para.**

paranam, adv. *formerly.* Bh. 1. 13. hya paranam bardiyam adānā, *who had known Smerdis formerly;* so Bartholomae. As an adj. Gray (AJP, 21, 15) *the former Bardiya,* and ed. Acc. sg. n. of adj. fr. para, *before.*

pariy, prep. with acc. *about, concerning.* Bh. 1. 13. pariy gaumātam, *concerning Gaumāta.* Av. pairi (New Pers. par-, Bal. pir), Skt. pari.

paru, adj. *many.* Nom. sg. n. paruv, Bh. 4. 8. Gen. pl. m. parūnām (written p^{a}r^{u}uv^{a}n^{a}am^a in Dar. NRa. 1; Art. Pers. a. b. 1). For gen. pl. f. parūnām, Dar. Pers. e. 1. YAv. pouru (Bartholomae, Grundr. 298, 3. Middle Pers. pur), Skt. puru.

paruva, adj. 1) *former.* Nom. pl. m. paruvā, Bh. 4. 9. 2) *eastern,* loc. sg. n. paruvaiy, Dar. Pers. e. 2, *on the east* (written p^{a}r^{a}uv^{a}iy^a by stone-cutter's blunder for p^{a}r^{u}uv^{a}iy^a; cf. Bartholomae, Altiran. Wb., 872, n. 8). YAv. paurva, Skt. pūrva.

paruvam, adv. *formerly,* Bh. 1. 4, 10, 14. Acc. sg. n. of paruva.

paruviyata, adv. hacā paruviyata, *from long ago,* Bh. 1. 3, 12. *paruviya, *first, before.* GAv. paouruya, Skt. pūrvya + suffix ta.

paruzana, adj. *containing many kinds of people.* Gen. pl. paruvzanānām, Dar. Elvend, 2; (written paruv | zanānām in Xerx. Pers. a. 2; ca. cb. 2; Van, 2: paruvzanānām in Xerx. Pers. b. 2; da. db. 2; Elvend, 2). paru (q. v.) + *zana, *man,* Skt. jana; fr. *zan, *give birth,* YAv. zan (New Pers. zāyaδ), Skt. jan.

parga (Elam. parrakka), m. Nom. sg. parga, Bh. 3. 7. Thus written instead of paraga of KT and ed.; cf. Foy, KZ, 35, 13. New Pers. purg.

parθava (Elam. partuma; Bab. pa-ar-tu-u), m. *Parthia, Parthian.* Nom. sg. parθava. Loc. sg. parθavaiy. Instr. pl. parθavaibi[š], Bh. 2. 1. 96.

parsa, inchoative stem (s = I. E. xsx', Bartholomae, Grundr. 135; Skt. pṛcha-ti, Av. peresaiti, Turfan MSS. pūrsid, New Pers.

pursaδ), *to ask, examine into, punish.* Impv. 2 sg. **parsā**. Pret. 1 sg. **aparsam**.

—— with prefix **patiy**, *examine, read.* Subj. 2 sg. **patiparsāhy**, 3 sg. **patiparsātiy**.

pārsa (Elam. paršir; Bab. par-sa-a-a), 1) adj. *Persian.* Nom. sg. m. **pārsa**. Acc. sg. m. **pārsam**. Instr. sg. m. **pārsā**. Gen. sg. m. **pārsahyā**. 2) As subs. m. *Persia.* Nom. sg. **pārsa**. Acc. sg. **pārsam**. Instr. sg. **pārsā** (with **anā**, q. v.), Xerx. Pers. a. 3. Abl. sg. (with **hacā**) **pārsā**, Dar. NRa. 3, 4; Sz. c. 3. Loc. sg. **pārsaiy**. In addition to the places of occurrence KT record an omitted line, Bh. 3. l. 53; ima tya manā kartam pārsaiy | θātiy dārayavauš xšāyaθiya.

pasā, prep. with gen. *after.* Bh. 3. 6. pasā manā, *with me.* pasā is probably for *passa < *pasca, Av. pasca (New Pers. pas), Skt. paccā < *pas-ac-ā (instr. Whitney, Skt. Gr. 1112, e.); cf. Gray, AJP, 21, 8, and Grierson, ZDMG, 50, 25. Otherwise Bartholomae, Altiran, Wb., 879 and Foy, KZ, 35, 26.

pasāvā, adv. *thereafter, afterwards.* pasā (q. v.) + acc. sg. n. ava. According to Bartholomae's reference to Ménant and Daressy (Recueil de trav.) pasāva is to be supplied after aitiy in l. 10 of Dar. Sz. c. 3, though ed. show no lacuna here. For [pas]āva avadā kāram of ed. read [a]vadā avam kāram in Bh. 1. l. 88; cf. KT, 18. pasāva is wrongly supplied in ed. in Bh. 2. l. 29. "There is no gap here; the clause is not introduced by pasāva, the proper name dādaršiš being the first word in the sentence. All the signs in the line are clear upon the rock." KT. [pasāva] is also wrongly supplied by KT and ed. in Bh. 2. l. 49, where the corresponding word fails in Elam. and Bab. versions. Its omission would have an important bearing on Weissbach's interpretation of hamahyāyā θarda, *in the same year*, in Bh. 4. 2, 6, 7, 9, 12.

pitar, m. *father.* Nom. sg. **pitā**. Gen. sg. **piθ^{r}a**, Xerx. Pers. a. 4. tya manā kartam utā tyamaiy piθ^{r}a kartam; Pers. ca. cb. 3. Av. **pitar** (Turfan MSS. pidar, New Pers. pidar), Skt. pitr̥; cf. Wackernagel, Ai. Gram. 16.

pirāva, m. the river *Nile*. Nom. sg. pirāva, Dar. Sz. c. 3. adam ni[yaš]tāyam imām [yuviyā]m kaⁿtanaiy hacā pirāva nāma rauta, *I ordered to dig this canal from the river the Nile by name.* Foy (KZ, 35, 31) argues for a construction of an acc. with hacā and regards pirāva nāma as a bahuvrīhi compound. Thumb (KZ, 32, 129) makes the anacoluthon the equivalent of hacā rautā — pirāva nāma rauta — hacā adā; cf. Bartholomae, BB, 14, 249; Foy, IF, 12, 176.

pisā, reading of ed. and KT in Bh. 5. l. 24. According to Justi (IF, 17, Anz. 126), the instr. sg. (in collective sense) of pisa, *raft*, fr. piš (q. v.). pisā viyatarayam, *I crossed on rafts.* Cf. Foy, KZ, 37, 529.

piš. The primitive meaning of the root (I. E. peik̂) seems to be *cut, trim* rather than *farbig machen* which Bartholomae gives. A survival of this signification we see in such a passage as RV. 1, 161, 10, māṅsam ekaḥ piñcati, *the one carves the meat;* in Old Slav. piša, pisati, *to scratch in, write;* in Gr. ποικίλος as applied to work in metal, stone and wood, and πικ-ρός (nil grade), *cutting, sharp, stinging,* e. g. ὅθ᾽ ἔμπεσε πικρὸς ὀϊστός, *where the piercing arrow had fallen,* Δ. 217; θυγατέρες πικρὰς ὠδῖνας ἔχουσαι, *sharp pains,* Δ. 271 (cf. ὀξεῖαι ὀδύναι, ibid. 268). The transfer to the familiar *adorn* (Middle Pers. pēsīt, *ornamented*) which is the meaning of the root in YAv. is, of course, natural and seen in many of the cognates; e. g. piç, *to ornament,* Goth. filu-faiha translating πολυποίκιλος of Ephes. 3, 10. Tolman in Vdt. Stud. 1, 31.

—— with prefix niy, *cut (an inscription).* s- aor. 1 sg. niyapisam, Bh. 4. 15, 21. Inf. nipištanaiy, Xerx. Van, 3. Part. acc. sg. n. nipištam, Bh. 4. 8. Acc. sg. f. nipištām, Xerx. Van, 3. Note Turfan MSS. nibišt.

puⁿtiya, adj. name of a people. Nom. pl. m. puⁿtiyā, Dar. NRa. 3.

puθʳa, m. *son.* Nom. sg. puθʳa. Av. puθra (Turfan MSS. pûs, pûr, pûhr, New Pers. pusar, Oss. furth), Skt. putra.

F

fra, verbal prefix, *forth;* e. g., frābara (fra + abara). Av. frā. (Phl. fra, New Pers. far), Skt. pra.

fratama, adj. *first, foremost.* Nom. pl. m. fratamā. fra (q. v.) + superl. suffix tama.

fratarta, reading confirmed by KT in Bh. 3. l. 26. See s. v. tar.

frāda (Elam. pirrata; Bab. pa-ra-da-'), m. name of a Margian rebel. Nom. sg. frāda. Cf. Justi, IF, 17, Anz. 106.

framātar, m. *master, lord.* Acc. sg. framātāram, Xerx. Elvend, 1. aivam parūnām framātāram, *one lord of* (i. e. *over*) *many*, et passim; (written wrongly framātaram, Dar. NRa. 1, framatāram, Art. Pers. a. b. 1; cf. Bartholomae, Altiran. Wb., 987). New Pers. farmaδār, Skt. pramātr̥; fr. fra + mā (q. v.).

framānā, f. *command, precept.* Nom. sg. framānā, Dar. NRa. 6. Turfan MSS. framān, New Pers. farmān; fr. fra + mā (q. v.). Cf. Pedersen, KZ, 39, 344.

fravarti (Elam. pirrumartiš; Bab. pa-ar-u-mar-ti-iš; Gr. Φραόρτης), m. *Phraortes*, a Median rebel. See Tolman and Stevenson, Hdt. and Empires of East, 68 ff; Weissbach, ZDMG, 51, 517. Nom. sg. fravartiš. Acc. sg. fravartim. Gen. sg. fravartaiš.

fraš$_{am}^{ta}$ y(?)adayāmaiy, an emendation which I suggested in Dar. Sus. a. for the uncertain word.

fraharavam, adv. *altogether, in all*, Bh. 1. 6. Thus to be read instead of fraharvam of KT and ed.; cf. Bartholomae, BB, 13, 69; Foy, KZ, 35, 4. n. Acc. sg. n. of *fraharava, *all;* fra + *harava, cf. haruva (q. v.).

B

bāxtrī (Bab. ba-aḫ-tar), f. *Bactria.* Nom. sg. bāxtriš. Loc. sg. bāxtriyā. Cf. Foy, KZ, 35, 65, who discuss the proper name in reference to the Elam. (bāxtriš = pakturriš; *bāxθ^{r}iš = pakšiš). YAv. bāxδī (New Pers. bāxr).

baga, m. *god.* Nom. sg. **baga**. Nom. pl. **bagāha**. Instr. pl. **bagaibiš**. Gen. pl. **bagānām**. For plurality of gods see Jackson-Gray, JAOS, 21, 168; Tolman, PAPA, 33, 68. The polytheism of the Deirmenjik Inscription of Darius (τὴν ὑπὲρ θεῶν μου διάθεσιν, cf. Cousin-Deschamps, Bull. de corr. hell. 13, 530) is probably due to political considerations. The plural occurs once in YAv. (Yt. 10, 141), yet more frequently in Pahlavi. YAv. **baγa** (Middle Pers. **baγ**, Turfan MSS. bagîystôm), Skt. **bhaga**. Cf. Fick, BB, 41, 341.

bagābigna (Elam. **pakapikna**), m. name of the father of Vidarna. Gen. sg. **bagābignahyā**, Bh. 4. 18. **baga which may be connected with YAv. **baγā**, *apportionment,* + **bigna(?).* Otherwise Justi, ZDMG, 49, 682; Bartholomae, Altiran. Wb., 922.

bagabuxša (Elam. **pakapukša**; Bab. **ma-ga-bu-di-šu**; Gr. Μεγάβυζος), *Megabyzos,* one of the allies of Darius in the defeat of false Smerdis. Nom. sg. **ba[gab]uxša**, Bh. 4. 18. **baga** (q. v.) + **buxša*, fr. **buj, to free,* YAv. **buj** (Middle Pers. **bôxtan**).

bāgayādi (Elam. **pagiyatiš**), f. name of a month, Sept.–Oct. (Oppert, Weissbach). Gen. sg. **bāgayādaiš**, Bh. 1. 13. **baga** (q. v.) + **yāda, worship,* fr. yad (q. v.).

bāji, m. *tribute,* Acc. sg. **bājim**. New Pers. **bāz**; fr. **baj, to allot,* YAv. **baj** (Middle Pers. **baxtan**), Skt. **bhaj**.

baⁿd (I. E. **bhendh*), *to bind.* Part. nom. sg. m. **basta** (I. E. **bhṇdh-to-s*), Bh. 1. 17; 2. 13, 14. YAv. **band** (Turfan MSS. **bast**, New Pers. **bandad**), Skt. **bandh**.

baⁿdaka, adj. *subject;* as subs. *servant, subject.* Nom. sg. **baⁿdaka**. Nom. pl. f. **baⁿdakā**, Bh. 1. 7. **baⁿda, bond,* YAv. **banda** (New Pers. **band**), Skt. **bandha**, + suffix **ka**; lit. *he who is in bonds.*

bābiru (Elam. **papili**; Assyr. in oldest documents **babilu, babili**, *gate of god;* in later documents **babilāni**, *gate of the gods,* whence Gr. Βαβυλών), m. *Babylon, Babylonia.* Nom. sg. **bābiruš**. Acc. sg. **bābirum**. Abl. sg. (with **hacā**) **bābirauš**. Loc. sg. **bābirauv**.

bābiruviya, adj. *Babylonian.* Nom. sg. m. **bābiruviya**. Acc. sg. m. **bābiruvi[ya]m** (thus read in Bh. 3. l. 86 in place of **bābirauv**

of ed.; cf. KT, 58). Nom. pl. (as subs. *the Babylonians*) bābiruvīyā, Bh. 3. 14. Acc. pl. bābiruvi[y]ā, Bh. 3. l. 88. bābiruvi[y]ā aja^n, *he smote the Babylonians* (thus read in place of bābirum agarbāya of ed.; cf. KT, 58).

bar (Pres. bara-, Bartholomae, Grundr. 123), *to bear, sustain, esteem*. Act. ind. pres. 3 pl. bara^{n}tiy, Dar. NRa. 4. Pret. 1 sg. abaram. 3 sg. abara (written ar^{n}r^a by stone-cutter's blunder in Bh. 3. l. 67; cf. KT, 54). 3 pl. abara^n. Impv. 3 sg. baratuv. Mid. ind. pret. 3 pl. abara^{n}tā, Bh. 1. 7. Av. bar (Turfan MSS. būrdan, New Pers. baraδ, Gīl. bardan, Kāš. bartan), Skt. bhṛ.

—— with prefix patiy + ā, *bring back, restore*. Pret. 1 sg. patiyābaram, Bh. 1. 14.

—— with prefix parā, *bear away, take away*. Pret. 3 sg. parābara, Bh. 1. 14, 19. Part. nom. sg. n. parāba[rta]m, Bh. 1. 14.

—— with prefix pariy, *protect, preserve*. Pres. subj. 2 sg. paribarāhy (paribar- to be read in place of parikar- in Bh. 4. ll. 72, 74, 78. "The character b is certain." KT), Bh. 4. 17. yadiy —— [nai]ydiš paribarāhy, *if —— thou shalt not protect them*. Bh. 4. 16. paribarāh(i)diš. pari[ba]rā (subj. 2 sg., not impv.; cf. the preceding vikanāhy, q. v.), Bh. 4. 15. avaθāstā (KT) pari[ba]rā, which Hoffmann-Kutschke (Phil. Nov. 3. 105) would understand; *so stehe da* (wie ich hier im Relief), *halt* (sic) *im Zaume* (= *gefesselt*).

—— with prefix frā, *proffer, grant*. Pret. 3 sg. frābara.

barataya, reading of ed. and confirmed by KT in Bh. 5. l. 23, where Foy would emend [xaudā]m tigrām bara^{n}ty, (Scythians who) *wear the pointed cap*, but KT's cuneiform text reads sakām in l. 22 which makes this theory impossible (unless we ascribe a blunder here to the work of the two English scholars).

bardiya (Elam. pirtiya; Bab. bar-zi-i-a), m. *Smerdis*, brother of Cambyses. For the prothetic σ in Σμέρδις of Hdt. (cf. Μάρδος, Μάρδις, Aesch. Pers. 765) see Kretschmer, KZ, 29, 440. Nom. sg. bardiya. Acc. sg. bardiyam. Cf. YAv. bərəzant, *lofty*, Turfan MSS. būrzist. Bartholomae, ZDMG, 48, 155; Foy, KZ, 37, 536; Justi, IF, 17, Anz. 103.

bū (Pres. bava-, Bartholomae, Grundr. 123), *to be.* Ind. pret. 1 sg. abavam. 3 sg. abava. 3 pl. abavaⁿ. Subj. 3 sg. bavātiy, Dar. NRa. 4. Opt. 2 sg. bīyā (Tolman, Vdt. Stud. 1, 33; Weissbach, ZDMG, 61, 729; Bartholomae, WZKM, 22, 88). 3 sg. bīyā (I. E. bhu-ī-iē-t, Bartholomae, Grundr. 143). Av. bū (New Pers. buvaδ), Skt. bhū.

būmī, f. *earth.* Acc. sg. būmim (written būmām in Art. Pers. a. b. 1). Gen. sg. būmiyā. Av. būmī (New Pers. būm), Skt. bhūmī.

brātar, m. *brother.* Nom. sg. brātā, Bh. 1. 10, 11. Av. brātar (New Pers. birādar, Kurd. barā, Oss. arvāda), Skt. bhrātr̥.

M

mᵃ in Seal Inscr. e. mᵃ xaršādašyā. According to Justi, IF, 17, Anz. 112, the expression for *seal,* *māraka, New Pers. mārah.

mā, prohibitive ptcl. *not;* 1) with opt., Bh. 4. 11, 17; Dar. Pers. d. 3; 2) with injunctive, Bh. 4. 10, 14; Dar. Pers. e. 3; NRa. 6. Av. mā (New Pers. ma), Skt. mā. Cf. Delbrück, Vgl. Syntax, 3, 288.

mā, *to measure.* Av. mā (New Pers. āzmāyaδ, Oss. amain), Skt. mā.

—— with prefix ā, *extend* (i. e. *be of ancient lineage*), or *prove oneself.* Part. nom. pl. āmātā, Bh. 1. 3; Bh. a, where Andreas-Hüsing would emend ādātā, *noble,* i. e. *of ancient family* (KZ, 38, 255. Cf. also the supplement of Bab. [mar]-bānūti which, however, renders fratamā in Bh. 23, 77, 83, 88); Yet KT's cuneiform text plainly gives m in Bh. 1. 3.

ma, pron. stem. See adam.

maka (Elam. makka), adj. as subs. name of a people. Nom. sg. m. maka, Bh. 1. 6; Dar. Pers. e. 2. Hdt. 4. 175, οἱ Μάκαι.

magu (Elam. makuš; Bab. ma-gu-šu; Gr. Μάγοι), adj. as subs. name of a Median tribe celebrated in priestcraft (cf. Jackson,

Zoroaster), *Magian.* Nom. sg. maguš. Acc. sg. magum. Phl. magū. Cf. Justi, IF, 17, Anz. 103.

maciya, adj. as subs. name of a people. Nom. pl. maciyā. For the reading iyam maciyā in Dar. NRe., see s. v. iyam. Hdt. 4. 191, Μάγves.

mātya, conj. with subj. *that not, lest, not.* Bh. 1. 13; 4. 6, 8, 15. mā + tya (q. v.).

maθišta, adj. 1)*the greatest.* Nom. sg. m. maθišta. 2)As subs. *chief, leader.* Nom. sg. maθišta. Acc. sg. maθištam. Superl. to *maθ, *great*, YAv. mas (Middle Pers. mas, New Pers. mih, Horn, NS, 42, 2).

māda (Elam. mata; Bab. ma-da-a-a; Gr. Μῆδοι), 1)adj. *Median.* Nom. sg. m. māda. Acc. sg. m. mādam. Instr. pl. māda[ibi]š, Bh. 2. 6. Loc. pl. mādaišuvā, Bh. 2. 6. 2)As subs. *Media.* Nom. sg. māda. Acc. sg. mādam. Loc. sg. mādaiy.

man (Pres. maniya-, Bartholomae, Grundr. 147), *to think.* Mid. subj. 2 sg. maniyāhay, Bh. 4. 5; Dar. Pers. e. 3; NRa. 4; so Bartholomae for maniyāhy of ed. 3 sg. maniyā[taiy], thus read in Bh. 4. 1. 50. The ā is attested by KT's examination. Jackson (JAOS, 24, 89) feels less certain, for he remarks that "despite syntactical grounds" there is no space for ā. Av. man, Skt. man.

man (Pres. mānaya-, Bartholomae, Grundr. 151), *to remain.* Pret. 3 sg. amānaya, Bh. 2. 9, 11. amāniya, Bh. 2. 6 (cf. KT, 26). Av. man (New Pers. māndan).

māniya, n. *estate* (?). Cf. Turfan MSS. mânbêd. Acc. sg. māniyam, Bh. 1. 14. Some of the meanings which have been proposed for this doubtful word are the following: *dwelling places* (KT); *les maisons* (Darmesteter, Étud. Iran. 2. 129); *le case* (Rugarli); *das Wohnen* (WB); *liegende Habe* (Bartholomae); *real estate* (Gray, AJP, 21, 16; cf. YAv. nmāna); Justi (IF, 17, Anz. 108) translates, *Hauskomplexe* (māniya von māna, *Haus,* wie nāviya, *Flotille,* von *nāu, also Plätze wo etwa Gewerbetreibende oder Händler, Reprāsentanten der bürgerlichen Untertanen, wohnen). Cf. Tolman, Vdt. Stud. 1, 13.

[mᵃnᵘuvᵃtᵃmᵃ, a proposed reading of Jackson (JAOS, 24, 93) for KT's ₊ ₊ tᵘnᵘuvᵃtᵃmᵃ (q. v.). "The text is indeed much mutilated, but each of the letters u, v, t, m is legible. (The letter of) the first part of the word (is) apparently nᵘ—. The sketch made in my notes looks precisely like nᵘ. A further examination of the damaged part revealed an apparent m preceding this, so that we may assume that the word began with m." A possible comparison with Skt. manuvat, *wie Menschen* is suggested. Weissbach (ZDMG, 61, 729) reads naiy šakauri[m naiy ₊ ₊] nuvatam, *weder dem Findling noch dem Armen*. The Bab. apparently renders by muškinu. We might compare mânbêd of Turfan MSS. So Hoffmann-Kutschke who renders, *Knecht und Herr* (mānuvant).]

₊ ₊ ₊ ₊ mamaita (KT's cuneiform text; ₊ ₊ ₊ ₊ mamita, KT's transliteration), mutilated proper name in Bh. 5. 1.

mar (Pres. mariya-, Bartholomae, Grundr. 148), *to die*. Mid. pret. 3 sg. amariyatā, Bh. 1. 11. YAv. mar (Turfan MSS. mûrd, New Pers. mīrad), Skt. mr̥.

mᵃ ₊ ₊ ₊ (Elam. maruš; Bab. ma-ru-'), to be read māru, m. name of a Median town. Nom. sg. m[āru]š, Bh. 2. 6; cf. KT, 25.

mārgava, adj. as subs. *Margian*. Nom. sg. mārgava. Instr. pl. mārgavaibiš, thus read in Bh. 3. 1. 16 in place of mārgayaibiš of ed. "The sign is v not y." KT.

margu (Elam markuš; Bab. mar-gu-'; Gr. Μάργος, Μαργιανή), m. *Margiana*. Nom. sg. marguš. Acc. sg. margum. Loc. sg. margauv. YAv. marγu (New Pers. marv).

martiya, m. *man*. Nom. sg. martiya. Acc. sg. martiyam. Gen. sg. martiyahyā (written in Art. Pers. a. martihyā). Voc. sg. martiyā, Dar. NRa. 6. Nom. pl. martiyā. Acc. pl. martiyā. Instr. pl. martiyaibiš. Av. mašya (New Pers. mard, Kurd. mir), Skt. martya; fr. mar (q. v.).

martiya (Elam. martiya; Bab. mar-ti-ia), m. name of a Susian rebel. Nom. sg. martiya. Acc. sg. martiyam.

marda, doubtful word in Bh. 5. 1. 11. Foy (KZ, 35, 48) would emend utāšim amarda, *und vernichtete es*, connecting the word with

Skt. mṛd. KT record; utā daiy marda where one feels strongly tempted to read utā šiš amarda, *and he annihilated them*. Cf. Tolman, Vdt. Stud. 1, 36.

marduniya (Elam. martuniya; Gr. Μαρδόνιος), m. *Mardonius*, father of Gobryas. Gen. sg. marduniyahya, Bh. 4. 18.

mazdāh, see s. v. aura and auramazdāh.

maškā, *skin, float of skins*. Loc. pl. maškāuvā, text as confirmed by KT in Bh. 1. l. 86, who fail to appreciate the value of their record, since they attempt no translation and even suggest the possibility of taking the obliquely-meeting wedges of the cuneiform sign for u as the word-divider, thus giving maškā davā. The new reading proves the correctness of Justi's conjecture (IF, 17, Anz. 125; cf. Foy, KZ, 37, 533) as loc. pl. of maškā; cf. Assyr. maš-ku-u, *skin*, Aram. meškā. It is in Persian a loan word (New Pers. mask) and has reference to the manner of crossing the river, which has been in vogue from early times to the present day, i. e., on inflated skins or a raft or bridge supported by such skins. The Assyrian reliefs (e. g. Layard's Nineveh, fig. 52) show the method. Xen. (Anab. 2. 4. 28) speaks of the rafts as σχεδίαις διφθερίναις. The meaning of the passage is now quite clear and this reading supersedes the various attempted emendations (cf. KZ, 35, 35; AJP, 21, 20; ZDMG, 46, 244). Jackson (JAOS, 24, 85) records that the first part of the word looks more like mⁿyⁿ, but later writes in a personal letter to Justi: "Your conjecture is so brilliant that I am almost tempted to doubt my reading, but the y did seem quite certain in my notes, for I examined the word with great care." Tolman in Vdt. Stud. 1, 15.

māh, m. *month*, with gen. of the name. Loc. sg. (with postpos. ā) māhyā. Gray (AJP, 21, 14) returns to the older view of regarding māhyā as contracted from māhahyā (them. gen. sg.; cf. Skt. māsa) and thus avoids the "appositional genitive" of the name. For the seasons of the Persian months see Justi, ZDMG, 51; Oppert, ibid. 52; KT, xxvi; Prašek Beiträge z. alt. Gesch. 1901. Av. māh (Turfan MSS. pûr-māh, New Pers. māh, Oss. maya), Skt. mās.

miθra, m. the god *Mithra;* cf. Hillebrandt, Ved. Myth. 3, 128; Jackson, JAOS, 21, 169; Grundr. d. iran. Philol. 2, 40; Tolman, PAPA, 33, 69. Nom. sg. miθra, Art. Sus. a; Art. Pers. a. b. 4, (written mⁱtra, Art. Hamadan; cf. Bartholomae, Altiran. Wb., 1185, n.). Av. miθra (New Pers. mihr), Skt. mitra.

muθ (Pres. muθa-, Bartholomae, Grundr. 124), *to flee.* Pret. 3 sg. amuθa. Cf. Hüsing, KZ, 38, 258. This interpretation (which is favored by both Elam. and Bab. versions) is undoubtedly correct and supersedes the former view of regarding amuθa as an adv. Cf. Tolman, Vdt. Stud. 1, 21. In Bh. 3. l. 71 read am[uθa] in place of maθišta of ed.

mudrāya (Elam. muzzariya; Bab. mi-ṣir; Steph. Byz. Μύσρα), adj. as subs. *Egyptian, Egypt.* Nom. sg. mudrāya. Acc. sg. mudrāyam, Dar. Sz. c. 3. Abl. sg. [mudrā]yā, Dar. Sz. c. 3. Loc. sg. mudrāyaiy, Dar. Sz. c. 3. Nom. pl. mudrāyā, Dar. Pers. e. 2; NRa. 3.

Y

yautiyā (Elam. yautiyaš; Bab. i-u-ti-ia), f. name of a Persian district. Nom. sg. yautiyā, Bh. 3. 5.

yᵃu + + + +, read by Bartholomae (IF, 12, 132) yauda"tim (act. pres. part. f. to yaud, YAv. yaoz, *be in commotion*); by WB¹, yu[diyā], *in Aufruhr;* WB²², yau$_{\text{ia}}^{\text{di}}$ + +, Dar. NRa. 4. auramaz[dā yaθ]ā avaina imām būmim yᵃu + + + + pasāvadim manā frābara, *when Ahura Mazda saw this earth in rebellion, thereafter he gave it to me.*

yauna (Elam. iyauna; Bab. ia-a-ma-nu), adj. as subs. *Ionian, land of the Ionians.* Nom. sg. yauna, Dar. NRa. 3. Nom. pl. yaunā. Cf. Justi, IF, 17, Anz. 99.

yātā, conj. 1)*while, when,* 2)*until.* Cf. Delbrück, Vgl. Syntax, 3, 334.

yaθā, conj. 1)*as,* 2)*when,* 3)*because,* 4)*in order that, that.* Bartholomae, by reference to Mènant and Daressy (Recueil de trav.) reads avaθā yaθā for pa[s]āva in l. 11 of Dar. Sz. c. 3. Av. yaθā, Skt. yathā. Cf. KZ, 33, 423; ZDMG, 46, 297; WZKM, 3. 147; Delbrück, Vgl. Syntax, 3. 429.

yad (Pres. yada-, Bartholomae, Grundr. 123), *to worship.* Mid. subj. 3 sg. yadātai[y], thus read in Bh. 5. l. 34 (cf. KT, 83), confirming Bartholomae's conjecture (Foy, yadātiy, KZ, 35, 48). The same form I supplied (Vdt. Stud. 1, 36) in the lacuna of Bh. 5. l. 19, hya auramazdām ya[dātaiy]. Pret. 1 sg. ayadaiy, recorded by KT in Bh. 5. 2, who attempt no interpretation, yet I regard it as quite likely the root yad; cf. Vdt. Stud. 1, 36. I also would emend y(?)adayāmaiy, Dar. Sus. a. Av. yaz (Middle Pers. yaštan, New Pers. yazdān, cf. Horn, NS, 37, 2), Skt. yaj.

yadāyā, abl. with hacā of an uncertain word in Bh. 3. 5, confirmed by KT who translate, *from my allegiance.* This attested reading makes improbable Foy's ya[u]dāyā (*kampf.* cf. Skt. yodhana, + aya, *gang*) *vom kriegszug*, and hacā yutiyā (Or. Litt. Ztg. Nov., 1905).

yadiy, conj. 1)*if*, 2)*when.* For yadipatiy (sic) see s. v. patiy, adv. Cf. Delbrück, Vgl. Syntax, 3, 314. YAv. yeδi, Skt. yadi.

yāna, m. *favor.* There is now hardly any doubt as to the reading of this word and the lacuna in Bartholomae's Altiran. Wb., 1285 (yan + + m) should be removed. Jackson (JAOS, 27, 191) records: "There is a slight space between n and m, apparently due to an original defect in the stone, and not to any lacuna in the tablet. I could see no evidence of any letter being missing and I believe that the reading yānam may be accepted as certain." Stolze's photograph (Pers. II, 95) evidently shows simply this "defect in the stone" and makes Foy's proposed emendation yāniyam, *segen*, improbable. Acc. sg. yānam, Dar. Pers. d. 3. aita adam yānam jadiyāmiy auramazdām, *this as a favor I pray of Ahura Mazda.* Av. yāna.

yanaiy, adv. *whereon.* Xerx. Van. 3. yanaiy dipim naiy nipištām akunauš, *whereon he had cut no inscription.* Loc. sg. on instr. stem of ya; so Müller, WZKM, 7, 112; Bartholomae, Altiran. Wb., 1262; otherwise Foy (instr. yana + iy; KZ, 37, 501); Bollensen (yana naiy); Oppert (ya-naiy).

yam (Inchoative pres. yasa-, Bartholomae, Grundr. 135), *to reach, attain.* Av. yam, Skt. yam.

—— with prefix ā, *appropriate, take to oneself, seize as one's possession*. Mid. pret. 3 sg. āyasatā (Bartholomae, BB, 14, 246), Bh. 3. 7. kāram āyasatā, *he took over the army;* Bh. 1. 12. dahyāva hauv āyasatā, *the lands he seized as his possession;* Bab. ₊ ₊ ti a-na ša ra-ma-ni-šu ut-te-ir, *he took it for himself;* Elam. emituša tuman-e, *he seized as his possession.* Cf. Tolman, Vdt. Stud. 1, 11. Kern (ZDMG, 23, 229) read ayastā as nom. ag. with acc. Hoffmann (BB, 18, 285) regarded the word as instr. sg. comparing Skt. āyatta, *abhängig von.* Cf. Foy, KZ, 35, 33; Gray, AJP, 21, 14.

yāvā, adv. *as long as.* Skt. yāvat. Cf. Delbrück, Vgl. Syntax, 3, 334.

yuviyā, f. *canal.* Nom. sg. yuviyā, Dar. Sz. c. 3. Acc. sg. yuviyām, Dar. Sz. c. 3. Cf. Skt. yavyā (instr.), RV. 8. 98, 8. Phl. yōi, New Pers. jōi.

R

raucah, n. *day.* Nom. sg. rauca, Bh. 3. 1. 1 rauca θakatam (q. v.) āha, *one day was completing its course.* Acc. sg. rauca, Bh. 1. 7. xšapavā raucapativā, *either by night or day.* Instr. pl. (for nom. pl.) raucabiš, Bh. 3. 3. 23 raucabiš θakatā (q. v.) āha", *twenty-three days were completing their course.* Av. raocah (Phl. rōc, Turfan MSS. rōj, New Pers. rōz); fr. *ruc, *to shine*, YAv. ruc, Skt. ruc.

rautah, n. *river.* Nom. sg. rauta, Dar. Sz. c. 3. hacā pirāva nāma rauta, *from the river Nile by name;* for construction see s. v. pirāva. Phl. rōt, New Pers. rōd, Kurd. ro; Skt. srotas fr. sru, *flow.*

raxā (Elam. rakkan), f. name of a Persian town. Nom. sg. raxā, Bh. 3. 6.

ragā (Elam. rakkan; Bab. ra-ga-'), f. name of a Median district. Nom. sg. ragā, Bh. 2. 13. Abl. sg. (with hacā) ragāyā, Bh. 3. 1. YAv. raγi.

rad (Pres. rada-, Bartholomae, Grundr. 123), *to leave.* Skt. rah. Cf. Foy, KZ, 37, 564; Bartholomae, Altiran. Wb., 1505.

—— with prefix **ava**, *leave, abandon.* Injunctive 2 sg. **avarada,** Dar. NRa. 6. **paθim tyām rāstām mā avarada,** *leave not the true path.*

rād, f. see **avahyarādiy.**

rasa-, inchoative pres.; see **ar.**

rāsta, adj. *true;* so now Bartholomae (WZKM, 22, 88), comparing YAv. **rāsta,** Turfan MSS. **rāšt,** *true.* Acc. sg. **rāstām,** NRa. 6.

+ + + + **rtaiyiya,** text confirmed by KT in Bh. 4. 1. 44. I suggested (Vdt. Stud. 1. 30) the supplement [upāva]rtaiy, *I turn to* (i. e. *appeal to Ahura Mazda*) regarding + + + + rtaiyiya as dittography for + + + + rtaiy (cf. tyanā manā, Bh. 1. 8). For this meaning of upa + ā + vart in Skt. cf. examples quoted in PWb. and note Turfan MSS. vard. Elam. ankirir ᵃⁿuramašta-ra sap appa, *I state as a follower of Ahura Mazda.* See s. v. **auramazdāh.** Bartholomae (WZKM, 22, 69) suggests **auramazd[ā va]rtiyaiy** (or **āvart-** or **vavart-**; cf. New Pers. **āvar**), *may Ahura Mazda be my witness,* regarding the form as opt. 3 sg. of denom. to var built on nom. ag. in tay. Hoffmann-Kutschke (Phil. Nov. 3, 103) proposes **auramaz[dā baga ma]rtiyiya,** *Auramazda ist der Gott des Menschen,* wobei letzteres Wort wohl für **martiyahyā** vermeisselt wäre oder besser **martiyaiy** vw. μάρτυς, *Zeuge,* mit vorhergehendem **auramaz-[dām],** *ich rufe zum Zeugen an.* He interprets the Elam. ᵃⁿkirir ᵃⁿuramašta-ra, *der (einzige) Gott ist Auramazda.*

V

vā, conj. encl. *or;* **vā — vā,** Bh. 1. 7. Av. **vā** (Turfan MSS. vå, *and,* New Pers. **va**), Skt. **vā.**

vaina-, pres. of nā- class treated as thematic (Bartholomae, Grundr. 132; cf. YAv. **vaēnaiti,** Turfan MSS. **vēnēēd,** New Pers. **bīnað,** Skt. **venati**), *to see.* Mid. *to seem.* Act. ind. pret. 3 sg. **avaina.** Subj. 2 sg. **vaināhy.** Mid. pres. 3 sg. **vainataiy,** Xerx. Pers. a. 3.

vaumisa (Elam. maumiṡṡa; Bab. u-mi-is-su), m. name of a Persian leader. Nom. sg. **vaumisa**. Acc. sg. **vaumisam**. **va[h]u + misa** (cf. miθra).

vaθʳabara, reading of WB in Dar. NRd. who translate *Genosse* (?); Bartholomae, Altiran. Wb. and Justi, ZDMG, 50, 669, *Stabträger* (?). Otherwise Foy, ZDMG, 55, 509. It is, as Justi observes, clearly a title of a court official. If vaθʳa = New Pers. bār, *branch, bough*, as Horn suggests, I would favor the meaning *bow-bearer*.

vayam, Av. vaēm, Skt. vayam; see adam.

vāyaspāra (Elam. miṡpar ₊ ₊; Bab. mi-is-pa-ru-'), m. name of the father of Intaphernes. Gen. sg. vā[ya]sp[āra]hyā, Bh. 4. 18. Foy suggests the etymology vaya[t], *flechtend* (Skt. vayanti) + spāra, *schild* (Av. spāra.dāṡta, New Pers. sipar) which Bartholomae (Altiran. Wb., 1359) rejects because of the ā in reference to the New Pers. and σπαραβάραι in Hesychius. KT record vā-, not va-.

var (Pres. varnav-, Bartholomae, Grundr. 131), *to choose;* Mid. *to convince*. Mid. subj. 3 sg. varnavātaiy (thematic), Bh. 4. 8. māt[ya] —— naiṡa[iy] ima (Weissbach, ZDMG, 61, 728) varnavātaiy, *lest it does not convince him*. Impv. 3 sg. varnavatām (thematic), Bh. 4. 6, 10. Av. var. Skt. v\underset{o}{r}. Cf. Keller, KZ, 39, 176. Note Turfan MSS. nē varovâd.

varkāna (Elam. mirkaniya; Gr. Ὑρκανία), adj. as subs. *Hyrcania*. Nom. sg. varkāna. Cf. YAv. vəhrka, *wolf* (New Pers. gurg), Skt. vṛka.

[**vart**, *to turn;* with prefix upa + ā. 1 sg. mid. [upāva]rtaiy, *I appeal*. See ₊ ₊ ₊ ₊ rtaiyiya.]

vardana, n. *town*. Nom. sg. vardanam. GAv. vərəzāna, YAv. varəzāna (New Pers. barzan; cf. Nöldeke, ZDMG, 46, 442), Skt. vṛjana. Note also Justi, IF. Anz. 18, 39.

vasiy, adv. *much, to a great extent, in large numbers, utterly*. Phl. vas, New Pers. bas, Bal. gvas; fr. *vas, *to wish*, Av. vas, Skt. vaç. Gray renders etymologically, *at will*, AJP, 21, 15. For reading vasaiy (*uṋsxhai), see Foy, KZ, 35, 21; Müller's vasiya, *gewalt, menge* (WZKM, 7, 257; cf. Pedersen, KZ, 40, 134) is improbable.

vašdāsaka, uncertain word in Seal Inscr. c. vašdā saka, WB.

vašna, m. *will, favor*. Instr. sg. vašnā; vašnā auramazdāha, *Dei gratia* (Dar. Inscr. 41 times; Xerx. Inscr. 6 times; Art. II. Inscr. once). The divine right of kings is recognized not only in this phrase but in such expressions as auramazdā xšaθ^ram manā frābara (Dar. Inscr. 7 times); hya (mām) xšāyaθiyam akunauš (Dar. Inscr. 5 times; Xerx. Inscr. 6 times; Art. III. Inscr. once). Av. vasna; fr. *vas, *to wish*, Av. vas (Turfan MSS. vasnâd), Skt. vaç.

vazarka, adj. *great, mighty*. The word is probably thus to be read instead of the common transliteration vazraka (YAv. vazra, New Pers. gurz, Skt. vajra, *Indra's thunderbolt*) of ed. and KT. Cf. Tαννοξάρκης = Persian tanu-vazarka, *great in body*. Nöldeke argued against vazraka on the ground that it would give New Pers. *bazra or *guzra, not buzurg, yet I fail to see his phonetic reasons. Cf. Tolman, Vdt. Stud. 1. 7; Foy, KZ, 37, 537; Bartholomae, Altiran. Wb., 1390, n. Nom. sg. m. vazarka. Acc. sg. n. vazarkam. Gen. sg. f. vazarkāyā. Turfan MSS. vazurg, New Pers. buzurg, Paz. guzurg. Cf. Jud. Pers. buzurgān.

vahauka (Elam. maukka), m. name of the father of Ardumanish. Gen. sg. vahau[kahya], Bh. 4. 18.

vahyavišdāpāya, uncertain word in Seal Inscr. d. vahyavišdā pāya, WB.

vahyazdāta (Elam. mištatta; Bab. u-mi-iz-da-a-tu), m. name of a Persian rebel. Nom. sg. vahyazdāta. Gen. sg. vahyazdātahya (sic; cf. Bartholomae, Grundr. 412, n), Bh. 3. 6, 7. Acc. sg. vahyazdātam.

viy, verbal prefix. *apart, away*, e. g. viyakaⁿ (see kan). Av. vī (New Pers. gu-), Skt. vi.

viθ, f. 1)*royal court, royal race*. 2)*royal palace*. Cf. Turfan MSS. visbêd. Acc. sg. viθam (written vⁱθam in Bh. 1. 121). Instr. sg. (with patiy) vⁱθāpatiy, Bh. 3. 5. kāra pārsa hya vⁱθāpatiy (text as

ANCIENT PERSIAN LEXICON

confirmed by KT, thus setting aside Foy's emendation (KZ, 37, 556) viθiyāpatiy, viθiy + āpatiy, *zu hause* in opposition to the army in the field; cf. Tolman, Vdt. Stud. 1, 24). Loc. sg. (with postpos. ā) vⁱθiyā, Bh. 4. 13. martiya hya hamataxšatā manā vⁱθi[yā], *the man who aided my royal house*. Bartholomae (Altiran. Wb., 1446) takes viθiyā as gen. sg. of viθī with meaning of viθ. viθiyā, Dar. Pers. c. Av. vīs, Skt. viç.

vⁱθᵃibᵃišᵃ (read either viθaibiš or viθibiš), an adj. in instr. pl. agreeing with bagaibiš in Dar. Pers. d. ll. 22, 24. The commonly accepted view at present regards the word as viθa, *all* < visa < vispa (cf. asa < aspa). I do not attach to the Bab. phrase, Dar. Pers. g. 24, itti ilāni gabbi, *with all the gods*, the importance some scholars have given it. The polytheism of the Babylonians would obscure a distinctive Persian religious conception in the epithet. Note s. v. drauga, how the Bab. translation fails to reproduce the Persian thought. This meaning has also suffered through the correction vⁱθᵃbᵃišᵃcā (q. v.) in Bh. 1. l. 65, which cannot now signify *all*, as was formerly suggested. The older reading and interpretation viθibiš bagaibiš, *with the gods of the royal house* or, as Justi (IF, 17, Anz. 108) puts it, *mit den vom Stamm verehrten Göttern*, come again into prominence. So Foy (KZ, 33, 431), Rawlinson, Spiegel, WB, Tiele (*met de goden van den stam*), Bartholomae (Zum Altiran. Wb., 227). For a discussion of this epithet in reference to the θεοὶ βασιλήιοι of Hdt. see Tolman, PAPA, 33, 68. Cf. Gray, JAOS, 21, 181; ibid. 23, 56; Foy, KZ, 37, 533; Rapp, ZDMG, 19, 67; Justi, IF, 17, Anz. 108; Pedersen, KZ, 40, 133.

vⁱθᵃbᵃišᵃcā, text as confirmed by Jackson and KT in Bh. 1. l. 65. Cf. Turfan MSS. vîsbêd. The late discussions of the word have been based on the reading viθaibiš; cf. Gray, JAOS, 23, 56, who regarded the form as instr. pl. for acc. pl., translating *and all things;* See now Bartholomae, Zum Altiran. Wb., 227. Foy's viθabišaca-cā (ZDMG, 54, 349), *geschlechtsgefolgschaft* agrees more closely with the reading which we must now adopt. In Vdt. Stud. 1, 14, I suggested viθbiš (Av. vīzˡbīš) instr. pl. for acc. pl., *and the royal residences;* or as Justi (IF, 17, Anz. 108), *einzelne Häuser* (viθ ist in der Inscrift des Dareios palastes die Bezeichnung dieses Gebäude, nicht des ganzen Schlosses oder der Burg von Persepolis, welche in der susischen Bauurkunde an der südlichen Mauer halvarraš heisst). Gray in a personal letter to me suggests viθabiš (instr. pl. n.) *relating to the royal residences*, comparing Av. vīsan, *der ein Haus, Hauswesen hat*.

viⁿdafarnah (Elam. mintaparna; Gr. Ἰνταφέρνης), m. *Intaphernes*, name of ally of Darius against the false Smerdis, Bh. 3. 14; 4. 18; thus read viⁿdafar[nā], Bh. 3. l. 84, [v]iⁿda[farn]ā, l. 86, viⁿda-[far]nā, l. 88, text as confirmed by KT, which removes viⁿdafrā of ed. from the Persian vocabulary; cf. Tolman, Vdt. Stud. 1. 27. *viⁿda(t), act. pres. part. to vid, *find*, Av. vid (Turfan MSS. vīndād, Middle Pers. vindītan), Skt. vid, + *farnah, *glory*, YAv. x^varənah.

vidarna (Elam. mitarna; Bab. u-mi-da-ar-na-'; Gr. Ὑδάρνης), m. *Hydarnes*, name of ally of Darius against the false Smerdis. Nom. sg. vidarna. The restoration [ma]nā for vidarnahyā of ed. in Bh. 2. l. 25 is certain; cf. KT, 26.

viyaxna (Elam. miyakannaš; Bab. addaru), m. name of a Persian month, Feb.-March (i. e. Adar, twelfth month; cf. Bab.). Gen. sg. viyaxnahya (sic; cf. KT, 8, 54), Bh. 1. 11; 3. 11.

viyanā[sa]ya, text in Bh. 4. l. 66 as confirmed by KT, (*whoever*) *injured* (my house). Foy suggests viyanāθaya, *wer schadete* and regards the form as pret. 3 sg. caus. to *nas, *perish*, Av. nas (Middle Pers. nasītan), Skt. naç.

vivāna (Elam. mimana; Bab. u-mi-ma-na-'), m. name of a Persian. Nom. sg. vivāna. Acc. sg. vivānam.

visa, adj. *all*. Acc. sg. n. visam. vispa, *all* > vis(s)a > visa.

visadahyu, adj. *containing all lands*. Acc. sg. m. visadahyum, Xerx. Pers. a. 3. duvarθim visadahyum, "the hall where the representatives of the several provinces brought at stated times their homage to the Great King." Bartholomae. visa + dahyu (q. v.).

vispazana, adj. *containing all kinds of people*. Gen. pl. f. vispazanānām, Dar. NRa. 2. vispa, *all*, Av. vīspa (Middle Pers. visp), Skt. viçva + zana, *man*, Skt. jana; cf. paruzana.

vištāspa (Elam. mištašpa; Bab. uš-ta-as-pi; Gr. Ὑστάσπης), m. *Hystaspes*, father of Darius. Nom. sg. vištāspa. Acc. sg. vištāspam. Gen. sg. vištāspahyā. *višta (Middle Pers. višaδak) *depressed* (vi + had, *sit*, *settle down;* cf. Skt. vi + sad, *to sink, despond*) + aspa, *horse* (q. v.). As a poss. compound the name must mean, *he of spiritless horses*. Note New Pers. guštāsp, cf. Horn, NS, 27, 3. Written always v¹št- in Bh.

višpauzāti (Elam. mišpauzatiš; cf. KT, 41), f. name of a Parthian town. Nom. sg. viš[pa]uz[ā]tiš, Bh. 2. 16.

S

saka (Elam. šakka; Bab. mātu gi-mi-ri; Gr. Σκύθαι), adj. as subs. *Scythian, Scythia*. Nom. sg. saka. Nom. pl. sakā.

sakā, f. *Scythia*. Acc. sg. sakām, Bh. 5. 4. abiy sakām, *against Scythia*, text confirmed by KT.

[san, with suffix viy, *to destroy*, the reading of KT in Bh. 4. ll. 71, 73, 77. Better read vikan-, see s. v. kan, and Tolman, Vdt. Stud. 1, 34.]

sᵃrᵃ, an uncertain word in Dar. NRa. l. 52, [mā]m auramazdā pātuv hacā sᵃrᵃ + + +. The meaning is shown by Elam. mušnika and Bab. bi-i-ši, *evil*. Because of the correspondence of these words with gastā l. 58, Foy would emend hacā gastā, *from evil*. Jackson (JAOS, 20, 55) suggests a comparison with Skt. chala and translates (JAOS, 21, 171) *from treachery* (hacā sarā, abl.).

[sar, asariyatā, reading of KT in Bh. 3. l. 92. See akariyaⁿtā s. v. kar, and Tolman, Vdt. Stud. 1. 28.]

sikayauvatī (Elam. šikkiumatiš; Bab. sik-kam-u-ba-at-ti-'), f. name of a fortress in Media. Nom. sg. sika[va]uvatiš, Bh. 1. 13.

suguda (Elam. šuktaš; Bab. su-ug-du; Gr. Σογδυανή), adj. as subs. *Sogdiana*. Nom. sg. suguda. YAv. suγδa.

skuⁿxa (Elam. iškunka), m. name of a Scythian rebel. Nom. sg. skuⁿxa (thus read for skuⁿka of ed. in Bh. k.). In Bh. 5. l. 27

s[kuⁿ]xa is clearly to be supplied. The note of KT (later corrected) that the name cannot be restored is based on their wrong transliteration of the word in Bh. k.; cf. Tolman, Vdt. Stud. 1, 37.

skudra, m. name of a district. Nom. sg. **skudra**, Dar. NRa. 3.

stā (Pres. **išta**-, Bartholomae, Grundr. 127, showing transfer to thematic conjugation as in Av. **hištaiti** and Skt. **tiṣṭhati**; cf. Tolman, Old Persian Notes, 203), *to stand, halt*. Mid. Pret. 3 sg. **aištatā**. Av. **stā** (Turfan MSS. **ēstēd**, New Pers. **ēstādan**), Skt. **sthā**.

—— with prefix **ava** (Pres. **stāya**-, Bartholomae, Grundr. 147), *place, restore*. Pret. 1 sg. **avāstāyam**. Cf. KZ, 39, 44.

—— with prefix **niy** (Pres. **stāya**-, see above), *enjoin, command*. Pret. 1 sg. **niyaštāyam**. 3 sg. **niyaštāya**.

stāna, n. *place*. Acc. sg. **stānam**, Xerx. Van. 3. Skt. **sthāna**, New Pers. **-stān**; fr. **stā** (q. v.).

star (Pres. **starav**-, Bartholomae, Grundr. 141), *to sin*. Injunctive 2 sg. **starava** (thematic). Dar. NRa. 6, **mā starava**, *sin not;* so Bartholomae (Altiran. Wb., 1597) in defense of the old reading against WB's **stakava**, *sei nicht ungerecht*. WB[II] now read **starava**.

sparda (Elam. **išparta**; Bab. **sa-par-du**), m. name of a region; according to Lassen, *Sardis;* cf. Meyer, IF, 1, 326–29; Müller, WZKM, 2, 93; Gray, AJP, 21, 3. Nom. sg. **sparda**.

š

—— **ša**, abl. sg. pron. encl. in **hacā avadaša**, *therefrom*. YAv. **hō** (New Pers. **(a)š**). See s. v. **avadā**.

—— **šaiy**, dat. sg. pron. encl. GAv. **hōi**, YAv. **hē**. Bh. 2. 7, **avaθā[šaiy] aθaham**, *thus I said to him*, et passim. **utā nāham utā gaušā utā harbānam frajanam**, Bh. 3. 13, *I cut off both his nose and his ears and his tongue*.

šakauri[m], word of doubtful meaning in Bh. 4. 13, naiy šakauri[m] $_{+\,+\,+}$ tunuvatam (KT; manuvatam, Jackson) zūra akunavam. The Bab. renders lik-tu u muš-ki-nu. It seems to me possible that the Bab. lik-tu (= šakaurim) and muš-ki-nu (= $_{+\,+}$ t^{u}n^{u}uv^{a}t^{a}m^a) from their derivation may refer to the two lowest classes of the kingdom, lik-tu, *slave*, lit. *one received* (against *Findling*, Delitzsch, Muss-Arnolt) and muš-ki-nu, generally rendered *pauper;* cf. Muss-Arnolt, Assyrian Dictionary, 604, but note Johns: "I think it very probable that the class included the subject race, not propertyless, but of lower standing. It may have included freed slaves and foreign residents." Weissbach (ZDGM, 61, 729) interprets *dem Findling;* Hoffmann-Kutschke (Phil. Nov. 3, 108) *Knecht, Höriger, Gefolge*. Bang suggests that šakaurim is a Semitic loan word *šakōrīm, *einem Verleumder*. It is doubtful whether KT's translation of Bab. version *to the prisoner* (?) *and freed man* is correct. See s. v. $_{+\,+\,+}$ t^{u}n^{u}uv^{a}t^{a}m^a and m^{u}n^{u}uv^{a}t^{a}m^a (cf. Turfan MSS. mânbêd). The reading is attested by the recent collations of the text and the various attempted emendations (KZ, 35, 45; ibid. 37, 557; IF, 12, 130) are impossible.

—— šām, gen. pl. pron. encl., a re-formation to dat. sg. šaiy and abl. sg. ša after analogy of noun-stems, Bartholomae, Grundr. 251, n. Bh. 3. 10, avaθāšām aθaha, *thus he said to them*. Bh. 2. 4, hyašām maθišta āha, *who was chief of them*. Bh. 5. 1. 15, utā[š]ām auramazdā $+\,+\,+\,+$ ^{a} $+\,+\,+\,+$.

—— šim, acc. sg. pron. encl. YAv. hīm, Skt. sīm. Bh. 1. 13, xšaθ^{r}amšim adam adīnam, *I took the royal power from him*. Bh. 1. 14, adamšim gāθavā avāstāyam, *I restored it* (i. e., *the kingdom*) *to its place*. As acc. pl. n. Bh. 4. 1. 6, adamšim (text confirmed by KT for adamšām of ed.) ajanam, *I waged these* (i. e. *battles*), wrongly translated by KT, *I overthrew nine kings;* cf. Tolman, Vdt. Stud. 1, 28.

šiyāti, f. *well being*. Nom. sg. šiyātiš, Dar. Pers. e. 3. Acc. sg. šiyātim (written šāyatām in Art. Pers. a, b, 1; Foy, KZ, 35, 58 after Marquart, ZDMG, 49, 671, reads šāytām). YAv. šāti; fr. *šiyā, Av. šyā, *rejoice* (Turfan MSS. šād, New Pers. šād). Cf. Casartelli, La Religion, 41; Stave, Einfluss des Parsismus, 64;

Jackson (JAOS, 21, 166) compares Isaiah, 45, 7: "I am JHVH, and there is none else—who forms light and creates darkness, who makes welfare and creates calamity."

šiyu (Pres. šiyava-, Bartholomae, Grundr. 123), *to set forth, go.* Pret. 1 sg. ašiyavam. 3 sg. ašiyava. 3 pl.ašiyava^n. GAv. šyu. YAv. šu (New Pers. šavaδ, Oss. caün, Kurd. cīan), Skt. cyu.

—— šiš, acc. pl. pron. encl. YAv. hīš. Bh. 3. 8, avadašiš uzmayāpatiy akunavam, *there I crucified them.* Cf. Delbrück, Vgl. Syntax, 3, 47.

Z

zāzāna (Elam. zazzan; Bab. za-za-an-nu), m. name of a Babylonian town. Nom. sg. zāzāna, Bh. 1. 19.

zūrakara, adj. *doing wrong.* Nom. sg. m. zūrakara, Bh. 4. 13. naiy zūrakara āham, *I was not an evil-doer* (text confirmed by Jackson and KT). The word is also to be read in Bh. 4. 1. 68, hyavā [zū]rakara (text confirmed by KT), thus superseding the various attempts at emendation (stavaka, Justi; startā, Bartholomae; atartā, WB[1]) and confirming Müller's conjecture in WZKM, 1, 134; cf. Tolman, Vdt. Stud. 1, 33. zūrah + *kara, fr. kar (q. v.).

zūrah, n. *wrong, deceit.* Acc. sg. zūra (text confirmed by Jackson and KT). YAv. zūrah- (New Pers. zūr).

+ + + + y (Elam. zuzza; Bab. zu-u-zu), name of a town in Bh. 2. l. 33. "The name was composed of 5, possibly 6, signs, of which only the last is visible." KT.

zra^{n}ka (Elam. [zirra]nkaš; Bab. za-ra-an-ga-'; Gr. Δραγγιανή), m. *Drangiana.* Nom. sg. zra^{n}ka.

H

hainā, f. *army, hostile host, array of evil.* Nom. sg. hainā, Dar. Pers. d. 3. Abl. sg. (with hacā) haināyā, Dar. Pers. d. 3. YAv. haēnā (Middle Pers. hen), Skt. senā; fr. *hi, *bind*, Av. hi (New Pers. gušāyaδ, *he uncovered*), Skt. si.

hauv, demon. pron. nom. sg. m. f. (I. E. *so + u, Gr. οὗ-τος), 1)*that*. In Bh. 1. l. 29 written hauvᵃmᵃ (cf. KT, 6). Probably the -am, as Bartholomae suggests (WZKM, 22, 65), is to be compared with the suffix in adam, tuvam, iyam, but I believe it comes here only through analogy; cf. Prakrit tumam, *thou*, beside tum. Bh. 3. 10, hauv kāra ašiyava, *that army set forth*, et passim. 2)*that one, he, it*. Bh. 1. 12, hauv āyasatā, *he* (i. e. Gaumāta) *seized (the lands) as his own*. Bh. 3. 3, hauvmaiy hamiθʳiyā (sic; cf. KT, 44) abava, *it* (i. e., the land of Margiana) *became rebellious to me*. With encl. šaiy and ciy written haušaiy, hauciy. YAv. hāu, m. f. (as if an extension of the fem. I. E. sā + u, Gr. αὖ-τη), Skt. a-sāu, m. f. Note Turfan MSS. hô.

haumavarka (Elam. umumarka; Bab. umurga), adj. designating a part of the Scythians in Dar. NRa. 3. If the reading be correct, the word would seem to apply to a custom in regard to the use of *leaves* *varka, YAv. varəka for the drink of the *hauma, YAv. haoma, Skt. soma; cf. Hillebrandt, Ved. Myth. 1, 102; Foy, KZ, 35, 51. Should the last member of the compound be read varga (after the Bab.), the interpretation still remains doubtful. Foy suggests, *die Haumahemmenden* (cf. Skt. vṛj) or *die Haumabereitenden* (cf. Skt. vṛjana). Nom. pl. haumavar[kā]. Cf. Hdt. 7. 64, ἐόντας Σκύθας Ἀμυργίους.

haxāmaniš (Elam. akkamanniš; Bab. a-ḫa-ma-ni-iš-'; Gr. Ἀχαιμένης), m. *Achaemenes*; founder of the Achaemenidan dynasty. Nom. sg. haxāmaniš, Bh. 1. 2; Bh. a. 2. *haxā (nom. sg. in comp.), *friend*, YAv. haxi, Skt. sakhi + *maniš, Av. manah; fr. 1)man (q. v.). Cf. Bartholomae, Zum Altiran. Wb., 39. Note Turfan MSS. ḫašā-gərd.

haxāmanišiya (Elam. akkamannišiya; Bab. a-ḫa-ma-ni-iš-'; Gr. Ἀχαιμενίδης), adj. *of the race of Achaemenes, Achaemenidan*. Nom. sg. haxāmanišiya (written hāxāmanišiya in Xerx. Pers. a. 2). Nom. pl. haxāmanišiyā. For the Achaemenidan dynasty cf. Tolman and Stevenson, Hdt. and Empires of East, 73 ff.; Meyer, Gesch. des Altert. 1. 613; Prášek, Forsch. z. Gesch. d. Altert. 3, 24, vs. the extreme view of Winckler, Or. Litt. Ztg., 1898, 43; Nöldeke, Aufsätze z. pers. Gesch. 15; Justi, Grundr. d. iran. Philol. 2, 416; Weissbach, Assyriol. Bibl. 9. 86. haxāmaniš (q. v.) + suffix ya.

hagmatāna (Elam. akmatana; Bab. a-ga-ma-ta-nu; Gr. Ἐκβάτανα, Ἀγβάτανα), m. *Ecbatana.* Loc. sg. hagmatānaiy. New Pers. hamaδān, cf. Hübschmann, Lautl. 143.

hacā, prep. with abl. *from.* Bh. 2. 12, hacā bābirauš, *from Babylon.* Bh. 1. 11, hacā avadaša, *from there.* With tarsa-, Bh. 1. 13, kārašim hacā daršma^n atarsa, *the people feared his tyranny.* GAv. hacā, YAv. haca (Phl. aj, Turfan MSS. 'aj, New Pers. az, Kurd. až), Skt. sacā.

ha^{n}j (Pres. ha^{n}ja-, Bartholomae, Grundr. 123), *to hale to prison or inflict some form of penalty.* Skt. sañj; cf. Foy, KZ, 37, 547.

——— with prefix fra; Pret. 1 sg. frāha^{n}jam, Bh. 2. 13.

had, *to sit.* YAv. had (Turfan MSS. nišîyând, New Pers. nišastan), Skt. sad.

——— with prefix niy (caus. nišādaya-, Bartholomae, Grundr. 151), *place down, establish.* Pret. 1 sg. niyašādayam, Dar. NRa. 4.

hadā, prep. with instr. *with.* GAv. hadā, YAv. haδa (Turfan MSS. 'ad, Oss. äd), Skt. saha.

hadaxaya, an uncertain word in Seal Inscr. b, hadaxaya + + + + + θadaθa.

hadiš, n. *dwelling place.* Acc. sg. hadiš, Xerx. Sus.; Xerx. Pers. cb. da.; Art. Sus. Cf. had.

ha^{n}dugā, f. *proclamation, record.* Acc. sg. ha^{n}dugām, Bh. 4. 10, 11.

hapariya- (Bartholomae's conjecture, Studien, 2, 67 in Bh. 1. l. 23; cf. Skt. saparyati), *to reverence, respect.* Pret. 3 pl. āpariyāya^n (for ahapariya-), see s. v. dāta. Cf. Justi, IF, 17, Anz. 106; Tolman, Vdt. Stud. 1, 9. KT still read apariyāya; WB^{II} upariyāya(?).

ham, verbal prefix, *together,* e. g., ha^{n}gmatā, *assembled together.* GAv. həm, YAv. ham (Middle Pers. ham), Skt. sam.

hama, adj. *same, one and the same;* cf. Weissbach, ZDMG, 61, 724. Gen. sg. f. **hamahyāyā** (a re-formation of gen. of **a**- stem on masc. gen. suffix; cf. **ahyāyā**). See s. v. *θard*. Av. **hama** (Middle Pers.; New Pers. **ham**), Skt. **sama**. For +++++++ **āra hama amaxamatā** of KT in Bh. 4. l. 92, Weissbach (ZDMG, 61, 730) emends, **kāra hama amaxahya**ⁿ**tā**, *die Leute allzumal freuten sich;* cf. Elam. **taššutum-pe sapiš**.

hamātar, adj. *having a common mother.* Nom. sg. m. **hamātā**, Bh. 1. 10. **ham (ha)** + *mātar, Av. **mātar** (New Pers. **mādar**, Gīl. **māar**), Skt. **mātṛ**; or by haplography, as Bartholomae suggests, for **hama** + **mātar**.

hamapitar, adj. *having a common father.* Nom. sg. m. **hamapitā**, Bh. 1. 10. **hama**, *same* + **pitar** (q. v.).

hamara, m. *foe, enemy.* Acc. sg. **hamaram**, Dar. NRa. 4. [hac]ā **pārsā hamaram patiyajatā**, *far from Persia he fought his foe:* so Bartholomae. **ham** + *ara, fr. ar (q. v.).

hamarana, n. *battle, conflict.* Nom. acc. sg. **hamaranam**. Acc. pl. **hamaranā**. YAv. **hamarəna**, Skt. **samaraṇa**; **ham** + *arana, fr. ar (q. v.).

hamiθʳ**iya**, adj. *rebellious.* Nom. sg. m. **hamiθ**ʳ**iya**. Nom. sg. f. **hamiθ**ʳ**iyā**, thus read in Bh. 3. l. 11 (text confirmed by KT, which removes **hašitiyā** from the Persian vocabulary; cf. Tolman, Vdl. Stud. 1, 23). Acc. sg. m. **hamiθ**ʳ**iyam**. Nom. dual. m. (Bartholomae), **hamiθ**ʳ**iyā**, Bh. 2. 16. Nom. pl. m. f. **hamiθ**ʳ**iyā**. Acc. pl. f. [**hamiθ**ʳ**iy**]**ā**, Bh. 4. 4. Instr. pl. m. **hamiθ**ʳ**iyaibiš**, Bh. 3. 1. According to Justi, IF, 18, Anz. 36, **ha** + **miθ**, *paarweise verbinden*.

[**har** (Pres. **hara**-, Bartholomae, Grundr. 123), *to flee.* Oppert's supplement [**aharat**]**ā**, pret. 3 sg. in Bh. 1. 95. See s. v. 1)**ah**.]

haraiva (Elam. **ariya**; Bab. **a-ri-e-mu**), m. *Aria.* Nom. sg. **haraiva**. YAv. **harōiva**.

harauvatī (Elam. **arraumatiš**; Bab. **a-ru-ḫa-at-ti**; Gr. Ἀραχωσία), f. *Arachosia.* Nom. sg. **harauvatiš**. Acc. sg. **harauvatim**. Loc. sg. **harauvatiyā**. Skt. **sarasvatī**, *rich in waters;* *harah, *water,* fr. *har, *flow,* Skt. **sṛ** + suffix **vant**.

haruva, adj. *whole.* Nom. sg. m. haruva. YAv. haurva (Turfan MSS ḥarv, New Pers. har), Skt. sarva.

hᵃrᵃbāna, m. *tongue.* Acc. sg. harbānam, Bh. 2, 13. adamšai[y] utā nāham utā gaušā utā harbānam frājanam, *I cut off both his nose and his ears and his tongue.* KT record: "Of the signs r, b, and n traces are preserved upon the rock; the remaining signs are clear." Weissbach (ZDMG, 61, 726) suggests uzbāna, i. e. hu-zbāna. Note New Pers. zᵃbān, zᵘbān; cf. Horn, NS, 34, 5.

haldita (Elam. altita) m. name of father of Arkha. Gen. sg. halditahya (sic; cf. Bartholomae, Grundr. 412, n.), Bh. 3. 13.

hašiya, adj. *true.* Acc. sg. n. hašiyam, Bh. 4. 7. Av. haiθya, Skt. satya; fr. *hat (weak stem to *hant, pres. act. part. to 2)ah) + suffix ya.

hⁿdu, m. *India.* Nom. sg. hⁿduš. YAv. hindu, Skt. sindhu, *the land on the Indus.*

hya (I. E. *sio), rel. pron. (originally demon.), *who.* Nom. sg. m. hya. KT's cuneiform text and transliteration fail to record hya after martiya in Bh. 4. 1. 65, where I have restored it as in ed., regarding its omission as simply a blunder in copying. Nom. sg. f. hyā. Cf. tya. Skt. sya.

[hyā, regard by Bartholomae as abl. sg., *whence, hence* in Dar. Pers. e. 3, hyā duvaiš[ta]m šiyātiš, *hence for long time*, etc. It is more probably the nom. sg. f.; cf. Foy, KZ, 37, 561.]

hyāparam, adv. *thereafter, thereupon.* Bh. 3. 11, patiy hyāparam. hyā (abl. sg. n.) + *para, *later, beyond.* Cf. Bartholomae, Altiran. Wb., 1844. Skt. para.

Printed in Poland
by Amazon Fulfillment
Poland Sp. z o.o., Wrocław